GEOGRAPHIES: An Intermediate Series

EDITED BY PROFESSOR R. W. STEEL, M.A., B.Sc.

THE WORLD OF MAN

The World of Man

Ronald H. Buchanan, B.A., Ph.D.

Senior Lecturer in Geography
at the Queen's University of Belfast

LONGMAN

LONGMAN GROUP LIMITED
London
Associated companies, branches and representatives throughout the world

© Ronald H. Buchanan 1976

First published 1976 by The Educational Company of Ireland Limited

This edition Longman Group Ltd. 1976

ISBN 0 582 35151 0

Printed in the Republic of Ireland by Richview Press Limited Dublin

CONTENTS

Preface

The series, to which this volume is the latest edition, was designed to meet the needs of young geographers, particularly those in sixth-forms, nearly twenty years ago, and since then there has been a revolution in much of our thinking about the subject. Nevertheless, certain topics still constitute a fundamental basis for all geographical study, and the establishment of the principles of human geography and their study on a world-wide basis remains as important as ever.

As geography has become increasingly specialised, it has not been easy to find suitably qualified authors to undertake some of the more general surveys of branches of the subject, and there have been special difficulties about the production of a book concerned with the vital field of human geography. Several authors, independently or in collaboration with others, have embarked on the task but none has been able to devote sufficient time to it to complete a manuscript. After the publication of the late Dr R. Kay Gresswell's book, *Physical Geography,* in which he dealt not only with his own specialism of geomorphology but also with climatology and biogeography, it became even more important that human geography should have its proper place in this series. Almost by chance I discovered that Dr R. H. Buchanan was writing a book concerned with the spatial patterns associated with the distribution of man and his activities throughout the world. His study was designed for a series edited by Mr R. A. Butlin which was particularly directed to the needs of those studying geography in Irish schools. It seemed to me that the manuscript of *The World of Man* was what was needed for a much wider audience, and so, with the full co-operation of the author and the editor, and the publishers concerned, this book has been adapted to become a volume in the *Geography: an Intermediate Series.* It does not conform exactly to the format or the nature of the other books in the series but it provides an excellent background for the understanding of many of the economic, social and political problems that face the world today. Anyone studying the topics discussed by Dr Buchanan will be exploring the spatial patterns apparent in the distribution of different phenomena and will, therefore, appreciate something of their meaning while he will at the same time realise that, in Dr Buchanan's words, 'each people has its own patterns of culture, each place its distinctive environment.'

A few modifications have been made in this version of Dr Buchanan's book but many of the Irish examples chosen by the author have remained unaltered. Similar examples could have been taken from other parts of the British Isles but there seemed no good reason for ignoring the special knowledge of Ireland possessed by Dr Buchanan, a native of Ulster, and a member of the staff of the Department of Geography at Queen's University, Belfast, for many years. I am most grateful to him for his willingness to allow his work to become more widely known through the series in which it now appears; and my hope is that its use in schools and colleges will encourage many geographers and others to embark on the exciting task of seeking a deeper appreciation of the complexities and the challenges of 'the World of Man'.

University College of Swansea
University of Wales
1976

Robert W. Steel
General Editor

ACKNOWLEDGMENTS

My grateful thanks are due to the following people for their help: Mrs Elizabeth Purdy and Mrs Anne Kain for typing the manuscript, and my wife for her work on the illustrations.

The publishers would like to thank the following for permission to reproduce illustrations in this book:

Aer Lingus, Dublin; Aerofilms Limited; George Allen & Unwin Ltd. for diagram page 256, reproduced from J. Hawkes and L. Wooley, *History of Mankind*, Vol 1, and for illustration from Dr. Thor Heyerdahl, *Ra;* The American Museum of Natural History; Associated Press Ltd., London; Australian Information Service, Department of the Media, London; Belfast Library and Society for Promoting Knowledge, Linen Hall Library; Bord Fáilte (Irish Tourist Board); Bord Iascaigh Mhara, Dublin; British Broadcasting Corporation; The British Library Board, London; The Trustees of The British Museum; photographs by courtesy of the British Tourist Authority; Cambridge University Collection; Camera Press Ltd. (Text and Illustrations), London; John Moss/Colorific; R. Common, The Queen's University, Belfast; Countryside Commission, U.K.; Fox Photos; Commercial Attaché of the Embassy of France, Dublin; The Dean and Chapter of Hereford Cathedral; The Ministry of Agriculture and Fisheries, The Hague; *The Illustrated London News*; International Audio-Visual Resource Service (a UNESCO project in collaboration with I.P.P.F.); Israel Information, London; The Embassy of Japan, Dublin; K.L.M. Aerocarto, The Hague; N.C. Mitchel, The Queen's University, Belfast; Montana Historical Society; George Morrison; the National Film Board of Canada; The National Library of Ireland; The National Maritime Museum, London; The National Portrait Gallery, London; *Observer Colour Magazine*; M. J. O'Kelly, University College, Cork; Ordnance Survey, U.K.; Orion Press, Tokyo; Oxfam; Peabody Museum, Harvard University; Photo Researchers Inc. N.Y.C.; Popperfoto; Public Record Office of Northern Ireland; Radio Times Hulton Picture Library; Renault Motor Company, Paris; The Science

Museum, London; Frank Scovell; Spectrum Colour Library; Professor Nicholas Stephens, University of Aberdeen; John Topham Picture Library; Board of Trinity College, Dublin; United Nations Food and Agriculture Organisation; United Nations Relief and Works Agency photo by George Nehmeh; United States Department of Agriculture, Office of Information; United States Department of the Interior, National Park Service, photo by M. W. Williams; Figure 1.7 is after P. N. O'Farrell, redrawn from *Irish Geography*, Vol. 5, 1968, page 431, by permission of the Editor; Figure 6.3 is a redrawn version from *Geographical Review*, Vol. 48, 1958, copyrighted by the American Geographical Society; Figure 6.4 is reprinted from *Geographical Review*, Vol. 54, 1964, copyrighted by the American Geographical Society; Figure 6.7 is reproduced by courtesy of *The Countryman;* Figure 6.14 is a redrawn version of a diagram originally published by the Department of Housing, Local Government and Planning for Northern Ireland.

The publishers have not succeeded in contacting copyright holders in a few cases. However, they will be happy to make a suitable arrangement with them at the earliest opportunity.

THE GEOGRAPHER'S WORID VIEW

People today are probably more aware of the immense variety to be found in landscape and ways of life throughout the world than any previous generation. Television brings the world into the home in an immediate and personal way: we can see what the desert looks like and hear the narrator describe it in words; and the crush of people can almost be felt as the cameraman jostles his way through a crowded Arab bazaar. When we compare these distant scenes with our own familiar surroundings—or environment—and wonder why they should appear so different we are beginning to think like geographers; for geography is the academic subject which studies places and the way of life of the people who live there.

The world as seen from the Apollo 17 Moon mission in December 1972. Television pictures transmitted during Apollo missions brought the world into peoples' houses in the most immediate and dramatic way. In this photograph the continent of Africa is seen upper left with Madagascar about the centre. The South Polar ice cap at the bottom of the photograph and much of the southern hemisphere is covered with dense cloud

Places

An awareness of place and of the differences between places is part of everyone's experience in growing up. It is something we discover for ourselves as soon as we venture outside our home, into the unknown territory that lies beyond *our* garden or *our* street. The further we travel, on holiday to the seaside or even abroad, the greater the differences are likely to be. And when we return and try to tell people where we have been and what we have seen we are following in the footsteps of all the great explorers down the centuries, from Marco Polo and Christopher Columbus to the Apollo astronauts. We are trying to satisfy peoples' curiosity about the unknown worlds that lie beyond their immediate horizons.

'Where?' and 'what?' are two basic questions which geographers try to answer; and until the world had been thoroughly explored they were the most important. From the earliest times men have tried to devise means of locating places, to answer the question 'where?'; and the map is the visual method which has been used most often. Accurate maps are not easy to make. They require precise measurement of distances and angles; features to be mapped, like hills or rivers, have got to be reduced in scale from their dimensions in the real world without undue distortion of their shape and size; and perhaps the greatest problem of all, a world which is spherical in shape has to be represented on a flat surface. The Greeks and Romans of classical times solved some of these problems, but it was not until the sixteenth and seventeenth centuries that the major advances were made in cartography which resulted finally in the accurate maps we use today.

Figure 1.1
Changing views of the world, reflecting Europeans' knowledge of distant countries and the accuracy of their cartographers, are shown in these representative maps. On each map the sites of London (A), Jerusalem (B) and Colombo (C) are shown

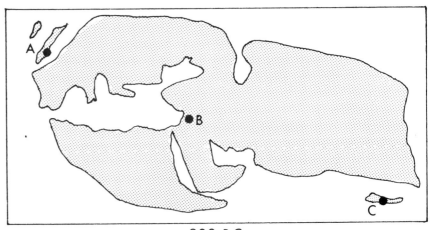

200 B.C.

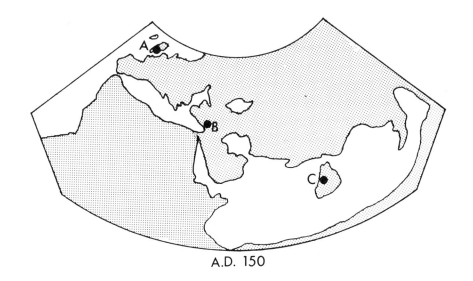

A.D. 150

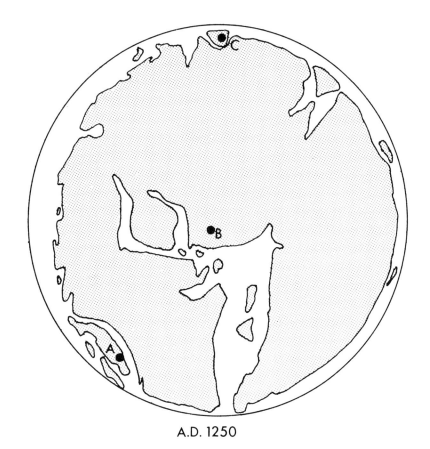

A.D. 1250

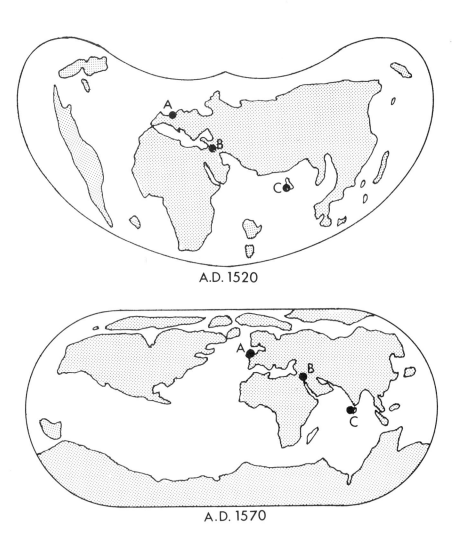

A.D. 1520

A.D. 1570

Travellers

Reliable descriptions of landscape and life in distant countries were also hard to obtain from the seamen and traders who sailed abroad. Travel by sea or land was slow, and first impressions were often dulled by journeys lasting months and sometimes years. Memory can be unreliable, and people often lack words to describe the things they see. Besides, travellers of all ages and times have been inclined to exaggerate their experiences, for there is a great temptation to use one's imagination when those who stay at home cannot check the facts for themselves! This is well illustrated in the following extract from an account of the British Isles written by the Greek geographer Strabo in the last century B.C.:

4

Ireland is a large island, of greater length than breadth, extending along the north side of Britain. We have nothing definite to say about it, save that its inhabitants are wilder than the Britons, being cannibals and coarse feeders, and think it decent to eat up their dead parents and to have open intercourse with women, even with mothers and sisters. But for these statements we have no trustworthy authority.

The last sentence shows a healthy scepticism towards travellers' tales which is not always apparent in the writings of early scholars. And the quotation itself illustrates a common dilemma: how to sift fact from fiction in providing accurate descriptions of the real world. For geographers, answering the question 'what is a place like?' has often been as difficult as showing where it may be found.

The British Isles according to Ptolemy. His *Geographia* was probably written about A.D. 150. The first printed edition was published in Italy in 1477, but this map is taken from the 1490 edition housed in Trinity College Dublin

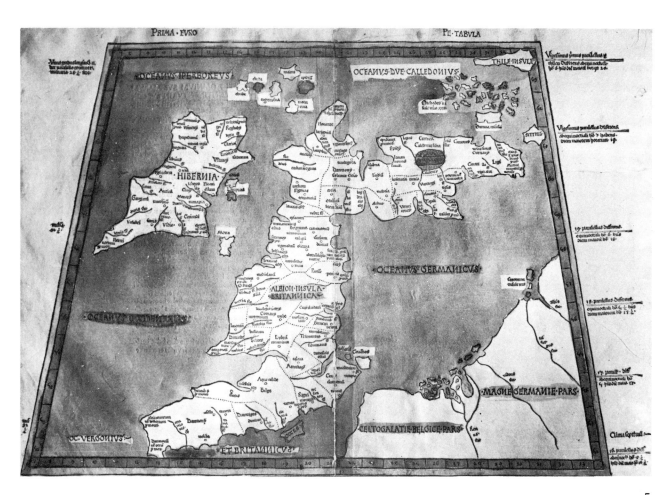

This is a section of a map of the world, drawn on vellum sometime about A.D 1300 and still to be seen in Hereford Cathedral in England. In the illustration, Great Britain is in the centre, Ireland lower left, France centre right and Spain bottom right. The cartographer's knowledge of Ireland was a little hazy—he represents the country as divided into north and south by two rivers, the Boyne and the Shannon; but he has judged correctly the relative positions of the four cities, Bangor, Armagh, Dublin and Kildare

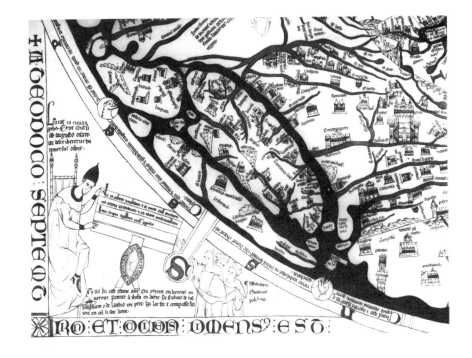

Information about the world increased enormously in the centuries after the great voyages of discovery undertaken by European seamen like Vasco da Gama, Columbus and Magellan towards the end of the fifteenth century. By 1800 land still unknown lay mainly in the continental interiors, especially Africa. From those who flocked abroad from Europe in increasing numbers—missionaries and merchants, colonial administrators and soldiers as well as emigrants—there came a steady stream of reports and letters. Scholars too began to accompany exploratory expeditions, like Charles Darwin who joined H.M.S. *Beagle* as naturalist on her voyage to South America and the Pacific in 1831. With new sources to work from, and so much material to examine and analyse, geography as a subject was completely transformed in the course of the nineteenth century. Formerly it had compiled information about different countries rather as one would collect words for a dictionary; now it became an academic discipline with its own distinctive aims, methods and philosophy. Once scholars were able to answer the questions 'where?' and 'what?' with some precision, they began to ask 'why there?', to seek explanations for the things they observed through scientific analysis.

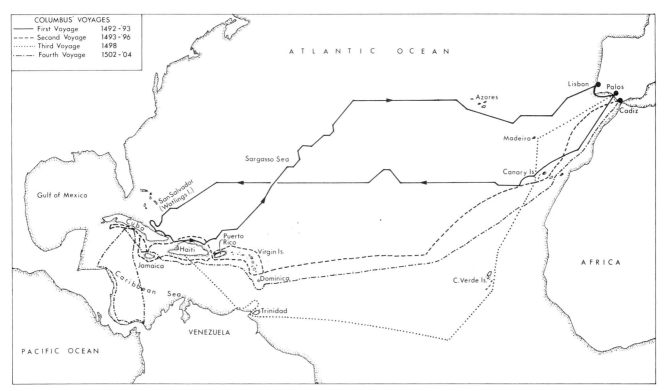

Figure 1.2
Christopher Columbus' four great trans-atlantic voyages, made between 1492 and 1504, opened the Americas to further exploration and colonisation by Europeans

Figure 1.3
Between 1497–99 the Portuguese seaman, Vasco da Gama, pioneered the eastern sea-route to India, exploring the east coast of Africa and finally making landfall near the town of Calicut in southern India

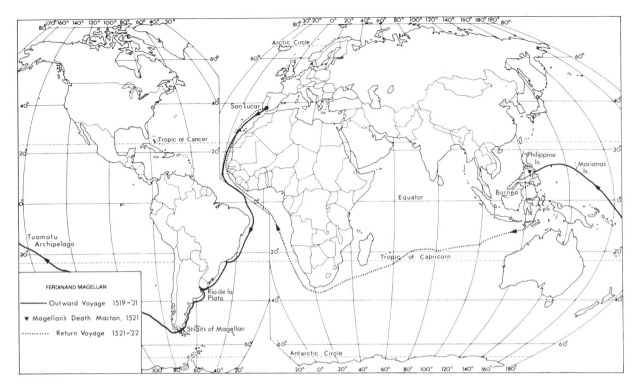

Figure 1.4
The expedition led by Ferdinand
Magellan was the first to sail right
round the world, beginning in
September 1519 and arriving
home exactly three years later.
Magellan himself was killed in the
Philippines, but he established the
western route to the Indies,
complementing the voyage
undertaken by Vasco da Gama
twenty years before

Charles Darwin (1809–82). (*Photo
courtesy of Radio Times Hulton
Picture Library*)

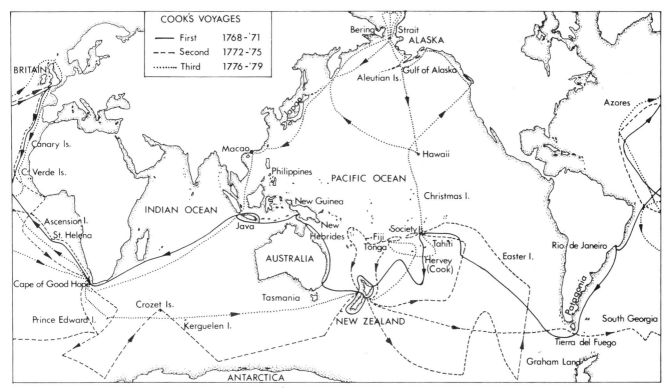

Figure 1.5
Cook's three voyages undertaken
between 1768 and 1779 gave
Europeans their first detailed
knowledge of the southern
oceans and in particular of the
island worlds of the Pacific

James Cook (1728–79), seaman,
explorer, navigator and
cartographer

Geographers

Alexander von Humboldt
(1769–1859)

These new developments began first in Germany, where two men in particular are regarded as the real founders of modern geography. Alexander von Humboldt (1769–1859), an explorer and scientist—he travelled extensively in northern South America between 1799 and 1804, and in central Asia—published one of the first systematic classifications of climate and vegetation on a world basis; and his contemporary, Karl Ritter (1779–1859), developed a regional approach to world geography which had a major influence on the later growth of the subject.

Much of this early academic work was concerned with the world's natural environment, with topography and landforms, vegetation and climate. In part this was due to the flow of information from the new generation of natural scientists, the geologists, zoologists and botanists whose work and growing interest in field observation had been so greatly stimulated by the publication of Darwin's *The Origin of Species* in 1859. In contrast, far less attention was given to the place of man in the world and to regional differences in his way of life. Not until nearly the end of the nineteenth century was any systematic attempt made to write a geography of man, first by the German geographer Freidrich Ratzel (1844–1904), and later by several French scholars, of whom the most outstanding was Paul Vidal de la Blache (1845–1918). These two men approached their subject from very different points of view. Ratzel and his students thought that adaptation to environment was the main reason why human life and activity varied so much throughout the world, a view very much in keeping with scientific thought of the post-Darwin period. This type of thinking is illustrated in the following comment, written in 1911, about the distribution of the American Negro:

The warm, moist air of the Gulf and South Atlantic state (U.S.A.) is attracting back to the congenial habitat of the Black Belt the negroes of the North, where moreover their numbers are being further depleted by a harsh climate, which finds in them a large proportion of the unfit.

Today of course, many American Negroes live in the 'harsh climate' of the north so the prediction made above has proved to be untrue. But the thinking behind the statement, which explains the distribution of a racial group solely by reference to climate, would be refuted by scholars like Vidal de la Blache. The latter believed that man's cultural heritage—the tools, techniques and experiences accumulated over many generations, were much more important than the environment in explaining the diversity of human life on earth. In the example quoted, he would contend that Negroes were to be found in the south-eastern states not because of climate, but because Europeans and Americans had the means of transport and the desire to bring people from Africa to work as slave labour on the plantations.

These conflicting views on the relative influence of environment and culture in shaping human life continued well into the present century, and they may have inhibited the early growth of human geography. Another reason was that the social sciences—subjects like anthropology, economics and sociology—developed at a much slower rate than the natural sciences in the early part of this century; and developments in geography have nearly always responded to the flow of information and ideas from sister disciplines. Thus new specialisms like geomorphology, climatology and biogeography developed quite quickly within physical geography, spurred on by work in geology, meteorology and botany. But only within the last thirty years has there been a comparable growth of specialist interests in human geography, as the social sciences have diversified their fields of study. Today the major subdivisions of human geography are economic, historical, political, social and urban geography, each with its own specialist field of research.

Academic Geography

Indeed there are so many specialisms that geography must seem a rather sprawling and structureless subject, poaching constantly on the fields of other sciences, and moving ever further away from its traditional purpose of describing and interpreting the many different environments and ways of life to be found throughout the world. The explanation for the development of geography in this way is to be found in the nature of the subject itself. Unlike most scientific subjects geography does not have a tidy bundle of facts it can call its own; instead it makes its contribution to knowledge in its viewpoint and method, in the way it looks at things and sees relationships between them. In everyday life, for example, it is quite possible for two people to look at the same object and see quite different things: a tourist looking at a mist-shrouded lake is disappointed because he cannot see the view, while a fisherman welcomes the day with these weather conditions for he knows the fish will rise to his bait. In much the same way an economist may examine an industry or a geologist a rock formation and see them in quite a different light from the geographer.

Perception of environment: this view of Bryce Canyon in Utah in the western U.S.A. delights thousands of tourists each year. But the pioneer farmer who first passed by saw it in a very different light. 'That', he is said to have remarked, 'would be the helluva place to lose a cow.'

In fact there is almost no limit to the range of geographical study, for anything which is part of man's environment and which occupies a part of the earth's surface can be studied geographically. Other disciplines in the physical, biological and social sciences each contribute their share of information about specific features of the earth or facets of human activity, while the geographer tries to integrate such findings as he considers relevant in presenting his view of the world. In practice, the geographer himself must specialise, for the flow of information from related sciences has been so great in recent years that no one person can really master all the available data. But whatever their specialism, geographers share a common aim: to explore the spatial patterns apparent in the distribution of different phenomena and to explain their meaning.

Location and Space

Location, the answer to the question 'where?', is the starting point in all geographical studies. One method of establishing location is by using a grid system such as the coordinates of latitude and longitude. Thus in reply to the question 'where is Dublin?', we can say it is 53° 20′ N. 6° 15′ W. Such a statement is useful to the navigator travelling over a featureless sky or ocean, or to someone looking at a world atlas. In everyday life, however, it is more usual to locate one place with reference to another in terms of distance, direction, time or some other unit of measurement. In this way we would say that Dieppe is 166 kilometres north-west of Paris, or it is a three-hour journey by car from Paris. This is called *relative location* and it is an important way of locating places because it defines the spatial relationship that exists between them. Where similar phenomena co-exist in such spatial relationships the term used is *distribution,* one of the most frequently used terms in the geographer's vocabulary. Any geographical distribution has three main aspects. Firstly, it has *density,* a term which describes the number of spatially-related objects within a given area. Thus the number of people living in Ireland may be given as the density of population per square mile/kilometre.

Figure 1.6
Location of a point by means of two co-ordinates. Here Dublin is shown to be 53° 20′ N measured from the equator, and 6° 15′ W of Greenwich. The equator and Greenwich provide the fixed points upon which the world grid is based—the latter because scientists at its observatory were originators of the scheme

Secondly, the objects cover a certain area in their distribution and are said to have a *dispersion*, as, for example, the dispersion of population which distinguishes inhabited from uninhabited areas. Thirdly, the word *pattern* is used to indicate the geometrical arrangement of objects within the area they occupy—often in conjunction with descriptive terms like nucleated or linear. Spatial patterns result from variations in the density and dispersion of objects: they pose questions like 'why are objects arranged in this way here and differently elsewhere?' They represent the sort of space relationships which modern geography tries to analyse and explain.

Patterns

Training the eye to recognise significant patterns in spatial distributions is part of the education of every geographer, whether the information is studied in the field or by means of maps and air photographs. Maps have always been the geographer's basic tool for spatial analysis and the presentation of results, but they do have limitations. For example, the interpretation of a certain pattern may require several correlations. These may be made visually, by overlaying a series of tracings showing other patterns which might explain the first —relating a settlement pattern, for instance, to that of topography, soils and field systems. This type of visual analysis can produce quite valid results, but it can also yield many different interpretations because it is subjective. As a result, geographers have recently begun to use a wide range of mathematical and statistical techniques which enable them to undertake analyses with much greater objectivity and using a far wider range of data than was possible before the advent of the computer. In this way geographers have also gained greater insights into the processes involved in the development of spatial patterns.

Knowledge of such processes is gained most easily by examining a particular pattern within a restricted local area. Patterns of land use, for example, may be related to spatial variations in topography and soils, and to the demands of local markets. Through field work, the interaction of these different components may be studied at first hand and an understanding of the processes involved can thus be achieved. Local studies can be regarded as an end in themselves, but the geographer is also concerned with the far more complex patterns he finds in the world at large. This change of scale involves a very big adjustment in thinking, but it is possible to relate the insights gained by studying the microgeography of a locality and its inhabitants to the macrogeography of mankind and the global environment.

Figure 1.7
Pattern. The distribution of settlements providing different categories of services in Co. Tipperary shows a spatial pattern typical of many analysed by geographers

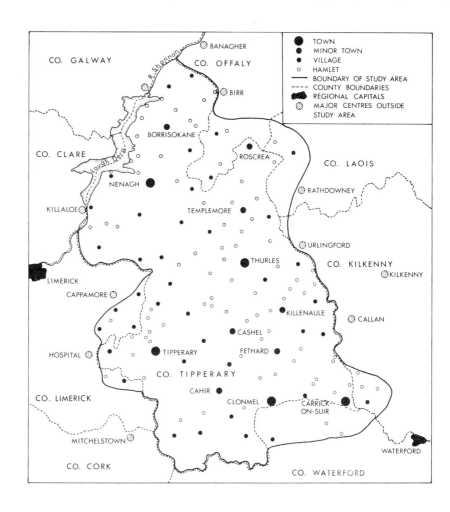

Models

Often this can be demonstrated most easily by models which simulate conditions in the real world by means of words, diagrams or mathematical formulae. Scientific models can rarely reproduce real world situations exactly, but they can greatly increase our understanding of processes, just as building a model car can show how its many components are put together. In geography, models such as the hydrological cycle or central place theory enable us better to understand the complex realities of the world in which we live. In particular they help to overcome the problem of scale, by showing that the same processes are involved in producing, for example, patterns of rainfall or settlement in places as different as Alabama, Antrim and Afghanistan.

Figure 1.8
Glenariff, Co. Antrim, showing
how air photographs may be used
in the preliminary stages of
interpreting the relationship
between land use, topography
and soils. (*Photo Aerofilms
Limited*)

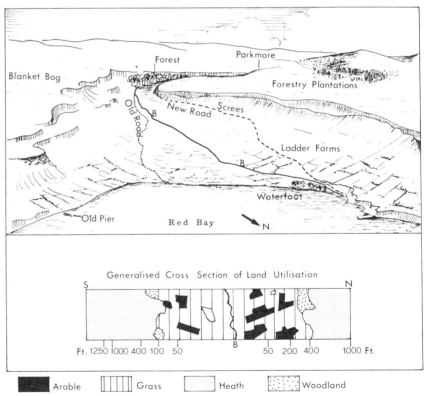

16

Figure 1.9
Diagrammatic representation of the hydrologic cycle

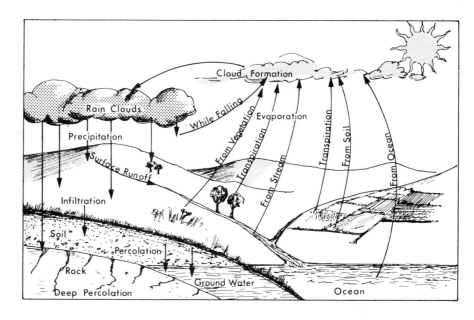

Time

In the real world, time is as important as space in shaping the pattern of life and landscape. One branch of geography—namely historical geography—is concerned specifically with this dimension. In particular it aims to reconstruct the spatial patterns of human activity in different places at earlier times, it studies changes in the man-made landscape, and it searches for visible influences of the past which may be traced in the present landscape. But in practice every branch of geography must take time and change into its reckoning, since nothing in our world is static; everything exists in dynamic relationships which are subject to change. For example, a city exists only as long as it provides its inhabitants with work, houses and services. It is likely to decline if it fails in any of these functions and may even disappear as a result of destruction by war or a natural disaster such as an earthquake. By including time as a necessary dimension in the study of spatial processes we can see not only how spatial patterns evolve but also predict the way they are likely to develop in the future.

Approaches to Geography

The analysis of spatial patterns visible in the natural environment and created by human action form one of the approaches used by geographers in their study of the world. A second approach is the ecological one, in which the relationships between man and environment are analysed within specific areas. This is a long-standing tradition in academic geography, but the legacy of environmental determinism has left human geographers wary of the sweeping generalisations made in the past about such relationships on a world scale. Today ecological relationships are being more rigorously examined at local level where they can contribute much to our knowledge, for example, of the problems associated with pollution of the environment. A third approach, regional studies, combines the results obtained by ecological and spatial analysis, to reveal the character of places as they exist in the real world. Regional description has long been considered the main work of geographers, a view that dates back to the topographical writings of an earlier time. It continues to form an important part of the geographer's basic training, but modern regional analysis has also a special interest in devising techniques by which regional units of different scales can be recognised, as well as in studying the processes and interactions which give them their distinctive character and coherence.

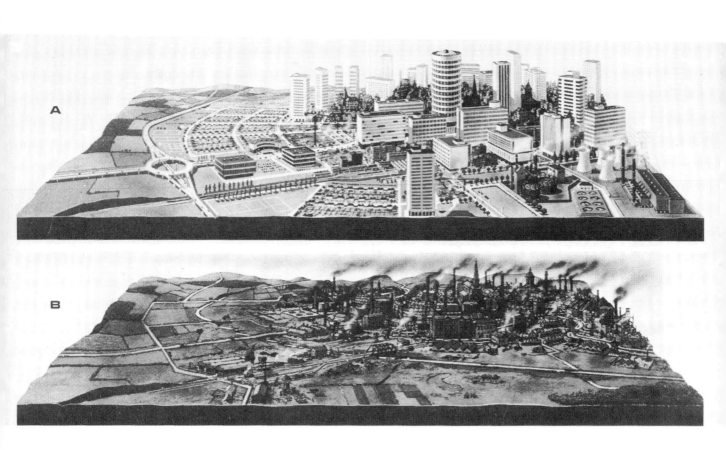

Change in the man-made landscape illustrated by the sequence of settlement in an English setting.
A Today's planned landscape of concrete and tarmac, high-rise building, motorway interchanges and sprawling suburbs hides older parts now being purposefully cleared. **B** 100 years ago the town was like a huge, smoky machine, largely unplanned, served by the new canals, railways, and by a rapidly growing population of working people living in mean back-to-back houses. **C** 200–300 years ago it was crossing the boundary between urban and rural and made a planned and balanced settlement with enclosed fields and straight roads, dominated by the church and the local landowner's house. **D** 750 years ago it was a neat medieval village grouped around a church as yet with no spire. A castle guarded the river and exercised authority over the countryside. Food was grown in rotation in open fields. **E** 2000 years ago and earlier the site looked untamed except for hill forts and a few fields. The forest was extensive, but trackways were in existence, whose line was to persist up to the motorway era

The World of Man

By studying spatial patterns relating to human life and activity in this book we are using the approach which is common to all systematic branches of geography. Our subject is immensely wide, and in an introductory study we must try to select only those aspects which are most relevant in creating regional diversty in the life and work of man throughout the world. For that reason we begin with the geography of man himself, with the diversity that exists in the distribution and composition of population on a world scale. Variations in these spatial patterns may be explained by differences in the way men make a living, through the economies which are discussed in Chapters 3 and 4. Race, language, religion and politics contribute to the cultural diversity which is outlined in Chapter 5, and the concluding chapter deals with settlement and communications.

2

POPULATION

The study of man's place in the world begins with human population. Answering the questions 'where do people live and how many are there?' leads us to speculate on the reasons why there should be such marked regional variation in man's distribution over the earth, explanations which take us to the core of human geography. These questions will be considered briefly now and developed in later chapters, but first we must establish the basic facts of population distribution and density and consider the dynamics of its growth and change.

Distribution and Density

Figure 2.1 World distribution of population

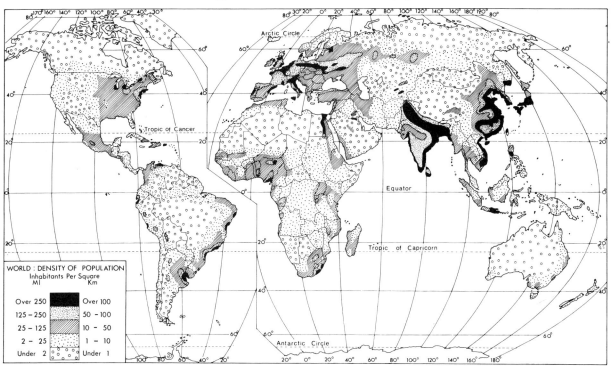

WORLD : DENSITY OF POPULATION
Inhabitants Per Square

MI	Km
Over 250	Over 100
125 – 250	50 – 100
25 – 125	10 – 50
2 – 25	1 – 10
Under 2	Under 1

Establishing exactly where people live is not as easy as it seems; it requires a fairly sophisticated government organisation to count all the people living in a given area at a particular period in time. Such enumerations were attempted in antiquity, for example within the Roman Empire and in China, but the first really comprehensive national census did not take place until 1749 in Sweden and was later followed in other European countries and the U.S.A. Periodic census-taking became more common in the nineteenth century, and nowadays it is normal procedure in practically all countries. But there are still many countries where the information is not wholly reliable, just as the accuracy of the census and even of population estimates decline the further back one goes in time. For many purposes census inaccuracies are a serious handicap but they are of minor importance at the world scale with which this book is concerned.

Table 2.1   1970 Population: U.N. estimates

Continent	Population (millions)	Density (per sq km)	Percentage of world population
Africa	353	12	9·8
North America	323	13	8·9
South America	190	11	5·3
Asia	2 081	47	57·7
Australia	12	1·5	0·4
Europe	649	62	17·9
World	3 600	24	100·0

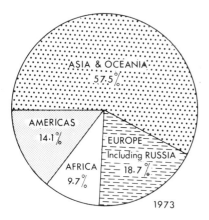

Figure 2.2
The proportion of the world's population in each of the major continents, data 1973

The world distribution of population is very uneven; vast areas are virtually empty whereas others are very crowded indeed (Figure 2.1). In fact nearly two-thirds of the world's population live on only 7 per cent of the land surface, while more than half of the land area is occupied by about 5 per cent of the population. Two further points can be made about the world distribution of population. Firstly, Europe and Asia together contain more than three-quarters of mankind, and Asia has 57 per cent of the total. Secondly, less than 10 per cent of the world's population live in the southern hemisphere, where of course there is far less land area and a much greater extent of ocean. If we consider this zonal distribution a little further, using latitude as the point of reference, we find that 50 per cent of mankind lives between 20° and 40° N., and a further 30 per cent between 40° and 60° N. Since this zone includes some very sparsely inhabited areas—the great deserts of the

Old World in Africa and Asia and the Alpine–Himalayan mountain chains—the concentration of people within its four main clusters becomes even more striking. These are: south and east Asia, Europe and north-eastern North America.

Figure 2.3
World population densities: The relationship between population and national territory illustrated on the same scale for different countries

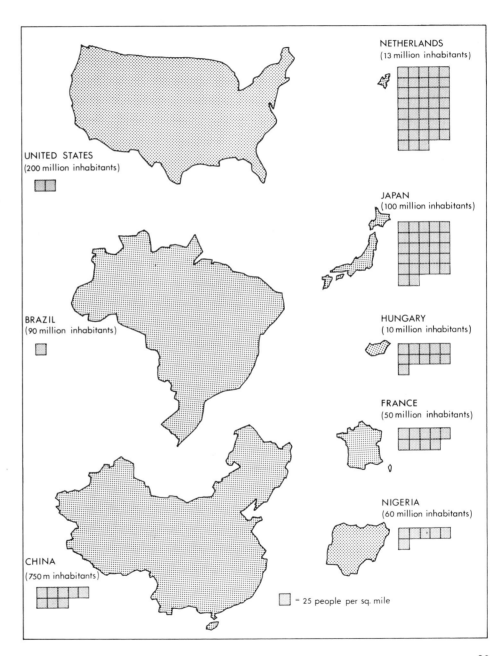

NETHERLANDS
(13 million inhabitants)

UNITED STATES
(200 million inhabitants)

JAPAN
(100 million inhabitants)

BRAZIL
(90 million inhabitants)

HUNGARY
(10 million inhabitants)

FRANCE
(50 million inhabitants)

NIGERIA
(60 million inhabitants)

CHINA
(750 m inhabitants)

☐ = 25 people per sq. mile

In using the word *concentration* with reference to population we introduce another concept to our study of distribution: namely, population density, or the number of people living in a specific unit area. Table 2.1 shows how greatly the continents differ in this respect: Australia is at the bottom of the world league with 1·5 people per square kilometre, and Europe heads the list with 62 people per square kilometre. Yet there seem to be some anomalies in these figures. North America, for example, has only 13 people per square kilometre, yet it contains one of the main clusters of world population. This is not apparent in the density figures because North America contains many sparsely populated areas in the mid-west and west which contrast with the concentration of people in the north-east. Crude population densities which relate total population to total national area can thus be very misleading, especially if the land includes extensive desert or mountain areas which are largely uninhabited. To find out how crowded one area is compared with another involves the use of more refined data—relating population not to total area but to land which is inhabited as opposed to waste, rural compared with urban, in pasture or in crop. In short the unit area is selected according to the question which is asked. In order to compare accurately the density of rural population in say, Ireland and Iran it is first necessary to establish what is meant by 'farm land' in both countries, and the different occupations that are included in the term 'rural'—are craftsmen, quarry-workers, fishermen and shopkeepers who live in rural areas to be included as well as farmers? In short, accurate enumeration can be quite complicated and it is wise to remember this when people remark, for example, that a country like the Netherlands is much more densely populated than India. This may be true for simple man/land ratios, but it ignores the point that the Netherlands is a heavily urbanised country which enjoys a relatively high standard of living whereas the population of India is predominantly rural. Moreover rural areas in India which have similar population densities to the Netherlands may be experiencing the acute shortages of food and capital which are associated with over-population. These cautionary remarks are intended to emphasise the fact that statistical comparisons are rarely as straightforward as they may seem. But having underlined this point we can now return to the distribution of world population, realising that regional contrasts in population densities would be even greater if more refined data were used than the crude population densities shown in Figure 2.1.

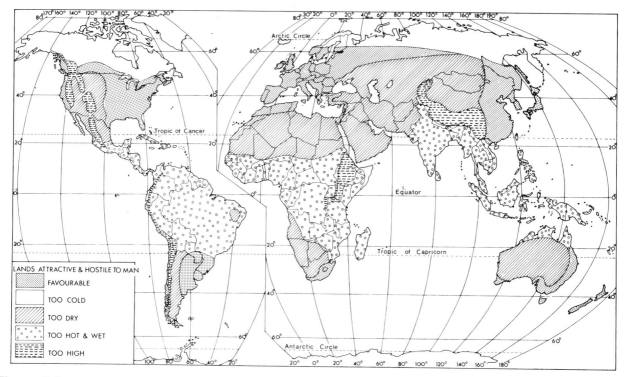

Figure 2.4
World environments which are
attractive and hostile to man

The lowest population densities in the world are found in three main latitudinal zones. First, the polar regions, around the Arctic Ocean from Canada to Siberia, where snow and ice predominate, giving way gradually to tundra and dense taiga forest as one moves from north to south. Secondly, almost equally low in density are the world's desert areas, lying roughly between 16° and 30° north and south. Those of the northern hemisphere include the Sahara in Africa, Saudi Arabia and the south-west of North America, and in the southern hemisphere much of western and central Australia, the Kalahari Desert in Africa and the Atacama in South America. Thirdly, there is the equatorial zone of tropical rain forest, which reaches its greatest extent in the Amazon basin of South America. Finally, and in addition to these zonal distributions of population, there are the great mountain chains of the Americas and Eurasia where topography as well as climate discourages many forms of organic life. Yet despite the difficulties presented by these environments none is totally uninhabited; scientists live in the Polar areas as well as Eskimo in northern Canada and Greenland, while mining engineers and oilmen share the desert with those hunters, nomads and

25

cultivators who still follow their traditional way of life in these harsh environments.

The densities of these sparsely populated areas contrast greatly with the four great regional clusters in Eurasia and North America in which most of the world's people actually live. Closer examination of these clusters reveals certain common features. With the exception of Japan, each is based on extensive lowlands, drained by great rivers and has easy access to the sea. In Asia this is particularly the case with dense populations along the Yangtse Kiang and Hwang Ho rivers in China and the Ganges in India. Both here and in the western clusters the significance of coastal lowlands and major islands as centres of population can also be noted. Not all these centres of world population are equally old. Those of India and China have existed from early times in man's history; Europe is less ancient, and its trans-Atlantic extension to North America has developed only within the last two centuries. But no matter how long they have been occupied by man, each of these lowlands has become rich farmland, based on crops such as wheat, maize or rice. Today, of course, an increasing proportion of the world's people live at the very high densities

Figure 2.5
World population: the major concentrations of population

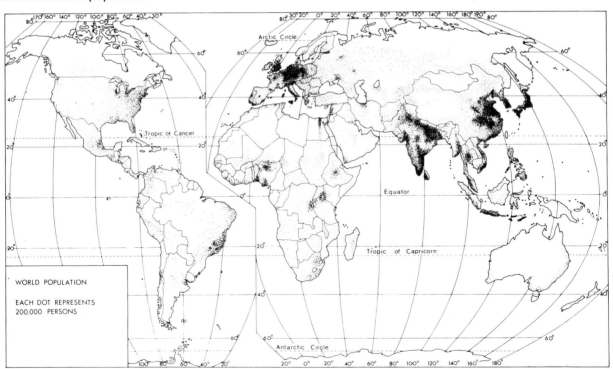

WORLD POPULATION

EACH DOT REPRESENTS
200,000 PERSONS

associated with urban life, and here there are important contrasts between the regional clusters of population. A majority of people in Europe and North America live in towns and cities, whereas in Asia the population is still mainly rural, even though some of the world's largest cities—for example, Tokyo-Yokohama with sixteen million people—and highest urban densities are found in Asia.

It has long been common to explain variations in population density at world scale in terms of topography and climate—indeed these associations were made almost automatically in describing the basic patterns outlined above. It seemed quite logical to an earlier generation of geographers to see these relationships as controls exerted by climate on human activities. Obviously such controls do exist: physiologically man works most efficiently within certain limits of temperature, rainfall, humidity and light—nobody feels really active on hot, sticky nights with the rain lashing down (Figure 2.6). Indirectly climate also affects food supply, by its influence on soil and vegetation. Consequently many geographers, notably the American Ellsworth Huntington, saw climate as the main determinant of world population distribution. Others, less certain of these arguments, sought other explanations—the type of economy for example: fewer people can be supported by nomadic herding than by intensive rice cultivation; and in the modern world it is easy to point to the location of mineral and energy resources such as iron-ore and coal as a major influence on the regional distribution of population.

In other words, simple correlations at world scale can give only a part of the truth: reality is very much more complex. In terms of population this is because man relates to environment through culture: he possesses the ability to make artifacts, develop techniques for using them and can communicate his experiences to those of his own generation and to others. Through culture man can ignore many of the laws of natural ecology which affect other living organisms—that is why the influence of climate is itself so greatly modified, enabling him to range more widely through the world than any other species. By a very early date he had occupied most parts of the world where his descendants are now found, though at densities which were only a fraction of some of those found today. The existing marked variations in world population densities have developed largely as culture itself has evolved,

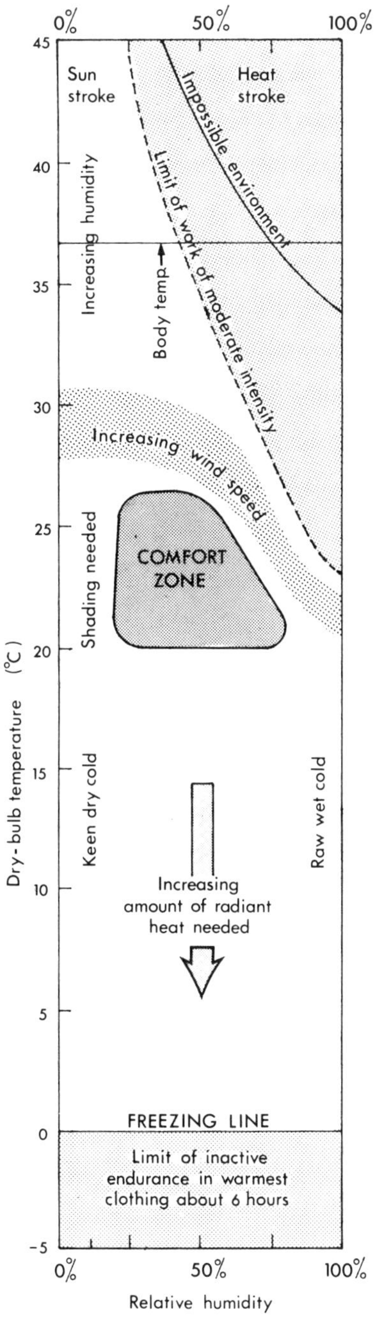

0%
50%
100%
Sun stroke
Heat stroke
Impossible environment
Limit of work of moderate intensity
Increasing humidity
Body temp.
Increasing wind speed
COMFORT ZONE
Shading needed
Keen dry cold
Raw wet cold
Increasing amount of radiant heat needed
FREEZING LINE
Limit of inactive endurance in warmest clothing about 6 hours
Dry-bulb temperature (°C)
45
40
35
30
25
20
15
10
5
0
-5
Relative humidity

Figure 2.6 Diagrammatic representation of the climatic conditions which white-skinned people find most comfortable

and the pattern has changed with major advances in culture. Two centuries ago, for example, both north-west Europe and North America were much more sparsely populated than today, the growth in their populations being associated with the development of the machine technology of the Industrial Revolution. Only by looking backwards in time, relating population growth to cultural development, can we really begin to understand why people are heavily concentrated in some parts of the world and sparsely distributed in others.

Population in History

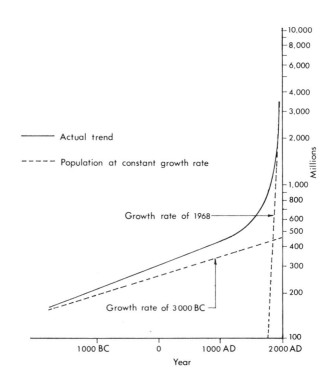

Figure 2.7
The growth of world population: trends based on logarithmic scale. The solid line indicates actual population growth, the broken line the trend that might be expected from the rate of increase estimated for 3000 B.C and A.D. 1968

For the greater part of man's history on earth, population numbers were small in total and increases were slow. Estimates of early populations are really little more than guesswork, but it seems unlikely that for most of the Paleolithic and Mesolithic periods, when men lived by hunting and gathering, numbers could have exceeded five million; and since they were widely distributed throughout the world, densities must have been very low indeed. The first major change began between 7000–6000 B.C. when man learned to increase his food supply, by inventing agriculture and domesticating animals. These new techniques of farming were responsible for the first clustering of population along the great rivers of the Middle East—the Nile, the Tigris and Euphrates, and the Indus; and rather later elsewhere, in China and central America. With farming, Neolithic man could increase the quantity of food available and ensure a more reliable supply than was possible in a hunting-gathering economy. This meant that local populations could grow in numbers, and marked fluctuations were less likely. Demographers thus think that world population may have reached between 250 and 300 million by the dawn of Christianity, and have doubled by 1650, reaching an estimated 500 million. By 1850 it had more than doubled again, reaching an estimated 1 262 million; and a century later, in 1950 it was 2 515 million, double the previous figure. The world estimate for 1970 was 3 635; and 70 million more people are being added to this total each year. By 2 000 there could be between 5 000 and 7 000 million people in the world. The real growth of world population then has occurred in modern times, reaching dramatic proportions during the past century and with implications for the immediate future that are difficult even to contemplate—the American ecologist Paul Ehrlich discusses them in a controversial book called *The Population Bomb,* an apt title which conveys the truly explosive proportions of world population growth.

Figure 2.8
Continental variations in the growth of world population since 1650

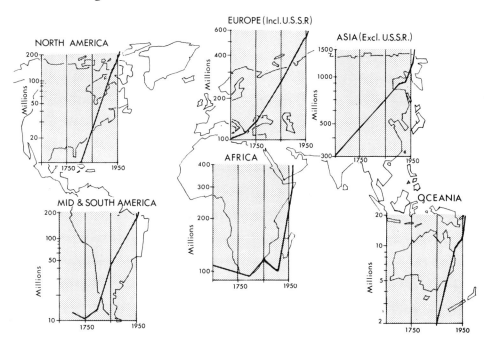

With this growth, regional differences in population density have also become more marked. We can see this at continental scale in Figure 2.8. Asians have long formed a majority of mankind, and their proportion of the total continues to increase. Two centuries ago Europe was the second major centre of world population, and although its numbers continue to grow, increases in Africa and Latin America are now very much greater. To understand why this should be so we must look at the demographic factors that are responsible for growth in population. These are natural increases—the difference between the number of births and deaths in a population, and migration—the movement of people between different places.

Age and Sex

Before examining these processes however it must also be noted that populations differ in their composition by age and sex, for these may affect both birth and death rates. Thus we would expect that a population with many elderly people would have higher death rates than one in which young married couples were in a majority; and one with a low proportion of married women should have a relatively low birth rate.

Figure 2.9
World sex ratios, 1965 data

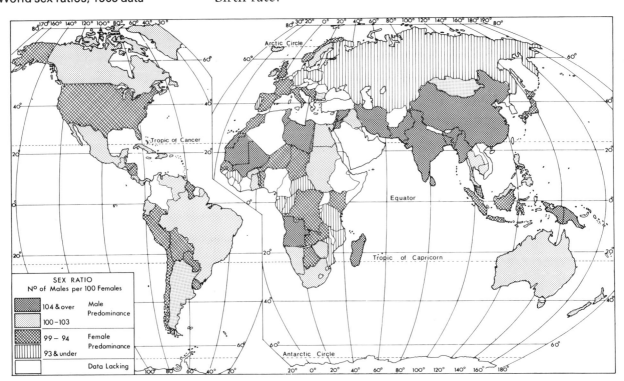

SEX RATIO
Nº of Males per 100 Females

104 & over	Male Predominance
100 – 103	
99 – 94	Female Predominance
93 & under	
	Data Lacking

In fact, populations differ much more in age structure than in sex, certainly at national level where the sexes are usually fairly evenly balanced. Male births exceed female in man as in most other mammals, but males have higher mortality rates from infancy on, and they do not usually live as long. World sex ratios, i.e. the number of women per 100 men, vary between 90 and 110 for different countries, but in some countries men predominate, for example, in China, India and Pakistan. This is explained by higher mortality rates among women, probably through child-birth, but in most countries local differences in sex ratio are more usually caused by migration. Men have usually moved from home more readily than women, with the result that men far outnumbered women in colonial areas in Canada or Australia during the last century. In the American gold rush of the 1860s, for example, the mining town of Bannock, Montana, recorded a population of 500 men and 10 women! Conversely, women were in a majority in areas of high emigration, a feature that was once characteristic of some Irish counties in the west. Today, however, it is much easier for women to find employment in towns and cities, and they now form a majority of migrants from rural to urban areas in most western countries. Most of the migrants are young, with the result that rural areas in Europe today have often more men than women, more old people than young and low rates of marriage. The age and sex structure of different populations can be easily compared by using a bar-graph called the *population pyramid* (Figure 2.10). The vertical axis of the graph divides

Figure 2.10
Population pyramids: the comparison between town and country in Ireland, 1966 data

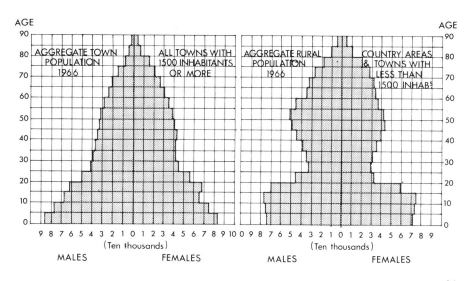

Figure 2.11
Population pyramids:
Mexico and Sweden,
1960 data

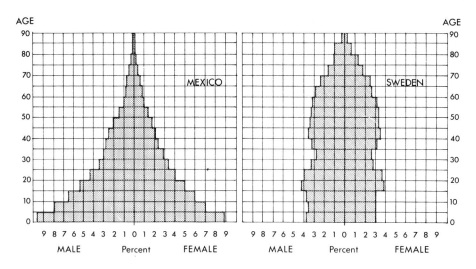

male and female, and is itself divided horizontally to indicate
the different age groups—usually at five year intervals from 0
to 80. The graph looks like a pyramid because there is little
difference in the proportions between the sexes at birth, and the
graph tapers towards the top as death progressively reduces the
number of people in each age group. Naturally the typical
pyramid rarely exists and there are many variations, the two
extremes being represented by the pyramids for Mexico and
Sweden illustrated in Figure 2.11. Mexico has a high birth rate
and many children, but the death rate is high in all age groups
and thus the sides of the pyramid slope inward at quite a sharp
angle. This is typical of many countries in Africa, Asia and
Latin America. The pyramid for Sweden, however, looks
more like a bell, with a narrow base, a middle-age spread, and a
slow tapering into old age. A similar shape is found in the
pyramids for most European countries and North America.
Notice that pyramids like these reflect minor fluctuations in
birth and death rates; in Ireland the effect of the Great Famine
of 1845–7, through death and emigration, is visible on
pyramids of the later nineteenth century; and the so-called
'baby boom' which followed the Second World War can be
seen in the pyramids for most European countries, including
neutral Sweden.

A further point to notice in the population pyramid is the
difference it reveals in age groupings between different countries, in particular the distribution between what are called the
active and the dependent groups. The former are those whose
activities support the latter, the actual range in age depending
upon the school-leaving and retirement ages which operate in

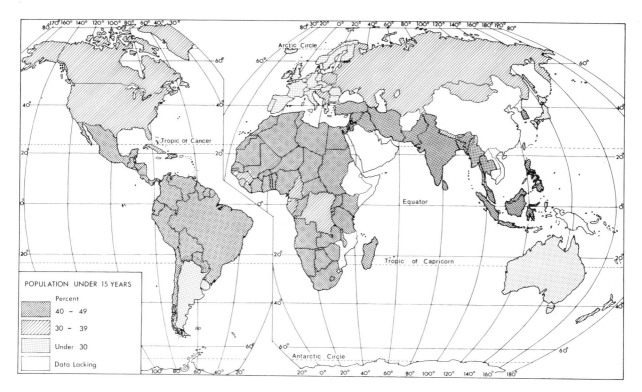

Figure 2.12
World population under 15 years,
1968 data

different countries. Of course in some areas this definition of an adult age group does not operate at all, but we can assume between the ages of sixteen and sixty-five as providing approximate limits. In fact the proportion of people in this adult age group does not vary greatly between most countries: the actual numbers do, for this depends upon national birth and death rates. But there are considerable regional differences in the dependent age groups, both among the young and the old. Where they are numerous in proportion to the active population they can represent quite a financial burden on national resources, making heavy demands on services such as education and welfare, in medical care and retirement pensions. In fact countries with a high proportion of old people are mainly found in Europe; those in which young dependents predominate are typical of Africa, Latin America and Asia. Hence the proportion of children under fifteen years can be as high as 40 per cent of the total population. These same countries usually have a much lower proportion of old people, because mortality rates are much higher than in Europe.

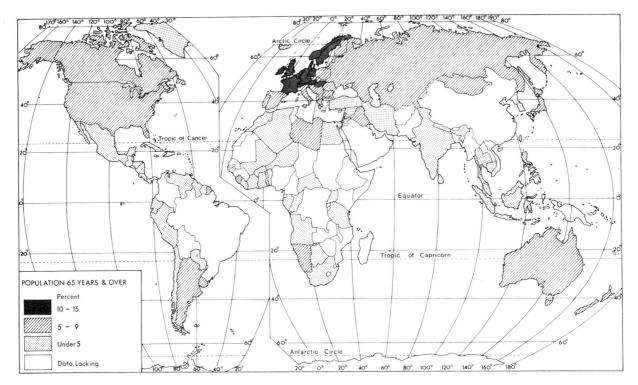

Figure 2.13
World population, 65 years and over, 1965 data

POPULATION 65 YEARS & OVER

Percent

10 – 15

5 – 9

Under 5

Data Lacking

Mortality and Fertility

Mortality and fertility are the terms used to describe the processes of death and birth in a population. We will look at mortality rates first because they tend to be more stable, fluctuating less than fertility rates, and are based on records which are more reliable and often go back longer in time. Moreover, mortality rates can themselves affect fertility, if deaths are numerous among women in the child-bearing age groups. Mortality can be measured in several ways, but for our purposes the *crude death-rate* is the most relevant index: it is the number of deaths per thousand inhabitants in a population in any one year.

In 1970 the world average death rate was 14 per thousand. Countries with lower rates include Australia, New Zealand, Canada, U.S.A., U.S.S.R. and most of Europe. Higher rates are found mainly in Africa, parts of Latin America and southern Asia, and sometimes they can be very high indeed, up to 300 per thousand in some areas. Much of this is due to a high incidence of death among infants and children, something that

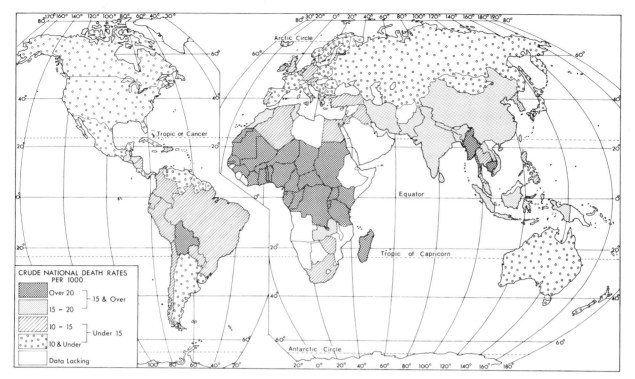

Figure 2.14
World mortality rates, based on crude death rates. Data 1968

was normal in our own society until nearly the end of the nineteenth century. But it also reflects a relatively low *life expectancy*. This term means simply the average number of years a person may expect to live when he is born. In this context we often think of the average span mentioned in the Bible—three score years and ten. This is now exceeded by a few years in most countries of western Europe and the U.S.A., but it is still much lower in most parts of Africa, Latin America and Asia. Incidentally this is an important spatial distinction between the European countries and their overseas derivatives in North America and Australasia, and the countries of tropical and north Africa, Latin America and Asia with the exception of the U.S.S.R. It recurs frequently in nearly all demographic data and in economic terms approximately the same regional groupings are implied by the terms *developed* and *underdeveloped* or *developing* countries.

In fact the low mortality rates of the developed countries are a relatively recent feature. Before the middle of the last century mortality rates in most European countries were similar to those of say Asia at the present time. Life expectancy had risen, but at a relatively slow rate during preceding centuries. For

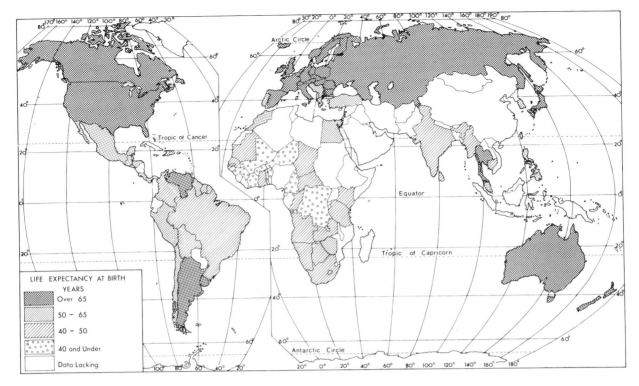

Figure 2.15
World life expectancy at birth,
1968 data

Figure 2.16
Changes in life expectancy over
the past 2000 years in selected
areas. In prehistoric times this is
thought to have been as low as 18
years; by 1789 it had doubled, as
seen in these figures for
Massachusetts and New
Hampshire in the U.S.A, and by
the 1950s it had quadrupled in
developed countries such as the
Netherlands

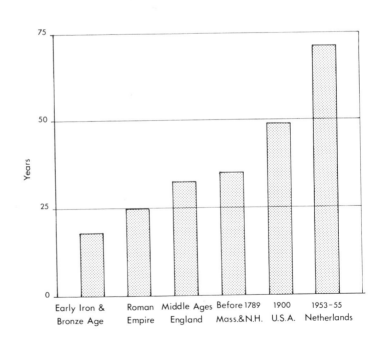

example a Roman born at the beginning of the Christian era had a life expectancy of 22 years; an Englishman born in 1650 could expect on average to live until he was 33. By 1840 life expectancy for the Englishman was still only 39, but by 1910 it had risen to 55, with a further substantial increase to 72 today. This increase, accompanied by a marked drop in the death rate, was largely confined to Europe and North America. It was brought about by a variety of economic and social changes—improvements in the quality and availability of food, better housing and sanitation and rising standards of living and working conditions. Improvements in medical science also helped to reduce infant mortality and to control formerly fatal diseases like plague, cholera and typhus. Life expectancy in the developed countries is now close to the biological limits of human age, and death rates have stabilised at a fairly low level.

Death control as it developed in the course of the nineteenth and early twentieth centuries affected only Europe and its associated overseas countries. In the rest of the world mortality rates and life expectancy remained at levels which Europe itself had experienced in earlier centuries. Only in the last few decades has it spread to the underdeveloped countries. Hence the downward trend in mortality is mainly the result of the wider application of medical knowledge and deliberate campaigns against infectious diseases. In most of these countries it has not yet been accompanied by the economic development which was an important cause of the increase in life expectancy in Europe a century ago. It seems probable that regional variations in world mortality will remain for some time to come, and nowhere is the decline likely to be so dramatic as to cause a major increase in population as a result of people living longer. In future, variations in fertility are much more likely to be the main cause of population growth.

By *Fertility rate* is meant the annual number of live births per thousand women in the child-bearing age groups—normally reckoned to be between fifteen and forty-nine years. Unfortunately fertility figures are not always very reliable, for birth statistics in many countries are highly inaccurate. But even bearing these limitations in mind there is a very considerable contrast in world fertility rates, much more so than with mortality; and once again the variation is most marked between the developed and underdeveloped countries. Thus the highest fertility rates, of 120 and over per thousand, are found in Africa, Latin America and south-east and south-west Asia. Conversely the lowest rates, 25 and under per thousand, are in North America, Australia and Europe, including the U.S.S.R.

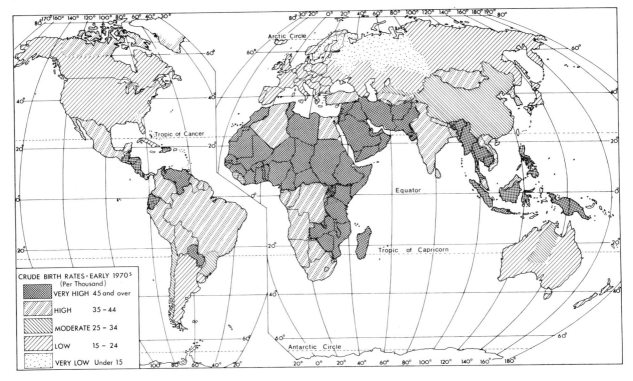

Figure 2.17
World fertility rates, based on
crude birth rates, data early 1970s

CRUDE BIRTH RATES · EARLY 1970s (Per Thousand)

VERY HIGH 45 and over
HIGH 35 – 44
MODERATE 25 – 34
LOW 15 – 24
VERY LOW Under 15

Since the highest fertility is found in the world's most densely populated areas, population increase here will far outstrip that in the remainder of the world.

Like mortality, there has been a downward trend in fertility rates but this has only been really marked in Europe and North America since about 1850. Fertility was lowest here during the 1930s, moving upward briefly in the so-called 'baby boom' at the end of the Second World War, but stabilising again since 1950. Elsewhere only Japan has experienced a similar drop in fertility, although everywhere birth rates are falling slightly and are liable to short term fluctuations.

The reason for these fluctuations is that fertility and birth rates are influenced by a wide range of social, economic, political and moral factors. Unlike death, birth is neither inevitable nor involuntary: most of us need not marry unless we want to, and even if we do we need not have children. Birth can be arranged in a way that death cannot, and voluntary limitation in the size of families is the main reason why birth rates have fallen in North America and Europe. Economic considerations are also important. People may postpone marriage or delay having children until they feel they can afford them and, consequently, periods of economic recession can be associated with lower fertility in developed countries.

Figure 2.18
Changes in crude birth and death rates between 1750 and 1950 in France and in England and Wales

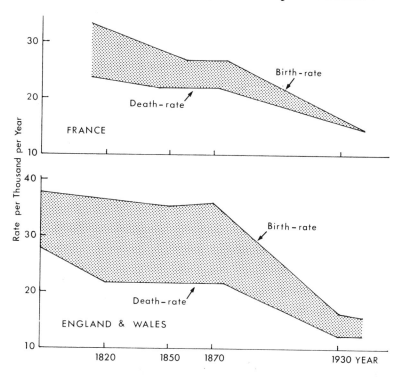

For these and other reasons regional trends in fertility are very difficult to predict, but what is certain is that trends in fertility will largely determine future patterns of world population growth. Death control is now fairly well established throughout the world and will be less subject to marked regional variations in future. Birth control is less widely practised, much harder to implement and far less acceptable; indeed it is rejected by many people on moral, social and practical grounds. The only other factor responsible for population growth is migration, but this has greatly declined at international level since the Second World War.

Migration

Migrations can be described and classified in all sorts of ways for they involve differences in distance, destination, numbers and motives. For our purposes, it is best to distinguish *international migration* which involves movements across state boundaries, and *internal migration* which takes place entirely within one state. International migrations vary in distance: they may

39

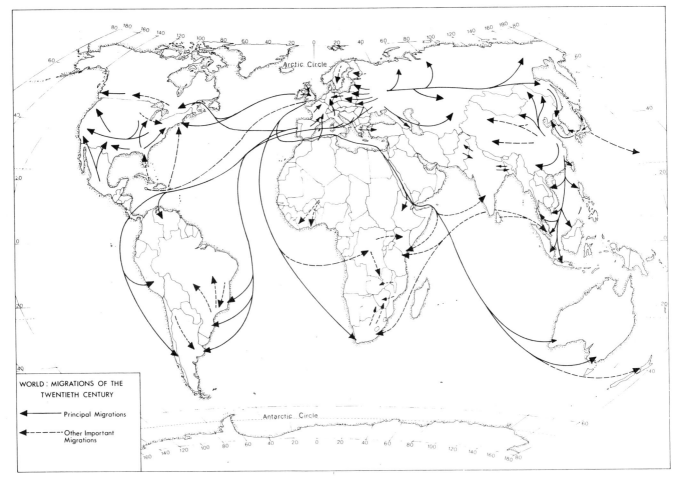

Figure 2.19
World migrations of the twentieth century

be simply between adjacent countries like Holland and Belgium, or between continents. On a world scale the latter are more important and it is with these that we are mainly concerned. Motives are also important, and can be considered under two main headings: *forced* migration in which the individual has little or no choice, and *free* migration where his decision is entirely voluntary.

International Migration
1 Forced Migration People may be forced to leave their homes and familiar surroundings through many circumstances, nearly all accompanied by considerable personal hardship and anxiety. These can be considered under four main headings.

40

(a) *Environmental Crises* were among the most important causes of migration in earlier times when men lacked the technology to cope with hazards such as floods, earthquakes or volcanic eruptions. The Bible is full of stories which illustrate this theme, like the legend of Noah and the flood. Crop failure and famine may be included in this category and there are many examples of migrations associated with such disasters in more recent times. We are well aware of the effect of the Great Famine of 1845–7 in Ireland which resulted from the failure of the potato crop in successive years. The modern world has also experienced similar movements, although on a less massive scale, for modern methods of transport mean that relief supplies of food and medicine can be distributed more easily. Despite this, recurring drought in the early 1970s forced herdsmen to leave their seasonal pastures on the edge of the Sahara and move to other parts of west Africa. Marginal environments like these are highly sensitive to ecological change, and some scholars believe that the loss of similar pasture in central Asia helped to trigger major population movements in late prehistoric and early historic times. These population movements had profound effects on the early history of China and India, and in Europe were one of the reasons which led to the collapse of the Roman Empire.

Emigrants leaving Cork for Liverpool, an engraving from the *Illustrated London News* of 10 May 1851

(b) *Population Pressure* may also result in forced migration, although it is often associated with environmental crises, either as cause or effect. In Ireland, for example, the migrations of the 1840s were a direct result of the Great Famine, but it is doubtful if the effect of crop failure would have been so severe if population had not already reached levels far greater than the land itself could support. Today population pressure is an important cause of migration in small countries where land for farming and job opportunities are severely limited, as, for example, in Caribbean islands like Trinidad or Puerto Rico.

(c) *Economic Pressure* Migration movements usually involve two sets of forces: a push mechanism which starts the movement, and a pull factor which draws the migrant towards a particular destination. Economic pressures include both these forces, although the prospect of better wages or brighter prospects elsewhere usually results in the type of voluntary decision associated with free migration. But forced migration resulting from economic pressures in

Figure 2.20
The Atlantic Slave Trade: the volume and destination of slaves shipped from Africa to the New World between 1701 and 1810, the period when the trade was at its height

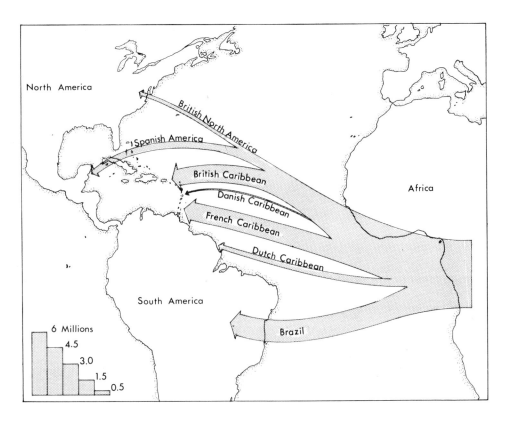

the past produced one of the greatest mass movements in history, the trans-Atlantic Slave Trade from Africa to the Americas. Here the motive was to satisfy a demand for cheap labour, which was unobtainable locally yet essential if the plantation economies developed in the New World were to survive and prosper. The Slave Trade began as early as the fifteenth century, reaching its peak in the late seventeenth and eighteenth centuries, and finally ceasing in the early nineteenth century. Estimates of the numbers of people forcibly moved during these three hundred years vary between five and fifteen million. Many died on the voyage: between 15 and 20 per cent was regarded as the average 'wastage', but it could rise as high as 50 per cent; and hundreds of thousands must have died before they reached the ships, on the long trek to the coast. The source of the American Slave Trade was the west coast of Africa, from Senegal to the Congo, although its ramifications spread far inland. To Africa it meant a major loss of population, in the active age groups; to the countries of the New World and the Caribbean it contributed new racial groups, economic wealth for some and misery for many others, cultural enrichment and political problems.

(d) *Political Pressures* are those in which the state is actively involved, either in the conduct of warfare or in the expulsion of citizens who have offended the government in power. All wars result in the destruction of property and the movement of refugees, but none had such a dramatic and tragic effect as the Second World War in Europe. The persecution of ethnic minorities, especially the Jews, forced labour movements and deportation, flight from the battlefront and invading armies and subsequent transfer and resettlement of refugees involved something of the order of sixty million people. This has had an immense effect on the economic and political structure of post-war Europe: for example, about a quarter of the population of West Germany—nearly ten million people—are officially recorded as refugees. It also spilled over into the Middle East in the resettlement of Jews in Palestine, a movement which began after the First World War and expanded rapidly after 1945. With the creation of the new state of Israel in 1948 a new stream of refugees began, the displaced Arabs settling in Jordan, Syria and the Lebanon. The number of refugees was small in comparison with Europe, or with the seventeen million people displaced during the partition of India

Figure 2.21
Migration of refugees from Eastern Europe since 1944. Most of the movement shown on the map occurred during or just at the end of the Second World War, but some migration has continued since, notably after the Hungarian uprising of 1956 and from Czechoslovakia in 1968

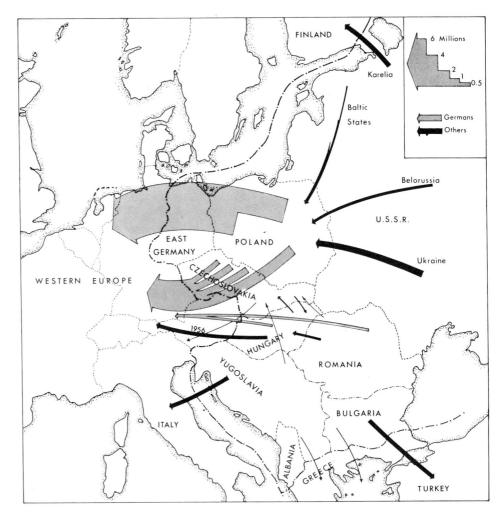

and Pakistan in 1947; but the resultant political problems remain a very live and explosive issue.

2 Free Migration In modern times the number of people who have left their home of their own free will far exceeds those who have been forced to move. Generally individual emigrants move away in search of a better job or a higher standard of living. These economic motives are extremely important and they may involve a host of subsidiary factors ranging from unemployment and redundancy, to government inducements on the part of the receiving country such as financial assistance, transport and guaranteed jobs. Governments may also encourage emigration themselves, by such indirect means as high taxation rates—an important factor in

44

Palestine Arab schoolboys returning to their homes in a refugee camp in east Jordan. This camp houses nearly 40,000 refugees who fled from the West Bank and the Gaza Strip as a result of the Arab-Israeli conflict of June, 1967

British emigration since the Second World War. But final decisions will probably be influenced by other reasons too—the desire for a better climate, search for a husband or wife, a feeling of adventure—all motives very difficult to classify but extremely relevant to the person concerned.

One final feature about free migration is that it is rarely an individual venture. Few people are real pioneers at heart although there are some in every community willing to face the hazards of life in new countries. The early colonists of North America included many people of this sort, like the hardy pioneers from eighteenth-century Ulster who settled in the wooded valleys among the Appalachian hills in Tennessee and Kentucky, and whose descendants became known as Hillbillies. More often free migration involves small groups of like-minded people who move deliberately to new environments, sometimes to preserve their religious beliefs. Thus many nonconformist sects moved from Europe in the eighteenth century to Pennsylvania, whose founder, the Quaker, William Penn, had guaranteed freedom of religious expression. One of the largest movements of this sort involved members of the Mormon Church in nineteenth-century America, although their migration was also stimulated by religious persecution. Theirs was an epic journey, in which some 20 000 people travelled more than 1600 kilometres across virgin land, from Illinois to the Rocky Mountains, where they established the new state of Utah in the 1840s.

Movements on this scale are truly mass migrations, and they are typical of the emigration which developed steadily from Europe to North America in the course of the nineteenth century. Irish, Italians, Poles and many other nationalities each established distinctive ethnic communities in the New World, and once begun the migration continued. Emigrants' letters home told of the hardships faced in the new country but also spoke of the opportunities, and it was these prospects which drew a steady stream of sons and daughters, nephews and nieces, cousins and grandchildren with each succeeding generation. In Ireland, migration which follows the paths already traced by kinsmen and people from the same parish has been endemic for more than a century, although its focus has shifted in the present generation from the U.S.A. to Great Britain.

Irish emigration to North America: advertisements like this, published in the *Belfast News Letter* of 30 January 1791, were very common in the press of the time.

30 January 1761

For the City of Philadelphia in America

The good ship *Joseph and Nancy*, burthen 250 tons, well victualled and manned, Captain James Taylor, Commander, will be clear to sail from hence by the 10th day of March next for Philadelphia aforesaid. Any person or persons that want their passage thither or that will go on redemption or as servants, or have goods to send on freight, may apply to Mr. Thomas Sinclaire, Merchant, or to said Captain at the house of Mr. Samuel Watt on the Hanover Kay who will agree with them on the most reasonable terms.

N.B.—She is a new ship and proves to be a prime sailer built this last summer, particularly designed for the accommodation of passengers; and as the Captain is known to be well experienced in that trade, those who take their passage with him may depend on the best usage. Such persons as have flaxseed sent them by said ship are desired to come immediately and receive it and pay the freight. Dated at Belfast 30th January, 1761.

Good new American flaxseed just imported to be sold by said Thomas Sinclaire.

Pattern The various pressures and motives which we have discussed are largely responsible for the modern patterns of migration which have had such an important effect on the structure and distribution of world population over the past three hundred years. They were also present in earlier migrations about which we have much less information, for the movements of pre-literate peoples are recorded only in the artifacts and folk-tales they leave behind. We can only speculate about the reasons which induced peoples of Mongol racial stock to migrate from eastern Asia to North America and thence through the entire continent, as far south as Tierra del Fuego; and about the voyages which peopled the island worlds of the Pacific. We can establish the direction and chronology of their movements, and recognise their cultural significance but as yet we cannot interpret their reasons for movement.

All that is certain is that the numbers involved in early migrations were only a fraction of those who moved to new countries in recent times. Among these the trans-Atlantic migration from Europe to the Americas is by far the most important. Beginning with small colonies of French, English, Spanish and Portuguese in the sixteenth century, the movement expanded steadily over the next two centuries, with Britain providing the bulk of the migrants, amounting to perhaps two million people in all. But in the early part of the nineteenth century migration quite suddenly became a mass movement from many European countries. Population growth, the result mainly of a falling death rate, was itself a major stimulus, but the reorganisation of agriculture associated with enclosure was also important. Between 1840 and 1914, fifty million people entered the U.S.A. alone, the majority in the period after 1880 when for a time the exodus from Europe to all overseas countries reached nearly one million people a year. Canada and the countries of South America, southern Africa, Australia and New Zealand shared in this mass migration of the latter part of the nineteenth century, although in proportions which were very much less than that of the U.S.A.

This spread of Europeans to so many parts of the world was by far the largest migration in history, but it was not the only one during this period. Similar movements occurred in Asia, from India, China and Japan, all regions with high population densities and low standards of living, which provided two major causes for emigration. But although they had the motives, Asians were never as free to move as Europeans. With the exception of Japan they lacked transport, for the major shipping companies were European owned, and they had no

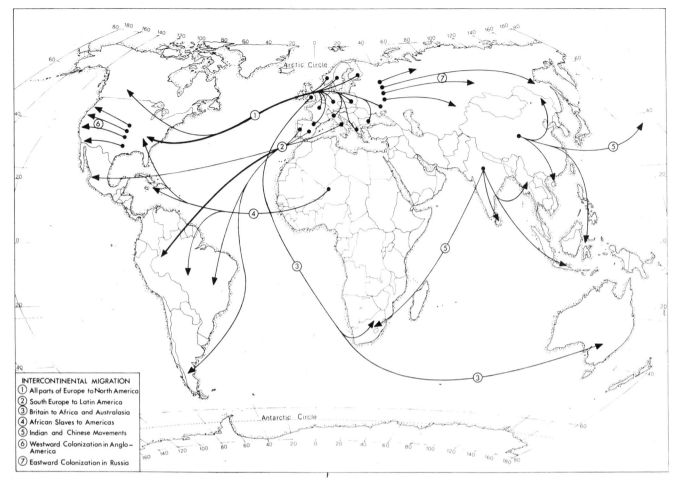

Figure 2.22
Intercontinental migration: a generalised map of the main movements since the early sixteenth century

INTERCONTINENTAL MIGRATION
1. All parts of Europe to North America
2. South Europe to Latin America
3. Britain to Africa and Australasia
4. African Slaves to Americas
5. Indian and Chinese Movements
6. Westward Colonization in Anglo-America
7. Eastward Colonization in Russia

tradition of long distance migration overseas to give them established links of community and kindred. Besides, Europeans were the first to reach the nearest 'empty lands', notably Australia, where they might have settled; and the Europeans did not want competition from Asians in land colonisation. Consequently when the Asians did migrate in any numbers they did so in the wake of Europeans, travelling on European ships and in most cases, working for Europeans.

This was especially the case with migration from India, a movement which mainly involved the indentured labourers known as coolies. The majority of these men who agreed to work for a fixed period for agreed wages, were initially employed in tropical plantations where crops like sugar need a

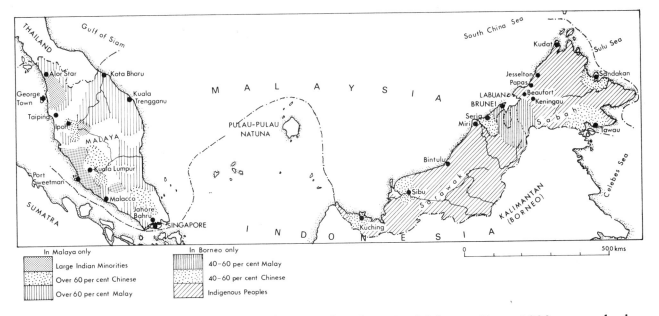

Figure 2.23
Malaysia: the proportion of Indians, Chinese and Malays in the different territories. Note that different percentages are used to designate the groups in Borneo from Malaya

large supply of acclimatised labour. From 1830 onwards they went to places like Mauritius and the West Indies, to Malaya and to east and south-east Africa where they worked first as labourers, later as shopkeepers and traders. Unlike the Indians who moved far from their traditional homeland, the Chinese tended to focus on south-east Asia, extending from Burma to the Philippines. Compared with the total population of China, the number of emigrants has always been small; in 1963 overseas Chinese were estimated to be about thirty million, compared with only five million Indians. Thus the Chinese form sizeable minorities wherever they settle and their influence is enormous for they are the real traders of the east. In contrast the Japanese appear as reluctant migrants, despite severe population pressures at home, and the political aspirations of a major industrial nation which by the early part of this century had become the equal of many European states. A sizeable number of colonists were settled in Manchuria and Korea well before the Second World War, with smaller numbers in tropical islands like Hawaii, and an interesting case, in Brazil. Resentment against Japanese occupation of so much of south-east Asia during the Second World War has meant that emigration virtually ceased after 1945.

This is also true of the world at large. Never again is there likely to be migration on the scale experienced by Europe in the nineteenth century, a movement which affected most parts of the world. Empty lands suitable for colonisation no longer

The Statue of Liberty, a gift from France to the U.S.A, erected in 1885 when transatlantic migration was still high. (*Photo courtesy of Radio Times Hulton Picture Library*)

exist, and more important, political restrictions against movement have been introduced progressively since the 1880s. Most countries in the world now operate stringent laws to regulate immigration. The U.S.A. was one of the first; its Act of 1882 was designed to discriminate against Asian immigration, a policy which was later adopted by Australia. In 1921 the Quota Act also curbed European immigration to the U.S.A., giving the words inscribed on the Statue of Liberty at the entrance to New York harbour a hollow ring:

give me your tired, your poor,
your huddled masses yearning to breathe free,
the wretched refuse of your teeming shore . . .

But although international migration is now actively discouraged and has virtually ceased, it was extremely important for two main reasons. Firstly, in terms of population it helped to postpone the inevitable problem of population growth for a time by redistributing a portion of the increase. Europe was the main beneficiary, not least because its population increase had begun to level off by the time migration ceased. Secondly, migration is selective: it is mainly late adolescents and young adults who move, and in earlier times women were fewer than men. At the peak period of emigration, this had an effect on the age/sex structures and the economies of sending and receiving countries, and it continues to do so in small countries like Ireland, or parts of Africa where migration continues and is largely male. But on a world scale the demographic effects of international migration are transitory. The scale of population growth is such that the redistribution of population achieved by colonising new lands a century ago has in no way slackened the natural increase in areas already densely occupied.

Much more important and more lasting are the cultural effects of population movement. When people migrate they take with them their language, customs, experiences and technology; all the attributes of their daily life are transferred to their new surroundings. Many of these are discarded as people adjust to a new environment and society, but others survive and a new way of life, often richer than the old for both native and migrant, develops through the fusion of the two. By these means cultures develop and cultural diversity is created. Migration plays a part in these processes, although its significance was greater in the past when movement took place mainly between lands already inhabited, involving peoples whose cultures were not greatly dissimilar. The great migrations of the last century, however, were to areas like North America or Australia, sparsely inhabited by people whose economy and technology was much simpler than that of the Europeans, and which as a result, has now largely disappeared. These same movements also brought Europeans to other lands though in smaller numbers, and it is in the links that they developed, in business, trade and politics that the great migrations have had a lasting effect. The colonial empires of Spain and Portugal, Holland, Britain and France which resulted from these movements have largely disappeared; in their wake has developed a host of economic and political problems, but there is also the legacy of contact and communication between peoples which has developed from the European migrations. If international migration has helped to create cultural diversity, it has also made mankind citizens of the same world.

Internal

Migration continues in the modern world, but it is now mainly confined within states where its effects may be much less dramatic than the large-scale international migrations of the past although no less important for the countries concerned. Internal migration is almost always voluntary, though forced migration may occur as a result of internal political crisis. Some 60 000 people, for example, were forced to leave their homes in Belfast as a result of violence and intimidation between 1968 and 1972.

Free migration takes place for much the same economic and social reasons as discussed above. The availability of jobs is nearly always the main reason, although many other factors will influence the individual, ranging from the quality and availability of local services such as schools and houses or recreation facilities, to the presence of friends and relatives. Certain communities have also a tradition of migration: this is very much the case in western Ireland and southern Italy, but it is also true of the urban population of the U.S.A. where it is estimated that one person in five changes home each year.

Internal migration usually assumes distinctive patterns, of which the most important are rural–urban and inter-regional, although it is not always possible to distinguish between the two. Movement from country to town is associated with industrialisation, and is the main reason for the rapid growth of cities in nineteenth-century Europe and in many countries of Asia, Latin America and Africa today. Usually the pull of employment opportunities in factories, the building trades, transport, shops and offices is increased by declining employment in rural areas resulting from the modernisation of agriculture, by pressure of population and low standards of living. Inter-regional migration is often an extension of this movement, with a drift of population from less prosperous regions to those more highly urbanised. The best example in Britain is the movement towards the south and south-east, where the London metropolitan region is the chief magnet, together with the smaller towns and coastal areas which are attractive as homes for commuters or for retirement.

Internal migration has two further aspects which should be mentioned. Firstly, neither of the types of movement described need be permanent; instead they can be seasonal or periodic in character. The former category could include the nomadic hunters and pastoralists of less complex societies than our own, and also the transhumance once widely practised by many European farmers, involving the movement of livestock to summer pastures in the hills. In Ireland this practice was known as booleying. Seasonal movement for employment is also found in many parts of Europe and the U.S.A. today, where certain types of crop such as fruit or grapes require a large labour force at harvest. In nineteenth-century Britain, seasonal labour was also needed for the hay and grain harvests, and it was provided by teams of men from Scotland and western Ireland who worked in Britain between planting and harvesting of their own crops at home. Often this type of seasonal movement leads the migrant to settle permanently away from home, or to return only periodically for short visits or on holiday. This type of movement is familiar in Ireland, in the mining areas of central and southern Africa, and in many countries of the European Economic Community which attract industrial workers from their less prosperous regions, as well as from adjacent countries like Algeria or Turkey.

Commuters: morning rush hour in Osaka, Japan

A second aspect of internal migration is that there are now many short-term movements which can be included in this category since they do involve major shifts of population. The most important of these are the journey to work and the journey for leisure, both resulting from the high mobility and living standards of modern industrial urban societies. The separation of work-place and residence can involve the urban commuter in long journeys by car or train, undertaken simultaneously with thousands of other people. Similarly, congestion of roads and high local densities of population on coast or in countryside results from modern demands for outdoor recreation. These movements are the most common types of migration practised in contemporary urban society.

World Patterns of Population Growth

Migration and natural increase are the two demographic processes responsible for population growth. Migration has been a major cause of regional population increase in the past, but in the world today variations in growth at continental scale are mainly the result of differences in fertility and mortality. By comparing these rates we can recognise five main categories of population increase:

1 Low fertility and low mortality resulting in a low level of population growth are characteristic of most countries in Europe, North America and Japan.
2 Higher but declining fertility with low mortality and a moderate population increase is found in a few countries, including Malaysia, Ceylon and Chile.
3 High fertility with fairly low mortality and a rapid growth rate is found mainly in tropical Latin America.
4 High fertility and high but declining mortality giving considerable population growth is common in most Asian countries where population levels are already very high, and in north Africa.
5 High fertility and high mortality is found in all the least developed countries, notably in most of tropical Africa. Population growth is therefore low, but these areas have the potential for substantial increases in population when mortality rates begin to decline.

Predicting future growth from these trends is no easy task, for as we have seen, fertility and mortality rates are influenced

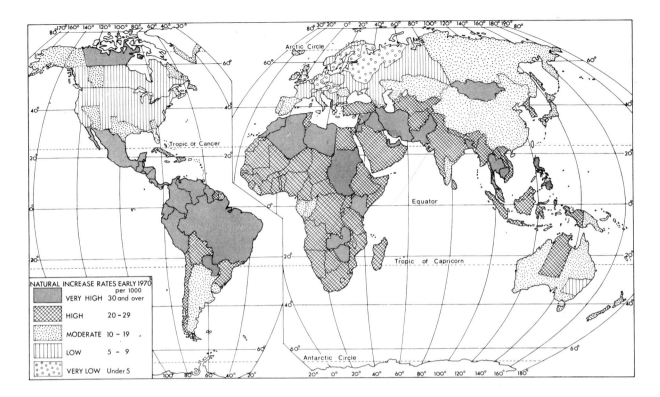

Figure 2.24
World: regional variations in the growth of population, data early 1970s

NATURAL INCREASE RATES EARLY 1970
per 1000
VERY HIGH 30 and over
HIGH 20 – 29
MODERATE 10 – 19
LOW 5 – 9
VERY LOW Under 5

by many factors. Mortality rates will almost certainly become fairly standardised throughout the world with little significant regional variation, but the timing of this is important in predicting levels of population during the remainder of this century. Likewise fertility should decline in those countries where it is high at present, but again the crucial question is—when? The countries of south Asia are especially important in this respect. Already they include the most densely populated areas of the world, and if their present fertility rates are maintained even for a few decades population growth will be enormous. Indeed on some reckonings the increase in Asia alone by the year 2000 could be equal to the number of people already present in the entire world. Tropical Africa and Latin America could also treble their populations by the end of the century. In comparison Europe, North America and Australia would experience a relative decline, with less than 20 per cent of the world's population in the year 2000 instead of the 30 per cent they contain at present.

No one is really sure what will happen, but many attempts have been made to devise models which would help to predict future growth. One such is called the *demographic transition*, a model which envisages that population growth will take place in four distinct stages.

Figure 2.25
The demographic transition, showing the four main stages

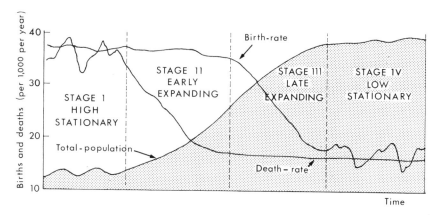

First comes a period of static or slowly increasing population characterised by high birth and death rates. Death rates fluctuate a great deal as a result of periodic famine and disease epidemics which affect all age groups, giving low life expectancy. This type of situation was formerly common everywhere in the world, and is found today for example in tropical Africa.

In the *second* stage death rates begin to fall with improvements in nutrition and health, and population enters a period of very rapid increase since birth rates remain high. This phase began in the early nineteenth century in Europe, and today is characteristic of much of tropical America.

At the *third* stage the rate of increase begins to slow: death rates stabilise at a fairly low level, and the birth rate also begins to decline, mainly as a result of deliberate limitation of the size of families. This occurred in Europe between 1880 and 1945, and is now happening in several Asian countries and in parts of Latin America.

The *fourth* and final stage begins when the population level is almost stationary: death rates are stable, but the birth rate is inclined to fluctuate slightly, giving a low increase in total population. This phase now applies to the urban, industrial societies of North America, Australia and Europe.

If the demographic transition is universally applicable, it should be possible to place different countries at their appropriate stage in the model and then predict their subsequent pattern of growth. For example, the countries of tropical Africa at present in stage one would then have to pass through two subsequent stages before their populations stabilised.

However, this may not happen in practice, for the demographic transition is based on the population history of Europe, and it does not follow that population growth in other continents will follow the same pattern. Indeed the contrary seems more likely. For example, several countries in Africa, Latin America and Asia have reduced their mortality rates much more quickly than in nineteenth-century Europe—in Ceylon the death rate dropped from twenty-two to ten per thousand between 1945 and 1952 following a very successful campaign for the eradication of malaria. Because of this, and since fertility remained high, population increases in these countries have been two and three times higher than in Europe at the equivalent stage. Fertility in Europe only began to fall with economic growth and higher living standards. So far this has not happened in the underdeveloped countries but with economic growth their fertility rates may drop too. Here it may be significant that the only non-European country which has followed the demographic transition is Japan, itself an economically advanced industrial nation.

But even if we cannot yet predict regional patterns of growth with any accuracy we can be certain that the level of population in the world by the end of the century will be very much higher than it is today. We can also be sure that the greater part of this growth will occur in the already dense concentrations of Asia, as well as in parts of Africa and Latin America.

For many people, this increase in world population is the really crucial issue of the twentieth century, a problem which is crucial to the future of mankind. The central issue is the relationship between population and resources: will population grow faster than man's capacity to produce food and the other resources necessary to maintain and improve standards of living throughout the world? Some believe that technological progress and a more equitable division of resources will make this possible, and that population will find its own level by natural means. Others are more pessimistic, foreseeing a world grossly overpopulated, with competition for resources becoming so great that widespread war, famine and disease will ultimately lead to a drastic reduction in numbers. People who predict this outcome usually look back to the eighteenth-century scholar, Thomas Malthus, who was the first to notice that numbers in a population had a tendency to increase at rates that were in geometric progression, whereas food production increased in arithmetic progression. Population growth must therefore at some stage exceed food supply, only to be checked by what he called 'war, vice and misery'.

57

Figure 2.26
Recent world trends in population and food production and in per capita food production. Note that per capita food production has levelled off because increased world food production has been offset by population growth

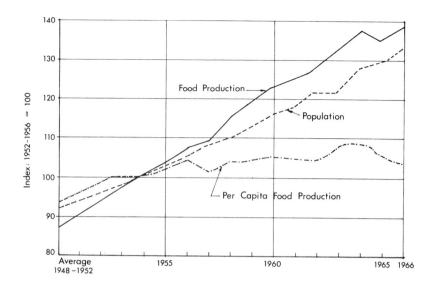

Many demographers and conservationists argue that the only way to avoid this ultimate catastrophe for mankind is to curtail population growth by reducing fertility. Many feel that this is only possible by government-sponsored programmes designed to encourage limitation in the size of families, although they recognise that birth control is far less acceptable than death control since it runs counter to many deeply held moral and religious beliefs. Nonetheless, family limitation is now official government policy in some of the world's most densely peopled countries, including India, although it is too early yet to gauge the effectiveness of these programmes in the long term.

Clearly some countries believe they must try to reduce their rate of population growth, but how far is this true for the world as a whole? Is there a maximum world population beyond which disasters of the sort predicted by Malthus will really take place, or are the scientists simply being pessimistic? In fact it is very difficult to answer this question objectively; resources by their nature are hard to quantify, and so are people's future needs and aspirations. For example, mineral oil was an unknown and unnecessary commodity for most people a century ago: now it is a vital ingredient in every industrial society, and a resource which appears to be diminishing very rapidly indeed. One reason for this is the use of the private car, virtually unknown as a means of transport even half a century

Family Planning in India: a woman waits to see the doctor at a state-sponsored clinic

ago but now regarded as a necessity of life in advanced industrial societies. If the car was to disappear through the exhaustion of the world's supplies of oil, people in Europe and North America would experience a very real decline in their standard of living; but a peasant farmer in India who never owned a car would not be greatly concerned, although he would be inconvenienced by the absence of trucks and buses. Oil is an example of one resource which will be affected by increasing demands made by rising standards of living and increasing population. There are others, even more relevant to the question of how many people can the world support. Food supply is an obvious example. We know from the papers that famines occur periodically in remote corners of the world, and various relief agencies remind us that many people in the world are hungry. How real is this problem, and where is it mainly found? Hunger can be measured objectively in two ways: by the amount of food we eat, in terms of calories; and by the balance between carbohydrates and proteins which our body needs to function properly. We usually think of the first when we say we are hungry—the technical term is *undernourished*; but the second is equally important since a balanced diet is essential to keep us healthy and full of energy. If the diet is unbalanced, we are said to suffer from *malnutrition*.

Comparable figures on nourishment and nutrition are difficult to establish accurately for different countries, but the problem areas of the world are clearly identified in Figure 2.27. In fact it is estimated that 20 per cent of the people in the low calorie countries have less than the average shown, and that 60 per cent lack one or more of the essential nutrients, usually

Figure 2.27
World: regional variations in nutritional standards, data from the 1960s

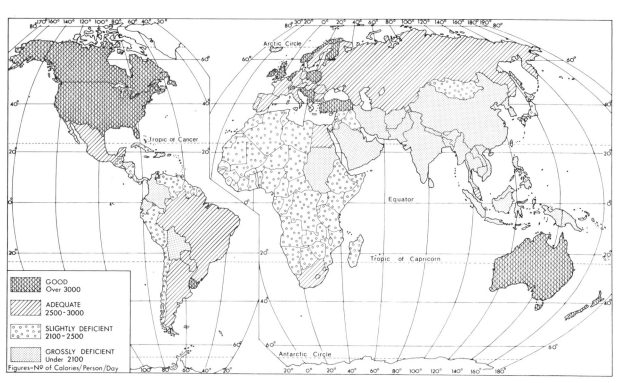

GOOD
Over 3000

ADEQUATE
2500-3000

SLIGHTLY DEFICIENT
2100-2500

GROSSLY DEFICIENT
Under 2100

Figures=Nº of Calories/Person/Day

protein. Moreover, undernourishment and malnutrition tend to go together.

If this is the position today, with perhaps one-third of the world's present population having insufficient food and inadequate diets, how can more people be supported? Scientists are confident that it is technically possible to increase world food supplies well above present levels. It is doubtful if the area cultivated can be greatly extended except at great capital cost, for example, through irrigation; but productivity could be increased, for example, by using higher yielding varieties of cereals. This is sometimes called the *green revolution*, and impressive results have been achieved, for example, with new strains of rice. But higher productivity also requires capital—for fertiliser among other things; and improved techniques need new methods of farming and systems of land-ownership, as well as new skills in management, administration and education. Unfortunately social, economic and political institutions are much more difficult to adjust and reform, and take far longer than the solution of technical problems. World food supply can be increased, but no one can predict if and when it will happen.

Figure 2.28
World population: projected growth to the year 2000. The shaded portion on the diagram indicates the range in estimates from low to high.

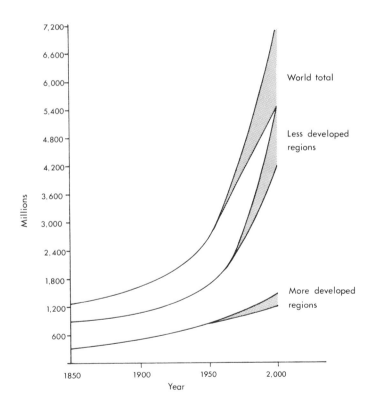

It is for reasons like these that it is so difficult to predict the consequences of world population growth as well as its future patterns. A better balance between population and resources cannot be achieved simply by limiting the size of families or by increasing the supply of food, essential though these both may be for man's future well-being. A greater priority is to devise means by which the world's resources can be shared more equitably, and distributed in such a way that all mankind has the opportunity to live at standards compatible with human dignity.

3

ECONOMIES

Making a living: a Peruvian Indian of the high Andes using a *tacla,* an implement very similar to the Irish *loy* or the Scottish *caschrom.* Like them it was used for digging the ground for the cultivation of potatoes, mainly for subsistence. (*Photo Carl Frank from Photo Researchers, Inc.*)

Where people live depends very much on how they make a living, that is the way they use the resources of an area to provide for their daily needs. The word *economy* is used to describe this very basic attribute of man's life on earth, but it is a term which covers an immensely wide range of human activities. For example, few of us today 'make a living' in the sense that we supply all our own needs. We rarely have to forage for our own food: we may shoot or snare the odd rabbit if we live in the country, go fishing or grow our own vegetables, but mostly we do this for fun, and not because we have to. Instead we buy our food from shops. Likewise we may make some of our clothes, but it is most unlikely that we will spin the thread or weave the cloth; nor are we likely to cut timber and quarry slate to build our own houses. We pay someone else to do these things for us, people with machinery and experience that we do not ourselves possess. So instead of 'making a living' most of us would say we 'earn a living', by selling our labour to an employer who pays us a wage or salary commensurate with the value he places on our skills, on the goods we make or the services we provide.

For much of human history, man has 'made a living' in the sense that his ability to survive has depended on his skill in

Earning a living: assembling organs in a Japanese factory. Most of the production is for export abroad

using local resources to satisfy his basic needs for food and shelter. But increasingly, more and more people have come to 'earn a living', by developing specialist skills and producing goods which are sold to others in return for commodities they need themselves. This sort of work requires a degree of commercial organisation to bring producer and consumer together for the exchange of goods, as well as efficient means of transport and communication. In short 'earning a living' represents a way of life different in many respects from that of people simply engaged in 'making a living'.

Our interest in economy in this book is derived from this last point, since we are mainly concerned with the study of spatial variations in the pattern of human life on earth. Differences in economic activities obviously have a major bearing on the patterns we seek to understand, and in this chapter we need some form of classification which will enable us to see how social organisation and economic activity are interrelated. From this we should be able to appreciate better the meaning of the terms *developed* and *underdeveloped* which were used previously in discussing population in Chapter 2, and which constitute one of the most significant divisions in the world of modern man. But first closer attention must be given to the word *economy* itself, in order to see it in terms of its constituent parts.

Economy

To survive as a living organism man needs a certain quantity of food and water each day. He needs to keep his body temperature within certain limits, and since his body is rather poorly insulated compared with other mammals he frequently has to supplement his natural covering of fat, skin and hair with clothing he makes himself. Finally, to protect himself further against extremes of temperature, precipitation and wind, and against predators, he often needs to build a shelter. These three are the basic needs which man must satisfy through the activities we call economic. They are based on converting resources into products, a process which involves expending energy and using implements or tools according to specified techniques, frequently with the organised labour of several people. Resources, technology, and social organisation are the main components of an economic system. They vary enormously in complexity and in the way in which they are interrelated in different forms of economic activity. For these reasons it is well to look at each in turn a little more closely before placing them in the context of the different economic systems practised throughout the world.

Food, clothing and shelter, man's basic needs illustrated in this painting of the camp of Algonkin Indians of north-eastern North America. Food is obtained by hunting, using the bow and arrow carried by the man in the centre, but maize is grown too and it is being ground by the woman left centre, using a wooden mortar. Clothing is made both from animal skins, prepared by the woman on the left, and by weaving, as in the loom on the right. Finally local resources are also used to make shelters, here made from elm bark. (*Photo courtesy of The American Museum of Natural History*)

1 Resources

Resources are derived from all the physical and biological materials that are found on earth—rocks, minerals, water, soil, vegetation and animal life. Some of these develop so slowly over geological time that their quantity is finite; for example, minerals like coal or uranium which can be exhausted through exploitation. Others are renewable in the sense that they recur through time although in quantities which may vary. Food crops are an example of this type of resource, their renewal being part of the normal biological cycle.

These material components of the environment are often called *natural resources* because their existence is due to natural processes which have nothing to do with man. But in fact they only become resources when man finds they are useful to him. They are a cultural concept, and their utilisation depends upon man's state of knowledge, his needs and his technological capacity at any one time. For example, coal was simply a soft, black stone until man learned that it would burn; but even then its use was restricted because major deposits were underground and thus largely inaccessible until man developed the tools and techniques necessary for their exploitation.

The level of technology is important for exploiting known resources—underwater drilling, for example, has made it possible to develop wells for oil and natural gas in offshore areas of the American Gulf coast and in the North Sea. In addition, technological developments can themselves create new resources from materials that already existed in the natural environment. For example, the rising demand for lubricants in the expanding machine technology of the nineteenth century led to the exploitation of mineral oil on an increasingly massive scale. In the 1840s 'Rock oil' as it was known in Pennsylvania, was thought to have some medicinal properties, and limited amounts were sold in small bottles. Forty years later, twenty-four million barrels of oil were produced in the same state for industrial purposes. The twentieth century has seen countless similar examples of the creation of new resources through technological development, from the use of uranium with the development of atomic power, to plastics and artificial fibres. Conversely, of course, some resources decline in importance through time to the point where lack of use means they are no longer considered to be a resource. Flint, for example, was one of the most important mineral resources of north-west Europe in prehistoric times, manufactured into a range of cutting tools, implements and weapons for which there were no human substitutes. Then came the momentous discovery of metal, first bronze and later iron, which rapidly made flint technology obsolete. Today only archaeologists can locate these sites of early industrial activity, and places along the Antrim coast in north-east Ireland which were major European industrial centres in prehistoric times through their abundant supplies of flint, are now of little economic significance.

Resources change therefore not only because reserves are depleted through exploitation, but also because of changes in man's needs. This in turn can profoundly affect the way of life of people whose livelihood depends upon the working of a particular resource. The flint-knappers of east Antrim were probably not greatly inconvenienced by the substitution of bronze and iron tools for the axes they produced in such quantities, for their society was unlikely to have been highly specialised and the majority of flint craftsmen were probably farmers as well. But the exhaustion of coal reserves and the development of open-cast mining techniques can have a profound effect upon specialist mining communities such as those of south Wales.

The location of natural resources is hence of critical importance, and since they are produced by natural processes, their distribution throughout the world is something over which man has no direct control. Moreover, their distribution is uneven, some regions being more richly endowed than others in terms of mineral wealth or biological resources. A British geographer, H J Fleure, recognised this many years ago when he divided the world into *human regions,* distinguished on the basis of the effort needed to maintain what he called 'the good life'—in reality, acceptable standards of civilised life. In some parts of the world, like the Arctic or equatorial forests, extreme environmental conditions made life difficult for the indigenous peoples. Even with great effort and considerable ingenuity people like the Eskimo could maintain only low levels of bare subsistence. In contrast, favourable conditions of soil and climate meant that relatively high standards of living could be enjoyed in Mediterranean Europe or Monsoon Asia

Figure 3.1
Lands whose environments are especially difficult for man because they are too cold, too dry, too hot and wet, or too high

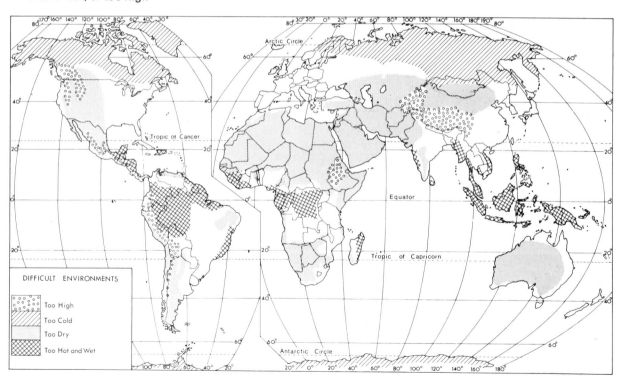

DIFFICULT ENVIRONMENTS

Too High
Too Cold
Too Dry
Too Hot and Wet

with comparatively little effort. And between these extremes were regions where men could prosper only by technological efficiency and a high input of energy.

In several respects this is an over-simplification of the relationship between man and environment in different parts of the world, but it underlines the point that natural resources are unevenly distributed. If man wishes to compensate for their absence he must develop the technical means to make the most of what is available locally; and if this is insufficient, he must seek alternative sources elsewhere. Through trade, the exchange of raw materials and manufactured goods, man has developed the means of redistributing resources which in nature are unevenly distributed. He has done so from very early times. The stone axes from north Antrim, for example, were traded widely in western and northern Europe; in the fifteenth and sixteenth centuries a much more complex pattern brought oriental spices to Europe to help preserve food and make it more palatable over the long months that separated one harvest from the next. This European example is especially important, for the spice trade stimulated the great voyages of discovery, which led Europeans to explore the world and eventually to develop its resources on a scale hitherto unknown.

2 Technology
Resources become important to man only when they are converted into goods or products that are useful to him. This is achieved by means of technology, which has three main aspects: tools, energy and techniques, the last being the ways in which tools and energy are used to produce specific goods or achieve certain goals. Energy is the basis of all technology, and man has searched constantly for ways in which to increase his own fairly limited resources—human muscle by itself can generate only about one-tenth of one unit of horse power, or seventy-five watts if we think in terms of units of electricity. Tools are one way in which he can do this, for they are simply objects devised by man to increase or transform energy and guide it in certain desired directions. The simplest tools are thus merely extensions of the human muscle: a stick used to flail grain increases the power of the human arm; a stone used as a hammer concentrates weight and adds force to the arm and hand. Many of the higher mammals use tools in this way, but only man makes them. No ape or chimpanzee has made a sophisticated implement like the long-bow which greatly increases human muscle power, transforms it by means of the

Caboche Indian, Brazil, shooting birds with a bow and arrow. The pose is unconventional to European eyes, but this nineteenth-century engraving illustrates the additional power and range which can be achieved with even a relatively simple artifact. (*Photo courtesy of Radio Times Hulton Picture Library*)

arrow and increases its range to cover considerable distances.

The bow is a more advanced artifact than tools like the hammer or knife which are direct extensions of human arms and hands. Like them it transmits energy, but it also magnifies the initial power enormously. Machines are artifacts which take this a stage further, transmitting and increasing energy but also changing its direction, as in the wheel which turns linear into rotary motion. Most primitive people have a wide variety of tools and implements in their technical equipment, but they usually have few true machines.

Once invented, tools and machines continue in use as long as they use energy efficiently. A blunt saw is less efficient than one newly sharpened; it will not cut wood as cleanly, and it will take much longer to do the job. Economy in the use of energy and time, and efficiency in use, are the main reasons why tools and machines are constantly being replaced by new inventions. But this does not mean they will be completely discarded: frequently they continue in use for a more restricted range of tasks than formerly. The plough, for example, is far more efficient than the spade for working in the field, but it is much too big and clumsy to use in the vegetable plot in the average garden.

Increasing efficiency in tool-making and a growing stock of implements and machines have characterised man's cultural development throughout history. Many of the really great advances in machine technology have occurred only in the last two centuries, but these in no way overshadow the technological achievements of prehistoric man. The use of the terms 'stone', 'bronze' and 'iron' to designate phases of prehistoric time underline this point, for they indicate periods when man learned new techniques of using raw materials to make tools more efficient than their predecessors.

The really great advances in technology have come when man has discovered new sources of power or devised new ways of harnessing known resources. Sometimes this has happened simultaneously with new developments in machine technology, as in the Industrial Revolution of the eighteenth and nineteenth centuries, but it has also occurred independently. Energy sources used by man may be *inanimate* or *animate*. The

Animal power: the drawing shows cattle yoked to a plough by their horns, taken from an Egyptian tomb painting of about 2000 B.C.

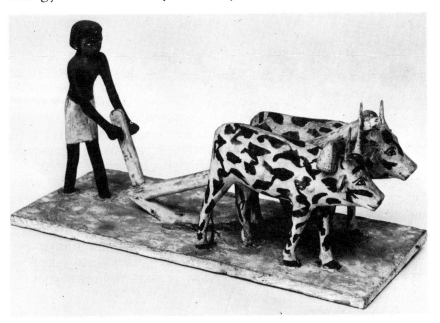

Making fire: an Australian aborigine rotates a long 'fire stick' against a piece of wood lying on the ground until it begins to heat. Dry moss placed alongside the wood then begins to smoulder and is blown until it ignites. (*Photo courtesy of Radio Times Hulton Picture Library*)

former have been much less important than the latter throughout human history, for man has found it much more difficult to control the power of wind or water as direct sources of energy. Instead his main sources have been derived from animate power, including both animals and plants, the latter being used either in living or fossil form. Fuels like coal and oil may be included in this category, since they are derived ultimately from living organisms, and are used directly as sources of energy. Living plants are more often used indirectly, providing energy for the animals which eat them, or fuel for fire.

Fire itself should not be regarded as a source of energy, but it deserves mention since its controlled use represents one of man's greatest achievements. Without fire, mankind would have been confined in early times to lands which never experience extreme cold; yet as far back as the second interglacial period, at least half a million years ago, he had spread right across Eurasia. Fire enabled man to range far beyond his tropical homeland, to have the benefit of light and warmth during long, cold nights, and to feel safe from predators. It introduced him to the art of cooking, the process by which the texture and taste of raw food is altered and made more digestible and palatable. In this way his range of foodstuffs was greatly extended, while the deliberate burning of vegetation further increased his food supply, by trapping animals and altering the character of plant growth, often to his advantage. Besides these many domestic uses, fire is essential in most forms of metal-working, and refinements in its use with different fuels have occurred at most stages of technological development.

The way man uses his environment is greatly influenced by his technology, and the amount and type of energy available to him sets fairly predictable limits on what he can or cannot do. For the greater part of his time on earth, man has had to rely on his own muscles for power, using simple hand tools; and in this low-energy economy his way of life was limited to a fairly basic subsistence. The first major development came when he learned to cultivate crops rather than gather seeds and fruit growing wild, and to domesticate animals instead of hunting them. We can think of this Neolithic Revolution, as it is called, as a revolution in the use of energy. Gradually animal power was substituted for human power in transport and in work on the land, and cultivated crops produced far more food than wild grasses in terms of the energy expended in harvesting them. Simultaneously, advances in tool-making gradually inaugurated a major new phase of technologcal development,

Figure 3.2

The Neolithic Revolution: the spread of farming in western Eurasia based on the distribution of the earliest known agricultural settlements in each region. Solid lines indicate positive evidence, hatched lines are conjectural. The periods represented are:
(a) up to 5000 B.C.;
(b) 5000–4000 B.C.;
(c) 4000–3000 B.C.

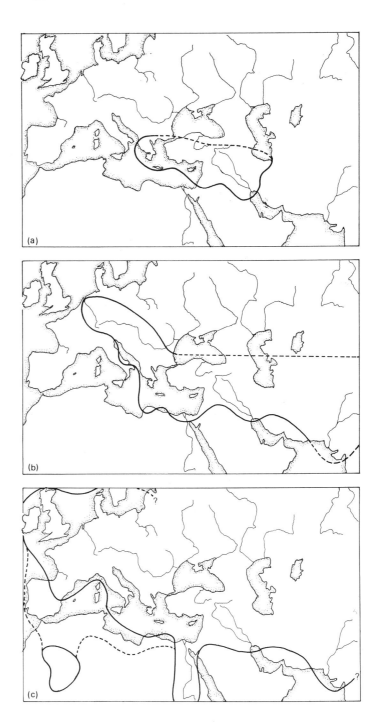

with social changes that soon became apparent. Population began to increase in numbers and in density now that a more stable supply of food was assured, and new and more complex forms of social organisation came into being. The village community replaced the family and tribe, farms began to develop with increasing specialisation in labour, and a whole range of arts flourished to form the basis of what we call civilisation. Of course many of these developments were foreshadowed in events that took place before the Neolithic; but it was only afterwards, and in a relatively short period of several thousand years that the first true civilisations were established—in that part of the Middle East known as the Fertile Crescent, stretching from the Nile to the Indus, in China, and later, in Central America.

Later technological developments in these areas were much less dramatic, although significant advances were made in the Mediterranean lands under the stimulus of Greece and Rome, and in China. But it was not until the eighteenth and nineteenth centuries that the rate of progress quickened, spurred on again by a revolution in the use of energy, this time based on coal and the use of steam. The Industrial Revolution, as it is often called, marks the beginning of this new phase of technological development in which we are still living. It initiated major changes in the processing of raw materials and manufacture of goods, created new materials and discovered new sources of energy in electricity and nuclear fission. At the same time labour itself was reorganised into large units of production as the multi-storey factory replaced the workshop, and management had to acquire a wide range of new skills.

The social effects of these changes were enormous and far-reaching; work became more specialised and locally concentrated with more and more people living in major clusters of population. Towns and cities coalesced to form conurbations, the major industrial centres being interlinked with complex networks of communication. The countries which first developed this new type of industrial, urban society soon had a way of life very different in style and standards of living from their contemporaries still in the low energy stage. And although the products of machine technology soon spread from the original centres in Europe and North America to most parts of the world, the earlier divisions persist, between the developed and underdeveloped countries. Differences in energy consumption provide a useful index of the economic gap that divides the countries of the world into these two major groupings, but it is important to remember that modern technology

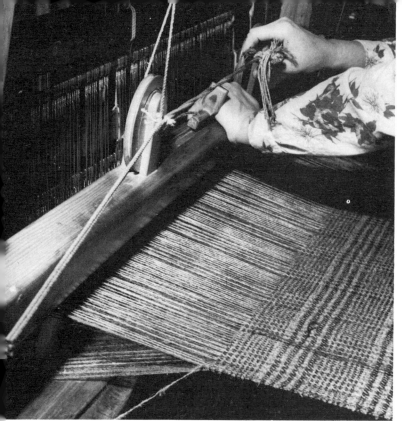

The Industrial Revolution: the contrast between animate and inanimate sources of power is well illustrated in the textile industry, between the hand-loom weaver of tweed cloth in the Hebrides, and the automated power looms of a factory in Twenthe Province, Holland

is only as secure as its energy sources. If the amount of energy available per capita were to diminish then living standards would begin to fall. Even a machine like the computer is a useless collection of metal and plastic without the electric power that makes it work.

Table 3.1 Income per head and energy production and consumption per head in selected countries, data 1956

| Country | *(in dollars and coal equivalent tons)* | | |
	Income per head	Energy consumption per head	Energy production per head
United States	2,078	8·58	8·28
Canada	1,493	8·25	5·77
Switzerland	1,195	3·18	1·75
New Zealand	1,135	2·81	1·97
United Kingdom	904	5·03	4·42
Denmark	823	2·62	0·10
Venezuela	664	2·18	29·41
Brazil	227	0·39	0·18
Iraq	175	0·48	8·41
Kuwait	80	1·54	359·27

3 Organisation

All forms of economic activity need some degree of organisation if technology is to be used efficiently to produce goods from raw materials. This is necessary even in the simplest operation. To make a stone axe, for example, early man had to locate a suitable rock outcrop, quarry the stone he wanted, and manufacture the axe on the spot or carry the stone away to work at home. And unless he was making it for himself or giving it away as a present, he would have to find someone who wanted an axe and was prepared to give him something in return. Every economic activity, whether it is manufacturing goods or producing food involves these three separate stages: locating the raw material or clearing the ground for cultivation, making the object or growing the crop, and distributing the finished product or produce. Of course the more complex the activity the greater the degree of organisation that is required. Making and selling a modern car is obviously a much more complicated business than fashioning a stone axe; it involves far more stages in manufacture, a highly sophisticated technology and the varied skills of a large labour force. And although production and distribution may progress through similar stages, there are some very major differences in the way in which these processes are organised, both in the manufacture of specific articles and in the economy at large. If we can identify these methods we should be able to understand more easily why societies also differ in their internal organisation, for economic and social structure are very closely related.

We can begin at the simplest level with economies based on hunting and food gathering. People in these societies usually try to satisfy only their immediate needs, and they require only simple procedures to achieve production and undertake exchange. Each member of the group undertakes much the same task in hunting and gathering, and each is responsible for making his own weapons and tools. He is essentially a Jack-of-all-trades, a non-specialist who learns all the skills necessary for his way of life in common with other members of the group. One can contrast this situation with the degree of specialisation necessary in modern industrial societies: a few years ago for example, a census published by the U.S. Employment Bureau listed more than 22 000 separate occupations.

In practice, of course, even very simple economies recognise some degree of specialisation, the most basic of all being the division of labour between the sexes. This is recognised in most societies, including our own, but it can take different forms. Normally women's work centres on tasks that can be

Work roles in tribal economies, illustrated from Indians of southern California. The men on the left are boring holes in shells to make into beads, while the women have been gathering acorns, The one in the centre has a carrying basket on her back: to the left another woman cracks acorns taken from the pile at her side, while to the right her companion grinds them into meal. (*Photo courtesy of The American Museum of Natural History*)

performed around the hearth and home—cooking, making pots and clothes and other jobs which can be done while minding children; but it can also include heavy labour in the fields, work which might seem more appropriate for men with their more muscular bodies. Advocates of women's liberation will be glad to know that there are no universal rules which divide the work of women from that of men!

Specialisation in work that is not directly related to sex or age tends to increase with greater variety in production and a wider range of implements and tools in daily use. Farmers, for example, need far more equipment than hunters and gatherers, and they may not always possess the skill and experience to make the tools and implements they need. For this they must rely on specialists, craftsmen like the wheelwright, the smith or the saddler. Craft work is often the first type of specialist

77

The country blacksmith, by far the most important craftsman in a traditional farming community since he has the skills needed to make the cutting tools and implements upon which most farming operations depend

occupation to develop when food gatherers become food producers. And when this happens societies must devise some method of arranging the exchange of goods between producers and consumers.

This is not as easy as it might seem: for instance, how are goods and services to be compared in value, and is the value to be fixed or allowed to fluctuate? Or put it another way: if a man is trying to exchange a spade he has made in return for food how does he establish its value in terms of eggs or meat or grain? Is the spade always to be worth the same quantity of food, or should it be worth more when food is plentiful but spades remain in short supply? Many methods have been used to overcome these difficulties of exchange in the past and some of these continue in use today; but the one most widely used today is the market system, in which goods are exchanged at prices determined by the law of supply and demand.

Trade in markets may be based on barter, as in the example cited above where the spademaker exchanged the implement he made for food (the word 'barter' means simply a business transaction in which no cash is involved). Trading by barter, however, can be very time-consuming: the spademaker who

Barter: a Canadian Eskimo exchanging pelts for groceries at a Hudson's Bay Company store. (*Photo by Richard Harrington, Camera Press*)

wanted a chicken would have to find someone who had surplus chickens and wanted a spade. Barter can work properly when only a few items are being exchanged, the work of a simple craftsman rather than the daily output of a factory; and thus it inhibits very greatly the volume of trade that can be conducted.

The alternative is to base the exchange on money. This can be used as a standard of value in the sense that every item for sale can be valued in money, thus providing an agreed system for the exchange of very different types of goods. But money has a further advantage in that it can be used as a means of payment: the spademaker is prepared to take cash rather than food for his spade because he knows he can use the money later to buy other goods of equivalent value. The use of money thus greatly simplifies the exchange and distribution of goods through markets. It has been used in some parts of the world for several thousand years, but Europeans were chiefly responsible for its increasing use over the past three centuries. Without it the expansion of world trade to its present levels would not have been possible, nor could modern technology have developed in the way it has.

Economies

Subsistence farming: the economy of the American Indians of Virginia as it appeared to the first Europeans to visit the area in 1590. Top left are seen hunters in the forest and on the right fields of young corn, together with pumpkins and tobacco. Materials used for making implements and weapons, building houses and making clothing were all derived from local resources. (*Photo courtesy of The American Museum of Natural History*)

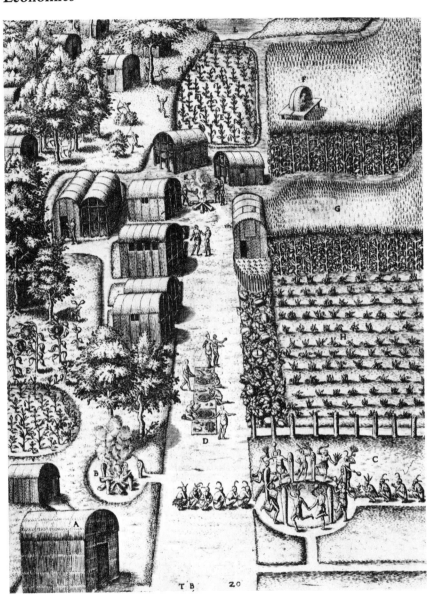

These differences in methods of organising production and distribution provide us with a simple basis for classifying world economies, and enable us to consider also their related forms of social organisation. At one end of the scale are *subsistence* economies, in which people rely almost entirely on their own resources, themselves consuming virtually everything that is produced, both food, artifacts and manufactured goods. Specialisation in work is minimal, for technology is simple and people have few possessions. Subsistence economies are associated with small groups of people, whose social relations are usually based on kinship. External contacts are few and their cultures tend to be stable and conservative: innovation is discounted for there is nothing to emulate and little to improve; and since numbers are limited there is little incentive to produce a surplus. When exchange takes place, it is based on barter. People in subsistence societies thus live lives that are independent of other social groups but in consequence are highly restricted, surviving only by means of their own effort and ingenuity. This means that life is insecure, often ending in food shortage, hunger and death.

This is much less likely to happen in advanced societies whose *market* economy fosters interdependence rather than

Market Economy: the type of commercial enterprise which has replaced Indian subsistence farming is exemplified in this photograph of a mixed arable and dairy farm on the shores of Lake Huron in Ontario, Canada

independence, providing commercial links between people possessing many different skills and ideas, exploiting various resources and using a wide variety of tools and facilities to produce a great range of goods. Specialisation by individuals and groups, by regions and even countries is the characteristic feature of market economies, in which the majority of people depend on industry rather than agriculture for their livelihood. All this is based on sophisticated systems of exchange, using money as the medium. In such societies kinship is of little importance, and social relations are governed by systems of law and contract rather than customary obligations. Often they are highly differentiated on the basis of wealth, which is unevenly distributed since each man earns a living according to the value society places on his skills. But although wealth and poverty exist side by side, living standards in advanced societies are immensely higher on average than among those whose economy is based on subsistence.

This woman from Lewis in the Outer Hebrides, with her solitary cow, illustrates the type of economy in which people produce a small surplus for the market but otherwise rely largely on their own resources. (*Photo courtesy of Radio Times Hulton Picture Library*)

Not all people in the world can be divided neatly into these two categories. Indeed the majority of mankind belong to an intermediate group who produce goods primarily to meet their own immediate needs, but also have a surplus available for exchange. This type of economic system is identified in particular with peasant societies. It is based primarily on agriculture and many aspects of its technology and social organisation resemble those of subsistence societies more closely than the urban-industrial complex of advanced nations. These economies vary greatly in detail, for they are widely distributed in the very different environments of Africa, Latin America and Asia; and of course formerly they were the norm

The plight of the rural migrant to the city: here Indian women scavenge in the company of vultures on the rubbish dumps of Delhi, framed by the electricity pylons which power the city's industries

in Europe too. But they all have certain common features: small-scale working units, few sources of power other than the muscles of men and animals, and only a limited surplus for sale in markets. Living standards are low, for agricultural produce is not sold for personal gain, but rather to pay rent for land and taxes. Historically, these commercial activities have helped to support small urban communities, but population increases during the present century have been greater than the land can accommodate, and many cities have grown rapidly in size, their population swollen by an influx of destitute people for whom there is little work available.

All three economic systems are at present undergoing change. There are now very few surviving subsistence economies which have not felt the impact of world trade, generated by the advanced industrial nations. Most peasant economies are in the throes of modernising traditional practices, spurred on by governments anxious to avoid the food shortages which are an inevitable consequence of population growth; and to develop industry as a means of diversifying their economic structure. In these circumstances it is perhaps misleading to use the terms 'subsistence' and 'peasant' to describe economic systems which are undergoing marked change. Instead some geographers prefer to use the terms *tribal*, *traditional* and *modern*. These are the ones we will use in this and the next chapter as we relate the general points we have been discussing to the types of economies practised in contemporary societies.

Types of Economy

There are so many ways of making and earning a living in different parts of the world that the categories used in any classification must be very broadly based. This is certainly true of the one used below in Table 3.2, which is intended to distinguish the main forms of livelihood followed by members of the three major social groupings we have already described. The activities themselves are divided into three main categories, according to whether they are based on the production of food or raw materials from natural resources (primary), involve further processing (secondary) or provide services for other producers (tertiary). In fact only in modern societies do these comprise well defined occupation groups involving large numbers of people. In each of the categories listed the type of activity is well defined, but the divisions are not rigid: any system of classification distorts reality by over-simplification, but this is necessary if we are to understand the complexity that exists in reality.

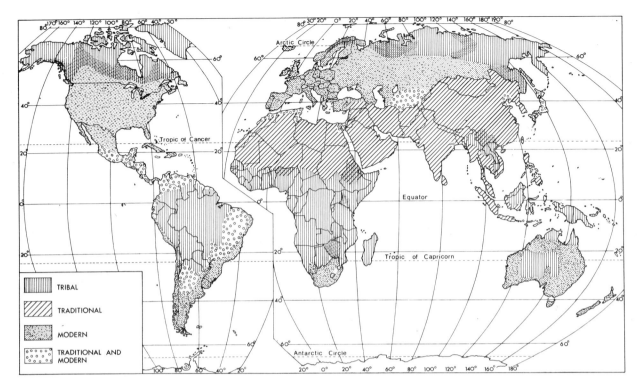

Figure 3.3
World Economies: this highly generalised map shows areas in which one or other of the three main types of economy is dominant. The divisions are rarely clear cut, and in many places different types may co-exist side by side

Legend:
- TRIBAL
- TRADITIONAL
- MODERN
- TRADITIONAL AND MODERN

Table 3.2 Types of Economy

Type of Society	Economic Activity		
	Primary	*Secondary*	*Tertiary*
Tribal	Hunting/gathering Herding Shifting cultivation		
Traditional	Intensive cultivation Pastoral Nomadism	Craftwork	
Modern	Mixed crop and livestock Crop farming Livestock rearing Plantation agriculture Forestry Fishing Mining	Manufac- turing	Distribution Finance Administration Personal Service

Tribal and modern economies meet here as New Guinea villagers lay a road using river pebbles, watched by the local District Officer

1 Tribal Economies

1.1 Hunting and gathering   Many people in modern societies hunt wildlife or gather berries in woods or from hedgerows, but very few people in the world today depend entirely on hunting and gathering for their subsistence. Except for fishing, people in modern and traditional societies are food producers, not food gatherers; yet this was the only form of economic activity known to early man until the dawn of the Neolithic some 9000 years ago. Today people who continue to follow this way of life are found only in the most remote and inaccessible corners of the world. In Africa they include the Bushmen of the Kalahari Desert and the Pygmy of the Ituri Forest in the Congo, probably the largest of the surviving groups; several Indian tribes of the tropical forests of Latin America; the Semang and Sakai of Malaya and Sumatra, and some other groups scattered in the forested mountain lands of upper Burma and Thailand. Even a century ago they were much more numerous: in the great plains of central North America and the south-western U.S.A., in Australia and Tasmania, and Latin America, as far south as Tierra del Fuego. Their distribution today is thus a survival of a time when hunters and gatherers were much more numerous and found in many different countries, not just in the marginal environments they inhabit today. For whenever their homelands were

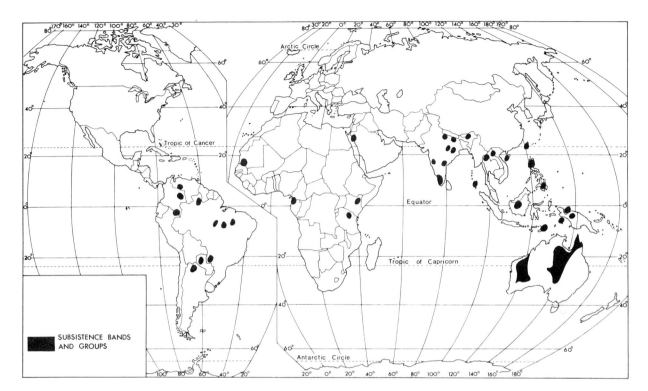

Figure 3.4
World distribution of hunting and
gathering economies in the mid
twentieth century

colonised by food producers, whether European, African or
Asian, they were either dispossessed or driven to extinction.
The reason for this is to be found in the structures of their
economy and society, which were more simple yet less flexible
than those of their successors.

The simplicity of food gathering economies is derived from
the fact that the group consumes whatever food it can collect
by hunting or gathering: there is no surplus for exchange and
nothing is made that is not used by its members. There is no
specialisation in labour except between the sexes: men are
usually the hunters, women the gatherers. Technology is simple, using a wide range of materials, but all derived from local
resources. Dwellings are usually little more than light shelters,
but tools and implements can be ingenious—like the Australian's boomerang, or the blow-pipe used both in south-east
Asia and Latin America. Possessions are few, however, and
equipment has to be light because food gatherers are always on
the move: since they have few domestic animals they must be
able to carry everything themselves. The one major exception
were the Plains Indians of North America who learned to tame

The Tasaday people of Mindanao in the south Philippines are a small band of hunters and gatherers whose primitive way of life was unknown to Western scientists until a few years ago. In this photograph the men are gathering food from the stream—crabs, shellfish, tadpoles and frogs. They also eat berries, bananas and roots, but the stream is their main source of food, as well as their principal highway. (*Photo by Helmut R. Schulze, Camera Press*)

and ride horses first introduced by the Spaniards in Mexico during the sixteenth century.

Hunters are mobile because they must move with the game and find new areas in which to gather food once local resources are exhausted. They make little attempt to process or preserve food: if a large animal is caught, or food is locally abundant they simply eat until it is finished and then move on. Living in the present in this way means that the search for food is constant; there is little conception of leisure and little security; and in times of scarcity people may have to go a long time without food. In these circumstances it is not surprising that mortality rates are high, and life expectancy low. The typical group has thus a much higher proportion of children than of adults, and very few middle-aged or elderly people.

Each group usually needs a large territory for its subsistence, although the area covered depends on the available resources. Contemporary hunters and gatherers live in marginal environments and population densities are thus very low: among the Kalahari Bushmen, for example, it is estimated at one person to every 8 square kilometres. Where environments experience a

Summer round up of buffalo by Cree Indians in Saskatchewan, Canada, drawn about 1800. The herd was surrounded by horsemen who then drove the animals between lines of tribesmen to a specially built corral where they were slaughtered. (*Photo courtesy of The American Museum of Natural History*)

marked seasonal rhythm with food resources abundant at certain times of the year, several groups may join temporarily to share the same territory. This was especially characteristic of the Plains Indians who followed the seasonal movements of the bison, congregating in the late spring and early summer as the animals moved from the foothills to gather in great herds on the fresh grass of the plains.

Rich food resources provided the basis for more specialised economies. They were found mainly in north-east Asia and North America, where besides the Plains Indians there were the Eskimo subsisting largely on sea mammals like the seal; and Indians like the Kwakiutl who exploited the rich fishing off the coasts of British Columbia, developing a culture which was perhaps the most advanced and elaborate of any non-agricultural people. Their range of equipment included many specialised weapons and tools, means of transport like the Indian travois, and the Eskimo kayak, sled, skis and snowshoes; and much more elaborate dwellings, ranging from the Kwakiutl timber-frame house to the tepee of the Plains Indians and the Eskimo igloo. Tribal people like these had more possessions than the more primitive hunters and gatherers, and they had the means of transporting them over land and water. They had more abundant food resources, and their greater efficiency in exploiting these led to the development of various methods of food processing and preservation. Life was less rigorous, more stable and settled and with a yearly cycle of seasonal activity in which periods of intensive hunting and fishing were succeeded by less strenuous times in which more leisured activities were possible. The fine wood carvings of the Coast Indians of British Columbia are familiar in their totem poles, while the Eskimo were expert in working ivory and 'soap stone'. Their high standards of craftsmanship show the extent to which specialisation in labour could develop in these richer communities, although they may not have had a formal pattern of exchange of goods and products.

Hunters and gatherers are often called 'primitive' because their way of life is much more simple than our own, and because their type of economy is the ancestor of all others. Its characteristic features are derived from an exclusive reliance on local resources for food and technical equipment, and this explains its main limitations. Such economies are finely adjusted to the natural cycle of plant and animal growth and regeneration, but they are highly vulnerable to natural disasters since they are so completely dependent upon their own efforts in obtaining food. Hunters and gatherers make no excessive demands in exploiting the resources of the natural environment, and their influence on vegetation and land forms is minimal. The one exception is their use of fire, which, it has been suggested, may have contributed to the development of some of the world's major grasslands, through the repeated burning of the original tree cover by hunters attempting to dislodge game from scrub and forest, or to increase grazing for herbivorous animals. But hunters and gatherers have made little impact on the world's landscape during the thousands of years when theirs was the main method of human subsistence. As their numbers have dwindled with the advance of modern civilisation many of the areas they formerly inhabited are now deserted, the old resources left largely unexploited or at least seldom used.

1.2 Herding Until recent times hunters and gatherers had no domestic animals except the dog, and it is generally accepted that animal domestication was first undertaken by cultivators. But in northern Eurasia, from the Arctic Coast of northern Scandinavia to the Bering Sea, a herding economy was practised by tribal peoples based on an animal, the reindeer, whose domestic form differed very little from its wild counterpart.

This reindeer-belt is one of extreme climate, and under natural conditions herds winter in the shelter of the taiga forest, moving north to graze the mosses, lichens and short grass of the tundra during the brief summer. Reindeer herders follow the same pattern: the Lapps in Scandinavia, for example,

moving from their winter settlements at the beginning of June to travel between three and five hundred kilometres in search of summer grazing. Further east, the Tungus migrate for distances of up to 1500 kilometres. Herds vary greatly in size between different tribal groups, from a few dozen animals owned by individual families to herds of several hundred head. But no matter the size of the herd, there is a constant search for grazing as the animals quickly use up available food and scatter over wide areas. This makes herding difficult, for at such times they are especially vulnerable to their main predator, the wolf.

Many tribes inhabit these harsh northern lands and there is considerable variation in their economies, which once included many hunters and gatherers as well as herders. Even the herders differ in the way they use the reindeer. In western Siberia it is used for driving with a sledge and as a decoy to attract wild animals in hunting. Further west it is used by the Lapps for milking, and in eastern Siberia for milking and for riding. The latter uses may have resulted from contact with horse and cattle herders further south, while the former may be derived from the techniques of people who were formerly hunters and food gatherers. But whatever the origin of reindeer domestication may be, all existing herders supplement their food supply by hunting and gathering, and use the domestic

Milking reindeer needs two people: one to hold and one to milk! (*Photo courtesy of The American Museum of Natural History*)

deer mainly for milk, taken both in liquid form and processed as cheese, and for transport. Very rarely are the domestic herds used as a source of meat, except for ceremonial feasts and in times of extreme food shortage. They are used, however, as a major source of raw materials for artifacts and domestic equipment, the bones for harpoons and fish hooks, sinews for string and thread, the hide for boots and leather clothing, and the hair for weaving into a rough cloth.

As with most hunters and gatherers, technology is simple, and tools and equipment are geared to a mobile life based on the migration cycle of the reindeer. The household with its herd is the main economic unit, living a very isolated life with only a few related families during the winter months when grazing is so scarce. In summer, however, much larger groups belonging to the same clan and tribe will foregather where grazing is plentiful, especially where other food supplies, like fish or berries, are available.

In its way of life, reindeer herding seems closer to hunting and gathering than to the pastoral economies of the nomads who herd sheep and cattle. Both rely heavily on their herds, but the domestic animals of the pastoralists are far further removed from their wild ancestors than the reindeer are from theirs, and the reindeer's habits in his particular environment resemble very closely those of his wild relatives. Thus the reindeer must range widely in his search for food, making supervision difficult, although at the same time close supervision is less necessary than with large domesticated herds of cattle or sheep. But reindeer herding also provides a much more precarious living. Reindeer are vulnerable to many predators, especially the wolf, and are frequently decimated by diseases like yellow anthrax. For that reason hunting and food gathering are essential to the herder's economy, the men engaging in hunting and the women looking after the herds when the men are away.

Life for the reindeer herder is precarious and food shortages are not uncommon. Indeed it is thought that some herders may have abandoned their former way of life and found other means of subsistence; for example, seasonal fishing communities living on the shores of the Sea of Okhotsk seem formerly to have been reindeer herders. Certainly herding as practised in northern Eurasia can support only a small and widely scattered population. Today the number of people who live in this way is fast declining, especially in the Soviet Union where new settlers have come to exploit the rich mineral and timber resources of Siberia. For the reindeer herder, such resources were largely irrelevant to his way of life.

1.3 Shifting Cultivation Farming, no matter how primitive, is a totally different way of life from hunting, gathering and herding, for it marks the transition from food collection to food production. This was the first decisive step towards man's control of environment, the means by which his numbers were to grow with a more regular supply of food, and settled communities were to be formed of increasing size and complexity. The impact of farming, in broadening the basis of man's supply of food, was made all the greater because the cultivation of plants was accompanied by the domestication of several species of animals and by technical improvements in tool making. The latter is represented by the replacement of flint tools by those made from polished stone which gave a much finer cutting edge; and since domestic animals provided a new source of energy as well as additional food supplies, these innovations helped to accelerate technological growth. For these reasons, the period when this all took place is often called the Neolithic Revolution.

These events of 10 000 years ago may seem very remote from the way of life practised by the tribal cultivators with whom we are concerned at present. But in fact some of their techniques of cultivation are little different from those of the first farmers of the Neolithic period; and many of the crops they grow, particularly in their regional variations, have changed little in the intervening centuries. Thus before we outline the characteristic features of tribal cultivation today we will look briefly at how agriculture itself is thought to have begun.

The way scientists have tackled this question of origins is to locate those parts of the world in which the wild relatives of cultivated plants are found under natural conditions. The assumption is that in those places man first learned the art of cultivation, although it is recognised that this process must have taken a very long time. Most of the main food crops grown in the world today are cereals, and with the exception of maize which originated in the New World, the wild grasses from which they were developed all belong to the Middle East. In this area of subtropical climate, marked by a long, dry season, and stretching from Syria through Anatolia to Iran, are found the wild varieties of grasses from which are derived most of the modern cereals: wheat, barley, rye, oats, millets and rice. From these same areas came the ancestors of sheep and cattle, the most important herd animals domesticated by man, with the horse from the steppes and the camel from the desert added a few thousand years later. The Middle East may not have been the only place where these animals were domesticated, but here

Figure 3.5
The Fertile Crescent: distribution of the wild grasses ancestral to wheat and barley,
(1) Einkorn; (2) Emmer; (3) Barley

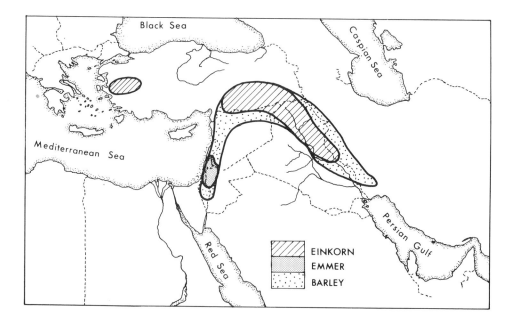

94

they were integrated with other farming activities from very early times. From elsewhere came the pig and fowl, probably from south-east Asia, and the dog which had almost certainly led a semi-domestic life from Palaeolithic times. The majority of domesticated animals thus came from Eurasia, with the New World contributing only the llama and the turkey as really significant additions.

The evidence of plant and animal geography, and of archaeological excavation suggests that the Middle East was the place where farming really began, about 10 000 years ago. But these sources do not tell us how it actually happened. Most scholars believe that some food gatherers, who collected seeds of wild grasses, accidentally discovered a variety whose seeds

Figure 3.6
Eurasia: distribution of the wild ancestors of modern domestic animals in the old world—pigs, cattle, goats and sheep, and the regions where they overlap

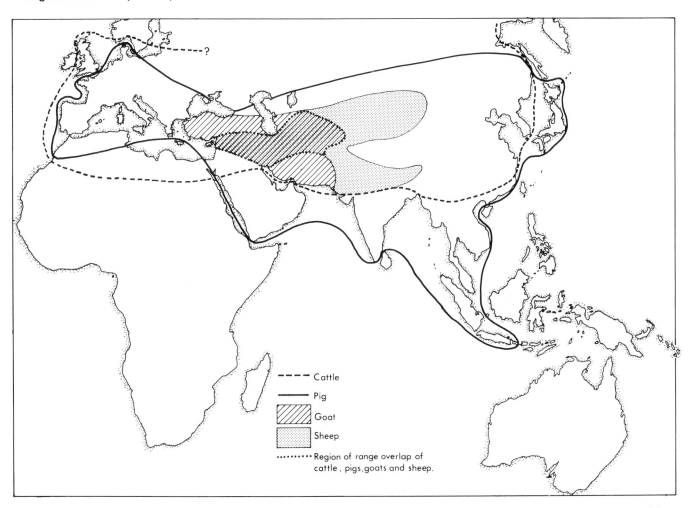

- - - - Cattle

——— Pig

Goat

Sheep

·········· Region of range overlap of cattle, pigs, goats and sheep.

did not explode and scatter over the ground as soon as they ripened. Instead they remained on the stalk long enough to be harvested, and this meant that they could be used much more effectively as a major source of food. From this chance discovery man gradually learned to breed a range of cereal crops, each adapted to different conditions of climate as knowledge of cultivation was diffused slowly to North Africa, Europe and India.

The main difficulty with this theory is that it is a very big step from collecting seeds of wild grasses to breeding new varieties of cereals and learning how to cultivate them so that they become productive crops. This led one scholar, the American geographer Carl Sauer, to suggest that farming did not begin with the fairly complicated task of cereal cultivation, but rather with the much simpler process of vegetative propagation. This means growing new plants from portions of the root or stem of existing ones, the natural process of reproduction in a great number of plants including the potato, and especially those which grow in the humid tropics or subtropics. Many such plants have edible roots, like the yam, taro and sweet potato which are widely grown as food crops in tropical countries today. And once man noticed how they were propagated, it was a fairly simple matter for him to encourage the natural process by planting on his own account. According to this view then, primitive cultivation began when man selected the plants he found most useful as sources of food, and planted them, using the same digging stick to dibble the holes for planting which formerly he had used to simply grub out the roots which grew naturally.

Sauer believes that farming originated in this way, and suggests two main locations where a wide range of suitable plants were found: in south-east Asia, including the mainland and associated islands, and the lands of central America which fringe the Caribbean. Cereal cultivation in Eurasia, he considers, followed later, developing on the margins of the planting economy in the Middle East—including the valleys of the Nile and lower Indus, Ethiopia and north China. In the New World, a similar sequence occurred, beginning with the cultivation of plants like cassava, squash and potatoes, with the later addition of a cereal crop, maize. Archaeological evidence for Sauer's theory has yet to be found, and it is by no means generally accepted. But it has the great merit of providing a more simple explanation for the origins of farming than much current theory, besides giving attention to the two basically different agricultural systems of vegetative planting and cereal cultivation which are of continuing significance in the modern world.

Many of the crops grown today are far removed from their Neolithic ancestors in appearance as well as in yield, but some of the techniques used in shifting cultivation would be quite familiar to Neolithic farmers. This term refers to a system of land use in which the area used for cropping is abandoned as soon as the soil shows signs of exhaustion and a new area developed instead. Typically the area is cleared by cutting and burning the natural vegetation, crops are sown or planted with the minimum preparation of the ground, and the growing crops are weeded and harvested by hand. Wood ash from the

Figure 3.7
Shifting cultivation: the changing pattern of land use during a seven year period at Fokole, Liberia. The village numbered about 1000 inhabitants, and the main crop was upland rice. Notice that there is about 6 acres in fallow to one under crop, and that by 1953 farmers had returned to land last cultivated in 1946

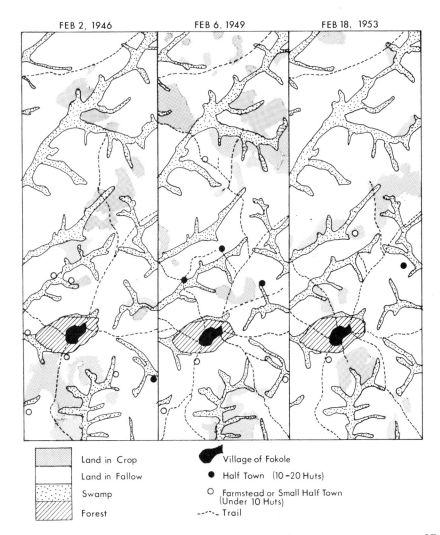

97

burnt vegetation provides a top dressing of soluble nutrients to assist plant growth, but no fertiliser is used to maintain soil fertility and after a few crops yields diminish, the plot is abandoned and the natural vegetation is allowed to regenerate. Meantime a new plot is cleared elsewhere and the cropping cycle begins again. Eventually the original plot may be cultivated once more, after a lapse of anything between five and twenty years after its initial abandonment. Shifting cultivation thus needs a fairly large area over which to operate if soil fertility is to be maintained by natural regeneration. Because it involves shifting the scene of operations, associated structures are often of a temporary nature: fences, for example, are rudimentary, and even houses may be abandoned if the distance between the settlement and the cultivation plots becomes too great.

Almost certainly this system is little different from that used by the earliest farmers, whether they grew cereals or vegetables, for it is based on a very simple application of the idea of crop rotation. In the world today, shifting cultivation supports perhaps 200 million people, so it is by far the most important of the economies we have classified as tribal. It is practised mainly in the tropical forest lands, in Latin America, Africa south of the Sahara, and the hill country of south and east Asia as well as many of the islands in the Pacific. It is also found on the savanna grasslands, especially in Africa; here clearance of natural vegetation is much less laborious than in the forest, but burning is more destructive of vegetation and soil, and regeneration takes longer, sometimes with a reduction in the number of plant species. Until the present century, shifting cultivation was also quite widely practised in the northern temperate lands of Eurasia, and surviving examples may still be found in Japan and Korea in the east, and Scandinavia in the west. Moreover, features reminiscent of shifting cultivation were found in the common field systems of Atlantic Europe, from Spain to Ireland, western Britain and Norway, suggesting that farming in these areas was derived ultimately from this system of land use. Many terms are used to describe it: 'slash-and-burn' and 'bush fallow' are commonly used as alternatives to 'shifting cultivation', while each language has its own word for the 'cleared plot'. Those often used by geographers include: *swidden*, an early English word meaning literally, a burnt over field; *milpa*, a term from central America and *ladang* in Indonesia.

The wide range of areas in which shifting cultivation is practised means that a great variety of crops may be grown within the system. They include roots like yam, sweet potato,

Shifting cultivation in central Sumatra. An area has been cleared of forest and the branches and undergrowth burnt. Later a crop of rice will be planted and after it has been harvested the land will be abandoned to the weed grass *lalang*

manioc and taro, and vegetables such as beans, peas, squash and melon. Trees are also grown, for example, banana and mango, and the coconut palm which is the most common of all. Tropical cereals include upland rice, especially in south-east Asia, millets and sorghums in Africa together with maize, though the last is most common in Latin America. Often one crop is regarded as the staple; where the climate is favourable it is often a cereal, as in much of tropical Africa where the millets and sorghums are by far the most important crops. But although one crop may dominate none is used exclusively; many different vegetables and cereals are usually sown together so that the cultivation plot provides crops in succession throughout the year. Generally there is little attempt at storage, the crops being harvested and eaten as soon as they are ready.

Despite the variety in crops grown, the techniques of shifting cultivation show many similarities wherever the system is practised. For example, there is no attempt to integrate livestock rearing with cropping as in the type of mixed farming familiar to farmers in Europe and North America. Livestock are kept by many shifting cultivators, especially in Africa where the savannas provide indifferent grazing for cattle, sheep and goats; but they are excluded from the cropped areas. Elsewhere in the tropics, domestic animals are mainly poultry,

99

duck and in Asia and the Pacific especially, pigs. No draft animals are kept, for the implements used in cultivation are based on human rather than animal power. This apparent omission may be explained by the scale and method of farming, for the hoe and digging stick are more useful than the plough for delving round tree stumps and weeding plants growing in small cultivation plots.

Generally the heaviest work in shifting cultivation is forest clearance. Farmers rarely have the implements to fell the largest trees, but even a simple stone axe can be used in ring barking while selective burning can reduce the tree to a trunk and transform the 'slash' and undergrowth to fertile ash in which the plants can grow. This is normally men's work, women being mainly responsible for the care of crops, undertaking most of the tasks of planting, weeding and harvesting. This involves constant labour since the different crops grown may ripen at different times; indeed shifting cultivation has none of the orderliness in planting or timing of harvest which is regarded as normal in farming in temperate lands. In addition women usually tend the small vegetable plots beside the settlement, which also contain fruit trees where the villages are semi-permanent. Women's life is certainly hard for besides work on the land and in the home they also gather wild fruits and berries to supplement their diet, while their menfolk engage in hunting and fishing.

Women's work! These hoe-wielding nuns at a Tanzanian mission are engaged in the traditional work of their lay sisters, although in this instance their hundred-acre farm is cropped by modern methods

Much of this labour involves the entire community of between fifty and two hundred individuals—the size varies greatly according to local resources and in some areas it may be very much larger. The individual household is the basic social unit, but cooperative work in forest clearance and cultivation gives the village community a special significance in economic activities, while the links of kinship give it further social cohesion. In addition, ownership of land is generally vested in the community rather than the individual: each household has a share in the crop rather than in the land.

The area to which the community lays claim depends on the length of time taken for forest regeneration after cultivation. A short interval between cropping cycles means that each community needs less land for its subsistence and this in turn depends on the crops grown, the fertility of the soil and the number of people in the village. It also depends on the pattern followed in shifting the cultivation plots: sometimes this follows a linear pattern, but it may also involve a circular movement. Again this depends on local conditions of topography and soil, although custom may also have an influence. The type of movement also affects settlement: where the sequence of cultivation moves in a circular path through the forest the settlement may be permanent, located near the centre of the village territory. If the movement is linear, the cultivation patches move further and further away from the village, involving long walks through the forest. When this occurs, temporary sleeping shelters may be built alongside the cropped land. Eventually, however, the village itself is moved to a new and more convenient site.

Shifting cultivation is a much more advanced system than the economies we have considered so far. It can support more people than most forms of food gathering and herding, though population densities are rarely more than twelve per square kilometre, and probably average much less. But it also has certain disadvantages which are becoming increasingly apparent in the modern world.

Firstly, food shortages and famine are not eliminated in this type of food producing economy, although it provides a much more secure basis for subsistence and a more balanced diet than among hunters and food gatherers. Cultivated plants are more susceptible to disease and to the ravages of insects and birds than those growing wild in the forest, while in the tropical environment shifting cultivators are as susceptible to the same range of infections and debilitating diseases which affect hunters and gatherers. Life expectancy is greater among the

Shifting cultivation in the Philippines. The trees in the foreground have been cut, the brushwood burnt and the ashes used as fertilizer for growing crops. However the top soil can be washed away during heavy rainfall since the plants which replace the trees are mostly shallow rooted and cannot bind the soil. Extensive forest clearance can thus lead to serious erosion, a problem that is here assessed by two forestry experts of the U.N. Food and Agricultural Organisation. (*F.A.O. photo*)

cultivators, but infant mortality in particular remains high, and few people survive to an advanced age.

Secondly, shifting cultivation is an efficient method of land use as long as the land can lie fallow long enough to restore soil fertility after cropping. The normal cycle of cropping and fallow is adjusted to maintain this ecological balance but it can be easily upset. For example, an increase in local population may mean that the cycle has to be shortened, unless there is enough empty land to establish a new community in an adjacent territory. Reduction in the length of the fallow period means that forest regeneration is not completed, and under tropical conditions of heat and heavy rainfall this can have an adverse effect on soil fertility. The level of plant nutrients in the soil is reduced, the growth of vegetation is retarded, and in extreme cases the soil itself may be reduced to a sterile laterite through leaching, or subjected to serious erosion.

Today most areas of shifting cultivation are under pressure to increase their productivity. Much of this is due to rising population as control of disease reduces mortality rates while birth rates remain high. But there is also a new incentive to grow commercial crops, partly as a result of internal demands for new implements or tools which can only be bought through markets; partly through external pressures, from government or major producers. In this way, for example, rubber seedlings may be grown in Indonesia, coffee beans in Latin America or oil palms in Africa. When crops like these are introduced, the total area cultivated must be extended if the level of food crops is to be maintained, and enlarged if demand increases; the traditional system of cultivation is gradually undermined, and the environment itself may suffer permanent damage.

The transition from shifting cultivation to cash cropping is represented here by coffee growing in Cameroon, west Africa. Here beans are cured at a co-operative mill

Ultimately shifting cultivation in the tropics must be replaced by more intensive methods of land use. This has already happened in other parts of the world—in Europe, for example, where the system was once part of normal agriculture. But the problems of rising population and of environment are much greater in the tropical lands today, and the transition to modern farming can only be achieved by major efforts on the part of the governments concerned, with help from various international agencies. Already the success of some experimental schemes in parts of east Africa and Nigeria shows that it can be done.

2 Traditional Economies

People who live in traditional societies are still concerned primarily with the basic problems of subsistence, of making a living using the local resources of the environments in which they live. But compared with tribal peoples, their economy is more highly organised and more productive, producing a surplus of crop or livestock which is exchanged through markets for a wide variety of goods and services. Traditional societies are thus more complex in their social organisation than those of tribal peoples, and where local resources are used efficiently, their economies can support far more people. Today the great majority of people live in societies organised in this way, and even modern commercial farmers are often only a few generations removed from their peasant ancestors.

2.1 Intensive cultivation Farming of this type is today most widely practised in east and south Asia, but similar economies predominate in the great river valleys of the Middle East, in Anatolia, and in Ethiopia—farther south they merge with the shifting cultivators of east Africa. In Central and South America, intensive peasant farming is found intermixed with large-scale commercial enterprise outside the tropical forest areas of shifting cultivation. In Europe, where true peasant farming was predominant until a century ago, some surviving communities continue the older methods of farming around the Mediterranean, in Italy and the Iberian Peninsula, and in parts of eastern Europe.

Traditional farming today is thus mainly associated with tropical lands, where the average temperature is consistently high and rainfall is seasonal, with a marked dry period. In the Old World, this climatic zone contains many different environments, but the main contrast is between the hills and the alluvial plains—especially those of the great river systems like

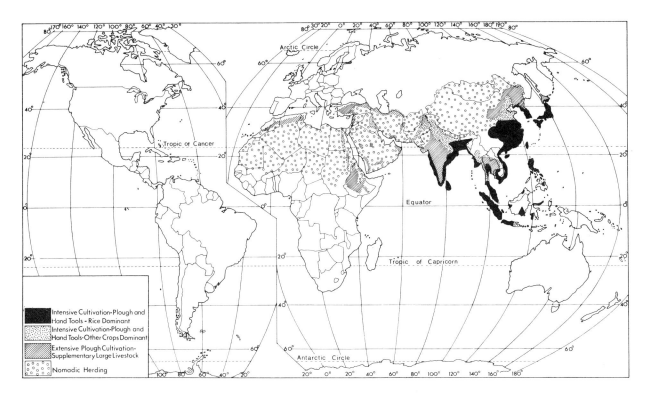

Figure 3.8
Old World: areas in which traditional economies still predominate

the Nile, the Tigris–Euphrates, the Indus and the Ganges and the Yangtze Kiang in China.

Almost certainly the type of sedentary farming with which we are concerned began in these same river valleys where it still flourishes. The crops grown throughout this zone vary considerably in response to different ecological conditions, but the different agricultural systems share some common features which distinguish them from the tribal economies based on shifting cultivation. Of basic importance is the fact that cultivation is permanent. Natural vegetation is cleared away, and the cultivated patches become permanent fields, often fenced to protect the growing crops from grazing livestock and demarcated to indicate ownership. With sedentary farming there is a problem of maintaining the fertility of the soil. This could be overcome quite easily in the flat river plains where annual flooding deposited rich alluvium on the fields after harvest; but elsewhere man had to learn to do this for himself if the land was to remain productive. He did so by using organic materials, derived from animal dung, human waste or compost. He also learned to conserve the soil, by letting fields lie idle for several years before cropping them again; or by alternating the crops grown in successive years. In most areas these two techniques, fallow and rotation, were used in conjunction with fertilisers.

Cropping in permanent fields means that the soil needs almost as much attention as the crops themselves, and for its preparation it needs more specialised implements than the axe and digging stick of the shifting cultivator. Probably the first to be developed were the hoe and the spade for working the soil, the sickle and the scythe to reap the crop and cut the hay, the flail and the winnowing tray to separate the grain from the chaff. These are all hand implements, but farmers in many areas soon began to use draft animals like the ox, the buffalo and the horse; and with their introduction came further innovations in the implements of arable farming. Of special significance was the plough, the universal symbol of the husbandman, which enabled the soil to be worked more efficiently than with hoe or spade. By using the plough a greater area could be cultivated, more crop could be grown and a bigger surplus produced. This in turn created a demand for better transport and storage, the use of wheeled vehicles and the development of a rudimentary road system. Obviously not all these things happened at once nor in the sequence indicated; but cereal

Reaping and stacking rice-sheaves by hand near Madras, India. (*Photo courtesy of Radio Times Hulton Picture Library*)

cultivation by means of the plough in permanent fields introduced a whole complex of related ideas and practices which spread quite quickly through the tropical lands of Eurasia, and northward to Mediterranean Europe. Wherever they went an artificial landscape of tilled fields and settlements was superimposed upon existing landforms and vegetation, creating lasting changes of far greater significance than the older methods of shifting cultivation.

The New World did not have the benefit of the plough or animal traction which so transformed the basis of agriculture in the Old World between six to seven thousand years ago. Yet here too agricultural innovations, based on the cultivation of maize with vegetables like squash and beans, helped to produce a food surplus which had far-reaching effects on economic and social organisation.

Livestock rearing has never been a major element in the agricultural systems of the tropical lands. In the Old World pigs and poultry are the most common domestic animals, scavenging around the village; and only land unsuitable for crop, or stubble is used for grazing cattle, buffalo or other draft animals. Fish provide the main source of protein, especially in east and south-east Asia, for peasant farmers are rarely hunters.

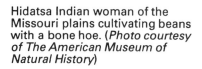

Hidatsa Indian woman of the Missouri plains cultivating beans with a bone hoe. (*Photo courtesy of The American Museum of Natural History*)

Terraced padi fields in Bali, Indonesia. This early morning photograph, taken in December, shows the fields flooded for planting rice seedlings. Notice how carefully the terraces follow the contours, and the intricate system of drainage channels

Cattle, sheep and goats only become economically significant on the dry margins of the tropical world and in Europe, where animal husbandry became fully integrated with arable farming at an early date.

Intensive peasant farming supports more people than shifting cultivation, but it also needs more labour and work is hard and constant for both men and women. The cultivation of lowland rice is particularly demanding, for the crop is grown in flooded fields. Consequently the land must first be graded, drainage ditches cut and the rivers embanked before the soil itself is cultivated. Seedlings are grown in carefully prepared seedbeds before being transplanted by hand, and the growing crop usually needs more fertiliser and frequent weeding before it is harvested. Moreover, several crops may be raised from the same plot of land each year. Men do most of the work in the fields, but labour demands are so heavy that women frequently help as well, especially at seed time and harvest.

Rice cultivation in particular is more like gardening than farming, but all peasant farming is small in scale compared with commercial cropping. Farms in the monsoon lands where rice is the main crop may be only a few hectares in size, and even then the land may be subdivided into a series of plots widely scattered through the cultivated land. In extreme cases fragmentation is so great that draft animals cannot be used efficiently, and the work is done entirely by hand.

Parcellement is the term often used to describe this process of fragmentation which is associated with peasant farming throughout the world. It results from the application of two separate principles, which in practice are often combined. One is that each farmer has a share in land rather than its produce—the principle usually followed in tribal economies; and therefore his share should be allocated according to differences in the quality of the soil. Each farmer should thus have a proportion of land that is good, as well as some of poorer quality. The second principle is based on the customs which decree how land is inherited. In some societies only one child may inherit his father's land, but in others all the sons and sometimes the daughters have an equal share, and the land is divided between them. Where this latter practice is followed, farms can become very quickly fragmented especially if population is also increasing. This happened in Ireland before the Famine, and is the present position in many of the tropical lands.

In peasant farming societies, the household is the basic economic and social unit, the farmer, his wife and children all working together on the farm. But land is vested in the community, and much of the labour in forest clearance and drainage as well as seasonal work on the land requires cooperation between its members. In this respect peasant villages resemble the settlements of shifting cultivators; and although they are usually much bigger, sometimes with more than two thousand people, the immobility of peasant families over many generations ensures a high degree of intermarriage. In such villages neighbours are often relatives, and the bonds of kinship make the village community a strongly integrated social unit.

Peasant villages, however, do not exist in isolation, for the surplus produced by the farmer is exchanged through markets which are often located in small urban centres. Urban development is not an essential attribute of peasant societies—periodic

Family labour: this photograph, taken in 1949 on the Aran Islands, off the west coast of Ireland, shows a farmer, his wife and son 'lashing' rye, to remove the grain from the straw

markets and fairs may be held in the open countryside; but where society is divided into several classes the market is often associated with the residence of a nobleman or landowner, and around it cluster the workshops of craftsmen and the stores of merchants. Very often peasant societies are stratified in this way; an upper class group owns the land which it rents to the farmers in return for produce or a cash payment. Indeed very often it is pressure of rent which is the main incentive for the farmer to produce a surplus for the market, and which ultimately forces him into a cash economy. Peasant society is thus organised in a much more complex way than the tribal cultivators discussed in the previous section.

The environments in which traditional peasant farming is practised are so varied that it is difficult to generalise about

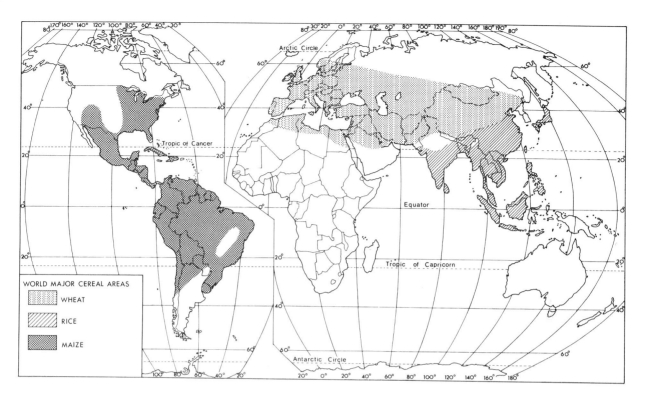

Figure 3.9
World: distribution of the three main cereals, wheat, rice and maize about A.D. 1500

farming techniques and the use of land. Even within the same region there may be major differences between hills and low-lands. Perhaps the greatest distinction is between arable farming based on cereals like wheat and millet, and the cultivation of rice, especially the varieties which are grown in flooded fields. The latter requires a whole range of sophisticated techniques for the control of water, as well as great care during the planting and growing season. Rice is a nutritious crop, and its intensive cultivation with multiple cropping plus an extensive use of vegetables supports some of the highest densities of rural population in the world, in China, Japan, south-east Asia and east India, the latter areas around the Bay of Bengal being the probable centre of its first domestication. With lower temperatures, less rainfall and poorer soil, rice gives way to more extensive farming based on wheat; and where rainfall is less certain the main crops are likely to be millets and sorghum, as in much of central India. Compared with rice, these cereals require far less labour in cultivation, for the land is ploughed dry, the seeds are sown broadcast, and usually only a single crop is grown. Wheat, however, is sometimes grown as a winter crop in the monsoon lands, to be followed by rice

111

planted during the wet months of summer. In the New World the cropping regime is different, for the main cereal is a native crop, maize, usually grown in association with beans and squash.

Today traditional farming throughout the world is changing through pressure of rising population and the influence of commercial farming. Population increases, especially in the monsoon lands of Asia, are among the highest in the world, and it is doubtful if they can be long sustained within the traditional system of farming. Intensive cultivation of paddy rice, for example, gives good crop yields per hectare, but productivity cannot be greatly increased without new techniques of farming and the reform of existing patterns of land holding. In addition, there is an urgent need for new sources of employment outside agriculture. A century ago Europe solved its population problem by agricultural reform, emigration and industrial development, and in the process its peasant cultivators became commercial farmers. Modern peasants in Asia and Latin America will find it much more difficult if they try to follow the same course.

2.2 Pastoralism Most people living in traditional societies are farmers, their main activity is raising crops and with few exceptions rearing livestock is of minor importance. But there are also people whose entire economy is based on domestic animals, which provide them with food and most of their basic needs. Their numbers are few today, but in the past these societies have been extremely important, especially where their pastoralism has brought them into contact with settled farmers.

Pastoralism is very much an Old World economy: the main domestic animals of the New World, the llama and alpaca, being kept for transport and wool respectively, and rarely used as a source of food. And in the Old World, the distribution of pastoralism is broadly zonal: reindeer herding in the sub-Arctic giving way to horses and sheep in central Asia, to camels in the dry zones of the Middle East and north Africa, and finally to cattle in the savannas of subtropical Africa. In each of these zones the dominant animal is the one which provides the main source of food, but there are usually others, used for subsidiary activities, as draft animals or animals for riding.

The distribution of pastoralism today is probably little different from that of earlier times. Once it was thought that pastoralism represented a transitional stage in economic development, between hunting and gathering and sedentary

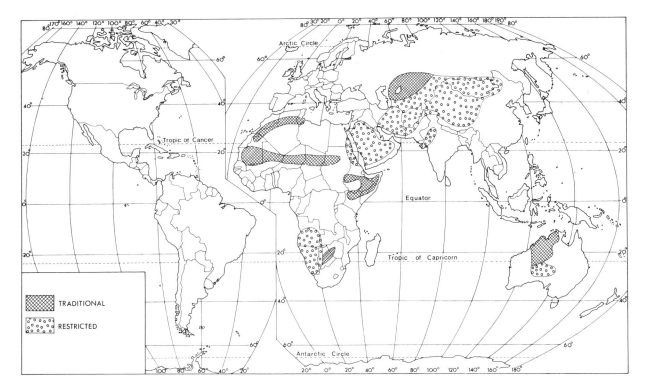

Figure 3.10
Old World: distribution of pastoral nomadism. In some parts of the world these economies retain most of their traditional features; elsewhere they have been absorbed into neighbouring and more specialised commercial economies. On this map the former are termed *traditional* and the latter *restricted*

farming; but it is now believed it developed as a specialist activity from cereal cultivation, probably in the Middle East where the main herd animals are thought to have been first domesticated. The biblical story of Cain and Abel relates the probable course of events, the shepherd leaving the arable land to exploit tracts of seasonal pasture which were too dry or too cold for successful farming.

The search for pasture dominates everything else in the pastoral way of life. The herdsman and the shepherd must be constantly on the move, searching for fresh grass and water for their animals. Their movements vary with the season; they are not made at random but follow routes prescribed by tradition yet sufficiently flexible to allow deviations in direction and length of stay according to the quality of grazing available in any one year. The pattern of movement may thus differ from one year to the next within the same environment, as it does between different regions. Some pastoralists, for example, may move quite short distances, especially those in uplands where differences in elevation may provide marked ecological contrasts between hill and valley. This is the case with the Masai who live in the equatorial highlands of east Africa. They may

Arab herdsmen with their camels, goats and sheep. Note the goat-hair tents

travel as little as 75 or 150 kilometres between their pastures, grazing their cattle on the short savanna grasses of the valleys during the wet season, and ranging more widely in the uplands during the longer periods of drought. On the other hand, the Kazak of Turkestan in central Asia may travel as much as eight hundred kilometres with their sheep and horses, across the dry plains before returning to the shelter of the foothills where they spend the winter.

Both the Masai and the Kazak are true pastoral nomads, but sedentary farmers may also use seasonal pasture for their livestock in the movement known as *transhumance*. In this the livestock, which are most often sheep and cattle, spend the winter on the home farm, but in late spring and summer they are driven to seasonal grazing in the hills and upland valleys and tended there by professional herdsmen, or by younger members of the farmers' own families. This type of movement is still practised in the European Alps, in several Mediterranean countries and Norway; and it was formerly a widespread custom in western Britain and Ireland.

The pastoral nomad, however, rarely grows crops; his way of life is geared to constant movement, and like tribal peoples he uses his livestock as a source of meat, their carcasses to make some of his artifacts, and their hair and wool as textiles. But in addition many pastoralists milk their livestock, make dairy produce, especially cheese, and use their animals as beasts of burden and for riding. Of course not all these practices are followed by individual groups: the Masai, for example, do not milk their cows nor do they use cattle as a means of transport —but they do use their blood.

Because pastoralists must be mobile, their possessions are generally limited and must be easily transported. Houses, for example, are usually portable, like the tent of the Bedouin camel herders of northern Arabia, or the Kazak's *yurt*—an ingenious felt-covered tent with a domed roof which is carried on a collapsible trellis-like frame made from flexible willow.

Typically, pastoral society is organised in small groups of kinsmen, a man and his sons with their families forming the main social and economic unit, travelling together with their flocks and herds. Such groups are usually fairly authoritarian in character, the head of the group wielding autocratic power like the patriarchs of the Old Testament. Herding groups are in turn combined in larger social units, the clan and the tribe, whose bond is recognition of a common ancestor. These larger groups rarely combine in normal pastoral activities; but grazing rights over specified territories are usually vested in them rather than in the herding groups. The institution of the clan thus provides a degree of social organisation in groups which are otherwise widely scattered, and which can take joint action to defend their territory if other groups encroach upon their traditional pastures.

Sometimes these associations for defence have assumed more aggressive postures. Pastoralists are not necessarily warlike, but their way of life gives them this capacity; their resources are mobile, and they are not encumbered by the fixed assets of farm and crop which root the farmer to his land. Consequently farmers living on the margins of cultivation have frequenetly been dominated by their pastoral neighbours. This is most notably the case in central Asia, where pastoralist and peasant have confronted each other down the centuries, and where names like Attila the Hun or Ghengis Khan testify to the political power of the pastoral nomads in history. Yet in the long run the plodding ploughman has had a more enduring influence on life and landscape in these areas than the nomadic warrior. The latter came from a wilderness which has remained little changed since he has gone, but the farmer remained and transformed the land with his fields and farms.

Farmers and pastoralists have also forged more peaceful relationships, for no herdsman has subsisted exclusively on his livestock and all have traded their produce of meat, butter, cheese, leather or wool for the farmer's grain, dates or tea. In the course of their migrations they could also obtain goods like salt, gum and resin which found a ready market in settled communities. Pastoralism and trade have thus been closely linked throughout history, not least because camels and horses provided a ready-made means of transport and the nomads' migration could easily be extended into an effective communication system.

In this respect the geographical position of the pastoral belt in the Old World was of crucial importance, dividing the temperate lands from the tropics. The pastoral nomads linked these contrasting regions in their normal movements, and local systems of trade ultimately developed into the great caravan routeways which brought Europe into direct contact with the Middle East, India and China. Where routes crossed or converged on the deserts' edge there grew towns like Baghdad and Damascus, Tashkent or Samarkand, existing solely on the trade developed and controlled by pastoral peoples. The pastoral nomads thus made a unique contribution to the development of urbanism and to the growth of civilisation in Europe and Asia, but their significance declined when the Portuguese,

Caravan in Saudi Arabia. (*Photo courtesy of The American Museum of Natural History*)

116

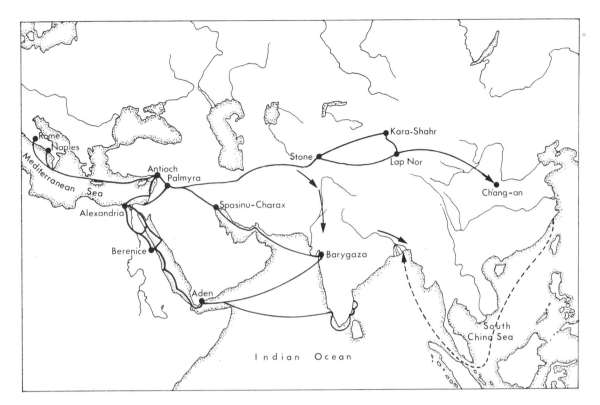

Figure 3.11
Eurasia: caravan routes used in
the silk trade c. 150 A.D. Land
routes were supplemented by sea
trade along the Red Sea and in the
Indian Ocean

and later the Dutch, pioneered the commercial seaways to the
tropical lands in the course of the sixteenth and seventeenth
centuries.

On its own, without the benefit of trade or commerce,
pastoralism can support only small numbers of people, living
at low densities. Life can be precarious, for the herdsman is
dependent on the quality of pasture in marginal environments,
and a severe winter or prolonged drought can wipe out his
entire herd. In this respect he resembles the tribal herder, but
unlike the latter he has external links with farmers and traders
which can ensure his survival even in the most difficult times.
Under normal circumstances he has the capacity to increase his
capital in a way denied to ordinary farmers, for his herds may
multiply and are readily exchanged for goods or cash, besides
furnishing an indirect source of profit by providing transport
for goods traded by merchants. Yet the pastoralist faces great
difficulties in adjusting to the new commercial world which his
earlier trading activities helped to create. For wandering
nomads are a frequent source of embarrassment to sedentary
nation states intent on demarcating their frontiers in sensitive

117

political areas of the Old World. Thus in the pastoral zone of central Asia, movement between traditional grazing lands has been disrupted along the long frontier between the U.S.S.R., China and Iran. Where the nomads have resisted such limitations, governments have sometimes introduced schemes for their enforced settlement, as farmers or ranchers. Elsewhere, in the Middle East for example, former grazing lands have sometimes been reduced by the encroachment of farming, based on irrigation. With the limitation of pasture has also come a reduction in the nomads' role in trade and transport, for the plane, lorry and railway have taken the place of the camel, and the caravan routes are no longer used. Not surprisingly, pastoralism as a way of life survives only in a few areas of central Asia, especially Mongolia, northern Arabia and east Africa: in other places the descendants of the nomads live on collective farms or work among the oil derricks of the Middle East.

2.3 Craftwork In traditional societies individuals within the family make many of the things needed in the house and on the farm, but most villages also support a number of craftsmen. A century ago, for example, an English rural community would have a blacksmith and perhaps a saddler and wheelwright; there would be a carpenter, a basketmaker and maybe a cooper, as well as a mason, slater and thatcher. Besides these crafts which cater for the farmer and the builder there would be a miller and a tanner, a weaver, tailor and shoemaker. Today these crafts have largely disappeared from the countryside, replaced by goods made in factories and bought in town shops. But craftsmen like these can still be found in the villages of traditional societies in Asia, Africa and Latin America. Chief among them is the blacksmith, the man who has mastered the mysteries of metal-working to produce the most important tools of all—those with a cutting blade. We will examine the significance of his work as an example of the role of craftsmen in traditional societies.

Almost certainly, metal-working was one of the first crafts to become a full-time occupation for it involves knowledge of several related processes, a high degree of skill, and time to manufacture different artifacts. Consequently, unlike some other crafts, metal-working is not easily combined with farming or other activities. This is particularly the case with the more useful metals: silver and gold are fairly easy to work; but copper and iron are usually found in ores that contain other chemical elements, and can be separated from them only by melting at very high temperatures. Once the ore is smelted in a

Craftsman: a blind basket-maker in Lebanon. (*Photo courtesy of Radio Times Hulton Picture Library*)

furnace, and the pure metal obtained, it must be shaped into the form required, by hammering on an anvil or pouring it in a molten state into a mould. Iron is particularly difficult to handle. It needs very high temperatures before it will melt, and even then it contains many impurities. The slag as it is called, can be removed gradually by repeated hammerings while the metal is still hot, but a quicker way is to add limestone in the furnace to remove the impurities, and harden the hot metal by dipping it in cold water. These basic processes can be outlined briefly in a single paragraph, but their complexities took several thousand years to master, and the skills and knowledge involved in producing metal tools help to explain why smiths were the first specialist craftsmen to appear in traditional societies.

Almost certainly early metal-working began in south-west Asia in the same areas where cereal cultivation first began. Gold, silver and copper were the first metals to be fashioned into trinkets and jewellery from finds of surface metals, but the real beginning of the smith's craft was the discovery of bronze, sometime before 3000 B.C. and probably in Syria or eastern Anatolia. Bronze is an alloy, made from copper and tin, the latter relatively scarce in the Middle East and a metal which had to be mined. Bronze-making thus involved knowledge of three separate processes—mining, smelting and manufacture; but its

A Greek smithy of the Iron Age
drawn on a vase and showing
some of the tools used

superiority over the softer metal, copper, ensured that knowledge of its working spread widely, north-west to Europe, and east to India and China, where it appeared about 1500 B.C. Iron working came later; its manufacture was a much more difficult process, discovered by the Hittites of eastern Anatolia about 2000 B.C. whose smiths first used it to manufacture ornaments and weapons like the sword and dagger. By 1200 B.C. iron-making was fairly well established in south-west Asia, but it did not reach China until about the fourth century B.C. and in Europe, classical Greece and Rome were the first major civilisations to make extensive use of iron. In the Old World, most of the basic discoveries in metal-working had been made by the middle of the second millennium B.C. but in the New World only the Incas of Peru had developed a knowledge of bronze when the Spaniards arrived in the sixteenth century A.D.

The introduction of metal had enormous significance for the economic development of traditional societies in the Old World. Each metal as it was discovered, was used initially for weapons and jewellery, for supplies were scarce and artifacts costly to manufacture. Thus stone tools and implements were still being used by Egyptian peasants a thousand years after the discovery of bronze; and in China bronze was used almost entirely for ritual vessels and weapons, rarely for tools. But gradually a whole range of tools and consumer goods became available as production increased, many little different in appearance from those in use today. Bronze smiths in Mesopotamia, for example, introduced the cold chisel, the rasp and the sledge hammer; and with the introduction of iron came tools like the hinged tongs and files in metal work, and farm implements like the axe, the hoe and the spade. Many of these had prototypes made from bronze or stone, but the greater strength and durability of iron, its finer cutting edge and eventual cheapness made it the metal for ordinary people, manufactured into artifacts and implements in everyday use.

Metal-working in the ancient world was sustained almost entirely by independent craftsmen, working with members of their own family in the way that blacksmiths continue to do in traditional societies. In some communities they lived semi-independent lives, living in their own quarters, marrying within their own group, and handing on their traditional skills from father to son. Something of these qualities remains in the itinerant tinkers of modern Ireland and Britain whose way of life bears some resemblance to that of their counterparts among the Bedouin or the Masai. Even in our own rural society, the blacksmith had considerable social standing, his strength and

Contrast the scale of the smith's shop in the photograph on page 120 with that of a modern factory

skill were proverbial, his forge was a social centre, and he was usually a man of substance.

For a long period, metal technology was conducted within this type of household industry, but larger and more specialised workshops did develop in Mesopotamia and China, and in Greece and Rome. This pattern of rural craftsmen and form of workshop continued in Europe until the Industrial Revolution at the end of the eighteenth century, when large-scale foundries were gradually developed to meet the demands of manufacturing industry. And at this point, the craftsmen of traditional society became the mechanics of the commercial age.

4 MODERN ECONOMIES

Modern economies differ from those we have discussed so far mainly in the way resources are used and distributed between different members of society. In such economies, people no longer rely on local resources to make a living: instead they use raw materials brought to their own community from many different parts of the world. A simple way to illustrate this is to glance around our own living room, or look at the food on the dining-room table. Few of the things we see have been made or produced in our own country, much less in our own home or garden. Yet a century ago most of the furniture and furnishings of the average home were made locally, and food, if not actually produced at home, was bought at the local market.

Irish farm kitchen, about 1888. Most of the furniture and furnishings seen in this picture were made by local craftsmen

Toyota cars coming off the
assembly line at the Tokyo plant,
Japan

There are many reasons for this change, but one of the most
important is that the technology used to provide the necessities
of life is now much more complex. Highly sophisticated
machinery, consuming enormous quantities of energy, converts a wide range of raw materials into finished products, and
requires skilled operators if it is to work efficiently. This in
turn means that work itself becomes increasingly specialised
and people more interdependent, at local level and in the world
at large.

Farmers, for example, no longer grow a wide range of food
crops, but concentrate instead on those products which fetch
the highest market prices. Regional specialisation is thus
characteristic of modern farming, as it also is of manufacturing
industry. Instead of a single craftsman working near the source
of his raw materials and completing all stages of manufacture

himself, the modern factory worker may make only a single part of the finished product which is assembled in a different factory. A car assembled outside Glasgow, for example, may use steel from south Wales, an engine built in Coventry and tyres moulded in Antrim.

Specialisation on this scale requires a complex system of transport linking areas where raw materials are produced, with those where they are manufactured into finished goods and eventually sold. These processes lead to concentrations of activity at nodal centres of communication, and the cities which develop in this way are the places where most people earn their living in commercial economies. Large cities are found in most countries of the world today, but the most urbanised societies are those of Europe and North America which pioneered the mass production of manufactured goods, and the commercial systems by which they were marketed throughout the world. Elsewhere, only Japan managed to absorb western technology and develop its own commercial organisation while remaining politically independent. In other parts of the world, European industrial nations established colonial territories which supplied them with raw materials and markets for manufactured goods. In this way, they gradually developed a world–wide economic system which they continue to dominate even though their former colonies are now politically independent. The activities which comprise this system are much more varied than those we have discussed so far, but although each is distinct and often spatially separated from others, all are interdependent.

1 Primary Activities

1.1 Agriculture and Animal Husbandry

Farmers in a commercial economy are less concerned with growing food crops for a local population than in producing whatever is most profitable from the range of crops and livestock that can be raised locally. Unlike the peasant, the commercial farmer is not limited by the experiences and resources of his own family and neighbours. Instead he has direct access to the specialist skills of many scientists through agricultural advisory services sponsored by governments. He can invest heavily in machinery, equipment and buildings, and in imported livestock, seed and fertilisers by means of subsidies and credit made available by state agencies, banks and farmers' cooperatives. Even marketing is often undertaken by specialised agencies working at regional and national level.

Commercial farming is usually characterised by marked

125

regional specialisation in crop or livestock rearing, the type of farming practised depending on local conditions of soil and climate which make certain activities more profitable than others, and on access to markets and prevailing world prices for different commodities. The system developed first in Europe where the growth of an urban industrial population created a rising demand for agricultural produce in the second half of the eighteenth century. This was met by the introduction of new methods of cropping and livestock rearing, reform of traditional patterns of land ownership and tenure, and the invention of new implements and machines like the swing plough and the mechanical reaper. All of these helped to increase productivity by improving yields and reducing the need for hand labour. They were especially important in opening up new lands for farming by European settlers in North and South America, southern Africa and Australasia, all of which are major centres of commercial farming in the world today. But in other parts of the world where traditional peasant farming was long established, older practices still prevail and the transition to a commercial economy is far from complete.

Figure 4.1
Land consolidation: an example from Guelderland Province in the Netherlands, in a scheme undertaken by the Dutch government

Old situation before 1952

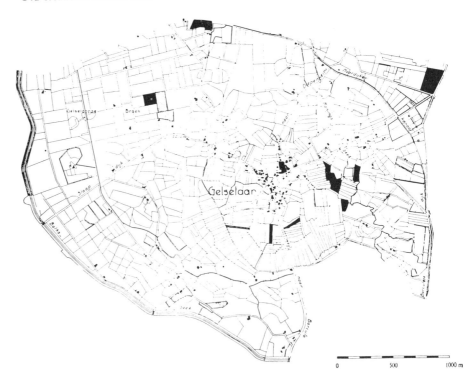

126

This is still the case in many parts of Europe, as well as in Africa, Asia and South America where the greatest barrier to change is often the prevailing system of land tenure with its associated small farms and fragmented holdings. Most countries consider that this is the crucial problem in modernising agriculture, and many have government agencies concerned specifically with land reform.

Where commercial farming is fully developed, rural families enjoy standards of living comparable in every way to those of city dwellers. Health, welfare and education services differ little between town and country, the car gives the farmer and his family a degree of personal mobility undreamed of a century ago, while the telephone, radio and television link him directly with the urban world. But because of his occupation the farmer usually lives at some distance from his neighbours, and young people often move to the city, seeking the more varied company and amenities of urban life. However, densities of rural population differ considerably with the type of farming practised, and we will now consider the different categories into which commercial farming can be divided.

New situation November 10th 1956

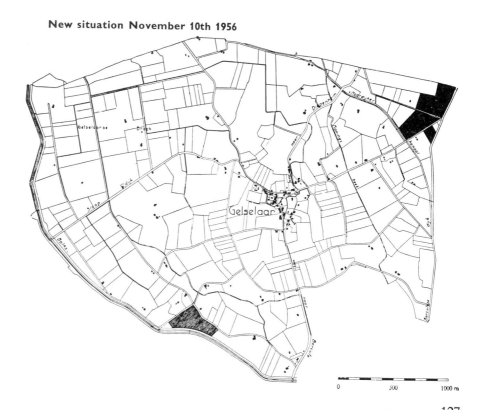

(a) **Mixed Crop and Livestock Farming** Farming which combines cereal cultivation with livestock rearing is traditional in northern and western Europe where the crop was used to feed the family and livestock, and surplus animals were sold as the main commercial product. This system is still practised in Europe where the main crops are wheat, barley, oats and rye, and in eastern North America where maize is the principal cereal. Root crops like potatoes and turnips are grown on both sides of the Atlantic, and income is mainly derived from the sale of fat cattle or from dairy produce. Specialised dairying occurs near large urban centres where there is a demand for liquid milk, but dairy farming is also characteristic of those regions where summers are too cool and moist for wheat and maize, and land is most profitably used as pasture. This applies to countries like Ireland and New Zealand which have no large urban populations of their own, but produce large quantities of butter and cheese for export by refrigerated transport.

Dairy farming requires a large capital investment in equipment and buildings, and is usually associated with large farms and a dispersed pattern of settlement. Traditional areas of

Figure 4.2
World: main types of commercial farming

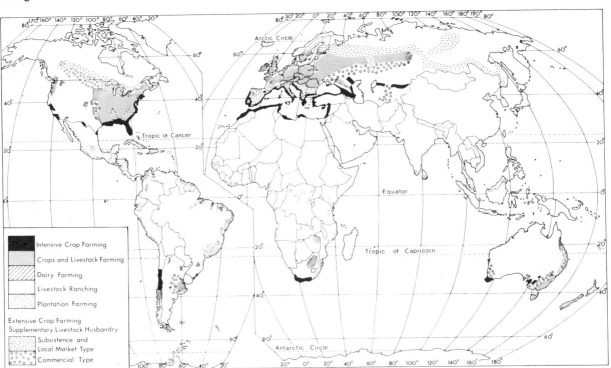

128

Upland areas attract summertime visitors: week-end traffic in Cheddar Gorge, in the Mendip Hills of Somerset

mixed farming contain many villages where farmers once lived, but with the reorganisation of agriculture over the past two centuries and the creation of individual holdings from common fields, most farmers now live in houses built on their farms.

Small towns are also numerous in these areas, for mixed farming generates a considerable volume of trade, which earlier generations of landowners did much to encourage by establishing markets as a stimulus to urban growth. Mixed farms today tend to be much larger than a generation ago—in England and Wales, for example, they average about thirty-four hectares; and they are increasing in size as farmers try to increase their productivity by making maximum use of modern technology. Larger farms and greater mechanisation mean fewer farmers and agricultural workers, with a consequent loss of population from country to town. In areas of marginal land, distant from major centres of population, there may be substantial unemployment in particular age groups, as, for example, in western parts of Ireland and Britain; but these same areas often attract a large seasonal population of tourists, since the environmental qualities which make them difficult to farm are increasingly valued by urban dwellers.

(b) Crop Farming Very different from the mixed farming of temperate Europe is the agriculture of the Mediterranean lands with its emphasis on cereals and perennials like the vine, fig and olive. Livestock rearing plays little part in Mediterranean farming, for summer drought limits pasture and it is more profitable to use the available areas of good lowland soil for intensive cropping. Hence olive oil replaces the butter and lard of northern Europe, just as wine is drunk instead of beer and milk. The animals that are kept are usually sheep and goats, providing wool, and milk which is normally made into cheese on the mountain pastures to which the flocks are moved during summer. Here they are cared for by professional shepherds, returning to the lowlands in winter.

Mediterranean farming is highly intensive, involving multiple cropping in lowland areas where water can be conserved by irrigation. Winter-sown wheat is the main cereal, but along the coastal fringes of southern Spain, crops of rice alternate with orchards of citrus and almond. Much of this farming is small in scale, and in its use of hand-labour it resembles the traditional farming of monsoon Asia more closely than the commercial

Commercial farming in a Mediterranean environment: an orange orchard at Riverside, California. (*Photo Aerofilms Limited*)

Commercial horticulture: these glasshouses in the Westland area of south Holland create a landscape very different from the traditional rural scene. (*Photo Aerofilms Limited*)

systems of temperate Europe. A high proportion of the population still lives by farming, and settlement is mainly in villages and towns of considerable antiquity. Yet large-scale commercial farming has existed in the Mediterranean for many centuries, notably in the Italian *latifundia* owned by the aristocracy and worked by tenants sometimes on a basis of share-cropping. Estates such as these were highly organised commercial enterprises, producing a marketable surplus which helped to support the great cities of mediaeval Italy such as Rome and Florence.

Intensive farming of a different type is the *commercial horticulture* which has developed with the growth of large urban populations in recent times. Most cities have areas of intensive market gardening on their outskirts, where vegetables are grown for the urban market using large quantities of imported fertilisers. Sometimes the crops are raised under glass to improve productivity, as in parts of south Holland where the resulting landscape of glasshouses, heating plant chimneys and family homes is scarcely distinguishable from the neighbouring

131

town. But modern transport has also made horticulture possible in areas remote from cities but possessing certain qualities of soil and climate which make them particularly suited for growing certain crops. Regional specialisation of this sort is especially marked in the U.S.A., where the Pacific coast states produce half the fruit and one-third of the vegetables for the entire nation. Other specialist areas occur on the Atlantic and Gulf coasts, but none of these matches California with its varied soils, long growing season and ample supplies of water for irrigation. The scale of operation here requires a large supply of seasonal labour, even with mechanisation, and farms are normally large, sometimes owned by companies which are also involved in food processing.

In Europe the scale of production is smaller, for before the advent of the E.E.C. tariff boundaries inhibited the free movement of produce between different countries. Hence horticulture is chiefly concentrated in small regional centres, the main specialist areas being Brittany and the Rhone valley in France, and the western Netherlands. Large-scale wine production might also be included in this category, the most famous vineyards being located in the eastern Paris basin, and the valleys of the Rhine and the Loire where wine is produced on large estates, which in some instances may date back to Roman times.

Another type of farming which developed in the course of the nineteenth century in response to the growth of urban population is large-scale *cereal cultivation*. This is found mainly in the American mid-west, Australia and the Argentine where land formerly occupied by indigenous tribal societies was gradually colonised by European farmers. With new implements like the reaper and the disc-plough they were able to cultivate increasingly large areas without the need of hired labour; and with the arrival of the railroad and the steamship to link the prairie farms with distant urban markets they were able to sell their grain in bulk at prices which undercut their European competitors. Indeed by depressing agricultural prices in Europe, American grain growers indirectly helped to precipitate the change from traditional to commercial farming practices.

Extensive grain growing has also developed in the U.S.S.R. during the present century, in the eastern Ukraine and southern Siberia. Here, as in North America, it occupies land which experiences considerable fluctuations in annual rainfall. Prolonged drought can be disastrous, both for the farmer and for his land; and the Kansas 'dustbowl' of the 1920s is a constant

Cereal cultivation on the Canadian prairies in Manitoba. The combine harvester works most efficiently in big fields—like this one which stretches away towards the horizon

reminder of the hazards facing the commercial grain-grower. However, it is recognised that this is a marginal type of farming. In good years it can yield higher profits per hectare than the livestock ranching which preceded it on the American prairies; but in neighbouring areas where rainfall is higher and more certain, farmers reduce their commercial risk by practising a mixed crop-livestock economy.

In the grain areas wheat is the principal and often the only crop, grown exclusively for cash and occupying enormous acreages. Little land is left in fallow, field boundaries are scarcely visible and the wheat seems to stretch endlessly towards the horizon. Yields tend to be low, averaging perhaps between 230 and 260 litres per hectare compared with 485 in Britain; but farms may be several thousand hectares in size and are highly mechanised. Great distances separate the individual farmer from his neighbour—population densities may be as low as 0·9 per square kilometre—and 'towns' are often little more than a few shops, a bank, church and school grouped near a grain silo which is sited on the railroad. Many farm-steads and even some of the towns are now deserted, for many grain-growers are now 'suit-case' farmers, visiting the farm only at seed-time and harvest and spending the rest of the year in a larger town where they may even have a second job in a service occupation. This double life helps to reduce the finan-cial risk of grain-growing in a marginal environment and enables the farmer and his family to enjoy more of the amenities of modern life.

(c) **Livestock Rearing** Livestock rearing as a specialised branch of farming has a very long history, but unlike the nomadic herdsmen of traditional society the American rancher or Australian sheep farmer graze their stock on fixed locations and raise their animals to supply commercial markets. Modern ranching has many affinities with commercial grain growing, for it developed in order to supply urban populations with food and animal products, and its growth was dependent on tech-nological innovations in transport and refrigeration to link the producer with his distant markets. Like wheat farming, ranch-ing is mainly found on the semi-arid margins of the continental interiors; indeed the rancher often preceded the farmer, his stock grazing the open range, exposed to the hazards of drought and blizzard but less vulnerable to the rigours of climate than the farmer, for stock could always search for fresh grass when drought threatened existing grazing land. Compet-ition for land from farmers usually led the rancher to retreat to land too dry for grain growing, and it is in the semi-arid areas of the Americas, Australia, South Africa and New Zealand that ranching is now most widely practised. In North and South America cattle are the principal livestock, but in Australia and New Zealand the emphasis is on sheep, in the former areas kept mainly for their wool, and in the latter as frozen lamb which is exported mainly to Britain.

The constraints imposed by climate mean that ranching is extensive in its use of land; it takes thirty hectares to support one steer in Nevada, and only two hectares in a mixed crop-livestock farm in the more humid climate of Nebraska. Indeed new, intensive methods of livestock rearing in mixed farm areas pose a considerable commercial threat to older methods of ranching, although world shortages of animal protein mean

134

Livestock rearing: a ranch in
Wyoming, U.S.A. (*U.S.D.A. photo*)

that fatstock prices should remain high. In North America cattle ranches are large; most are over 1000 hectares, some exceed 4000 hectares, while the average Australian sheep station is 8000 hectares. This scale of operation requires very substantial capital investment, especially in fencing and water supply, and modern ranches are often operated by business companies, many of them subsidiaries of meat packing and processing plants.

At the centre of these huge areas is the ranch or sheep station, itself a major complex of dwellings, farm buildings and paddocks; often it even has its own airstrip, for distances between ranches and towns are so great that the plane sometimes takes the place of the car for normal journeys. The landscape of ranching areas has thus few visible signs of human activity, for ploughed fields are few, fences are unobtrusive and dwellings and towns widely scattered. Life for the rancher can be lonely, and despite the facilities provided by modern technology and high standards of living the independent rancher has often to rely on his own resources.

(d) Plantations Farming for commercial markets is most highly developed in the world's temperate lands, but tropical agriculture has also been affected by the growing demand for its products from the major industrial nations. Of course trade in tropical produce was established long before the Industrial Revolution. Arab caravans and Venetian galleys brought spices like cloves, nutmeg and pepper to flavour and preserve the bland foods of mediaeval Europe, while explorers like Vasco da Gama and Columbus undertook their epic voyages to develop new routes to the Indies. But with the industrial expansion of Europe in the nineteenth century, demand for tropical produce increased dramatically: to the original spices was added a growing range of tropical produce—cocoa, tobacco, coffee, sugar-cane and bananas, cotton, ground-nuts, copra, rubber, jute, hemp, manila and sisal. Limited supplies of some of these crops were made available through traditional agriculture, but as the demand increased and diversified, new methods of production had to be found, and the tropical plantation was that most widely adopted.

In essence the plantation is a large farm, owned and often managed by foreign companies, which produces a limited range of crops for sale on world markets. It is worked as a business enterprise, employing its own labour force and quite distinct from native farms—indeed its locational needs may be quite different since the plantation requires a good system of external communications, preferably based on sea transport, and its crops may have special ecological needs in soil or micro-climate. A characteristic feature of the plantation is that it needs a large labour force, and since workers were often imported from abroad, plantation areas tend to have large immigrant communities which subsequently created a host of social and political problems.

The earliest plantations were in America where the Portuguese grew sugar-cane for export to Europe, using first native labour and then introducing Negro slaves from west Africa. Later, English and French colonists followed their example, the former growing indigo and tobacco on plantations in Virginia and adding cotton which eventually became the main plantation crop in the southern United States. In Asia the plantation economy developed slowly, until the opening of the Suez Canal in 1869 brought the East Indies almost as close to Europe as the West Indies. Soon the Dutch in Indonesia, and

Plantations: loading bananas at a railway siding on a Guatamalan plantation

the British in Malaya, India and Ceylon were growing large quantities of tea, coffee and rubber in plantations, using Indians and Chinese as indentured labour. Similar plantations were developed in east and south Africa, but these were much smaller in scale, for the remoteness of the tropical interior and difficulties of communication made investment here much less attractive than in Asia.

Political changes in the tropical lands after the Second World War have greatly affected the plantation system, for to newly independent states the plantation represents unwarranted foreign interference in the management of the national economy. Undoubtedly the system had its defects. Exclusive dependence on external markets means that the plantation is highly vulnerable to fluctuations in world prices; and while Europeans may withdraw their investment if prices fall too low, the workers remain. Alternatively, if prices for one crop prove uneconomic another may take its place—the West Indies, for example, have turned in succession over the years to sugar cane, cotton, coffee and citrus fruit. In the search for profitable enterprises the land itself may be over-exploited, leading to loss of fertility and erosion, while the local economy suffers by a succession of trade booms and slumps. However, plantations have also contributed much to the economic development of tropical lands, by providing the essential infrastructures of road, rail and sea transport, and building schools and hospitals. New crops introduced by European planters have been adopted by native farmers, broadening the base of the traditional economy, and encouraging new techniques in farming which are of benefit to agriculture as a whole. They have also provided the main and sometimes the only source of foreign exchange so vital for further economic growth. In these ways the plantation system has done much for tropical agriculture, although traditional farmers in tropical lands have yet to make the transition to a full market economy.

1.2 Extractive Industries

From food production we now turn to a group of activities which are based on the extraction of raw materials from natural resources. With fishing, the primary aim is to provide food, but forestry and mining provide raw materials for a wide range of industrial processes. Fishing and forestry are both normal activities in tribal and traditional societies, but since Neolithic times mining has tended to be a specialist occupation. In modern economies, all three are major commercial activities, and although the total number of people employed is small compared with those engaged in farming or industry, their way of life tends to be different from other occupation groups in contemporary society. For example, they often live in small settlements far distant from the main concentrations of modern population.

(a) **Fishing** Fish have been an important source of food for man from the earliest times—indeed some scholars have argued that human life began on tropical seashores. Here food was abundant at all seasons, man had few competitors or predators and had no need to pursue elusive game, and stones for toolmaking were close at hand. Today fishing is a highly organised industry in modern economies, yet the methods used have altered remarkably little down the centuries. Modern fishermen may use elaborate nets and sophisticated sonar equipment for locating shoals, but their approach to the resource is that of the hunter; fish-farming, practised for centuries by traditional farming communities in Asia, has yet to be developed on an extensive scale although it is technically feasible and may well be the only way to conserve resources for the future.

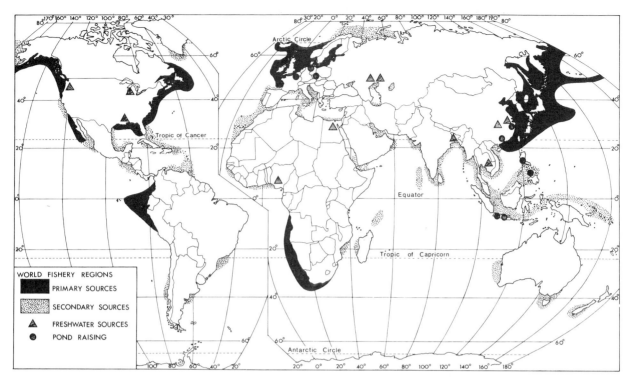

Figure 4.3
World: major fishing areas, data late 1960s

The great commercial fisheries of the world today are located in the northern hemisphere, where warm currents enter the northern seas along the continental shelves of Eurasia and North America. Tropical oceans may have a richer and more varied marine life, but neither in quantity nor quality can they match the herring, mackerel and cod found on the rich fishing grounds of the north Atlantic and the North Sea. From mediaeval times, fishing has been a specialised occupation among communities bordering the North Sea, with Dutch and English fishermen in particular following the herring as it migrates southward during the summer months. The Roman Catholic Church gave a powerful boost to a developing industry by promoting weekly abstinence from meat, and the herring, eaten fresh or smoked and salted, became a major staple in trade, and a source of mercantile wealth for many ports in the North and Baltic Seas. Herring fishing remained an important industry until the end of the last century, when the introduction of the steam trawler enabled fishermen to stay longer at sea. A little later, the introduction of refrigeration and cold storage meant that fish could be landed and marketed in fresh condition long after they had been caught; and thereafter

139

North Sea fishermen began to move north to new fishing grounds on the edge of the Arctic Circle and White Sea.

Further west, in the north Atlantic, cod have been fished on the Grand Banks of Newfoundland since the early sixteenth century. Men from the Azores and Portugal, from Brittany Normandy and south-west England sailed west in early summer, returning home in October to prepare their salted cargoes for market. They have been succeeded by modern trawlers and factory ships which process the catch on the fishing grounds, many of them belonging to the U.S.S.R. which has become one of the major deep sea fishing nations. In these same waters, European and American fishermen also pursued the whale so relentlessly in the early nineteenth century that it has now virtually disappeared from the north Atlantic. Thereafter the whalers moved to the Bering Sea, but again the slaughter was so extensive that surviving species are now mainly found in the southern hemisphere.

Modern off-shore fishing boats in port at Killybegs, Co. Donegal

As an organised industry, deep-sea fishing is mainly confined to the maritime nations of western Europe. Here fishermen live mostly in large ports like Aberdeen, Bergen or Grimsby, where the fishing fleets are based and special market facilities are available. Elsewhere in Europe, especially in the Mediterranean, in Japan, China and south-east Asia fishing is mainly conducted inshore. Sometimes it is merely a supplement to normal farming activities, as in western Ireland or the crofting districts of the Scottish highlands and islands. Sometimes it is a specialist occupation, based on small harbours and fishing villages, where neighbours share boats and gear and are closely related by ties of marriage and the common bond of facing the daily hazards of life at sea.

(b) Forestry   Forests are the natural vegetation cover in most parts of the world outside the tropical deserts and higher mountain ranges in temperate latitudes; yet today probably less than one-fifth of the total land surface is still clothed in woodland. This has resulted almost entirely from human activity, for the forests have provided man with a varied supply of food and industrial raw materials. Woodland clearance may have begun quite early in human history, as primitive hunters used fire to drive game from the depths of the forest—it is thought, for example, that some of the mid-latitude grasslands may have developed in this way. But systematic clearance began only after man had become a farmer, first making small clearings in shifting cultivation, later felling the trees and grubbing up their roots to make permanent fields. With the growth of fixed settlements, timber became an important material for use in buildings, as well as for making tools and implements, vehicles and ships. It was also widely used for fuel, in domestic hearths and as charcoal in iron-smelting. Today it provides a great range of industrial raw materials: wood pulp for paper and cardboard, cellulose for making plastics, resin used in glue, and as a source of tar, wax, oil, tannin and sugar. With this increased use, more and more timber reserves are being exploited; but at the same time, forests are being viewed as a major resource in themselves, and not simply as a source of raw materials. Slowly it has been realised that forests protect land from erosion, act as watersheds and help to conserve water supplies for large urban centres, besides forming attractive environments for the recreation of their populations. In addition they help to maintain the water balance in the atmosphere through transpiration.

Today the main surviving forest belts of the world are the

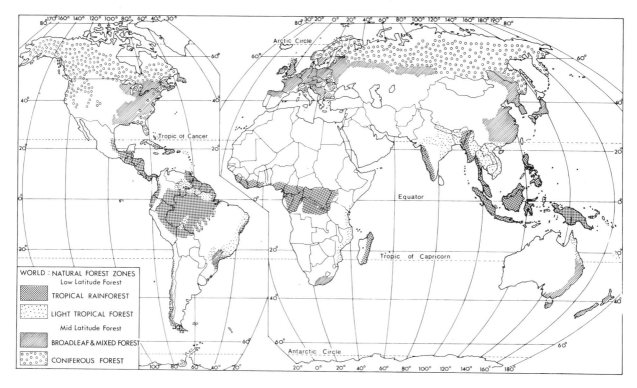

Figure 4.4
World: natural forest zones

coniferous forests of North America and Eurasia which consist
mainly of spruce, fir and different species of pine; and the
sub-tropical forests of Brazil, the Congo and Malaysia-
Indonesia. The latter contain many different species, but they
are mainly exploited for their hardwoods: greenheart and
mahogany from South America, gaboon and ebony from
Africa and teak from south-east Asia. Between these two
zones, the deciduous forests which once clothed much of
Europe and North America with species like oak and beech,
maple and hickory respectively, have largely disappeared and
they now produce little commercial timber.

Reaction to this wholesale clearance of native woodland has
eventually led many governments to develop national policies
for reafforestation and management, with timber planted,
maintained and felled by government agencies in a controlled
way, rather as a farmer uses his land for cropping. This
method is now accepted as almost the only way in which
timber supplies can be conserved against ever-increasing demand, and in this way forestry becomes an integral part of a
modern system of agricultural land use.

Norwegian coniferous forests are a major source of softwood. Felled in winter they are here being hauled downstream by tug boat to the sorting plants and sawmills, carried along this natural conveyor belt by the spring floods. (*Photo Aerofilms Limited*)

In Britain, for example, a Forestry Commission was established in 1919 in an effort to restore the dwindling areas of native woodland, whose exploitation had led to acute timber shortages during the First World War. Fifty years later there were 0·7 million hectares of forested land in Great Britain, with a target of 2·02 million hectares to be reached by the end of the century. Most of the trees planted are coniferous species such as spruce, larch and pine, because commercial demand is mainly for softwoods; while tropical forests provide most of the hardwood species. Softwoods also mature more quickly, and they have the added advantage of being able to grow on land too poor to support deciduous forests and also unsuitable for most types of modern farming. For these reasons, the largest areas of state forest in Britain are located on the hills of Scotland, Wales and northern England, where employment in farming is declining and forestry can provide an alternative source of income. In these areas forestry helps to maintain

143

roads, settlements and services which would otherwise decline, and although it supports relatively small numbers of people in direct employment, it makes an important contribution to tourism and recreation. State forests in Britain are being used increasingly for camping and other outdoor activities on a pattern already well established in North America. In this way land largely abandoned by farmers acquires new uses, in the production of commercial timber and as recreation centres for a largely urban population.

(c) **Mining** Unlike fishing and forestry, mining is based on resources that are non-renewable: once a mineral source has been fully exploited the miner moves on, abandoning his settlement and leaving the land scarred by his activity. As a specialist occupation, mining dates back at least to the early Iron Age, but large scale operations began little more than a century ago, steadily increasing in size and scale with the almost insatiable demand for minerals created by modern industrial technology. Yet as an economic activity, mining is very unevenly distributed throughout the world for it depends not only on the location of specific minerals but also upon a whole range of economic and technical factors which vary greatly between different countries and through time.

Rather more than two thousand separate minerals have been identified, but those that are important economically can be classified into four main groups. The first to be used by man were the *non-ferrous metals* like gold, silver, copper and tin, to which were added lead and zinc, and most recently, aluminium and magnesium. Most minerals in this group are produced in the Americas, with the exception of tin and gold, the latter being mined particularly in South Africa and Australia. *Iron* was discovered later, but it is the most important mineral of all and although it is mined in many parts of the world, the main producers are North America, western Europe and the U.S.S.R. *Non-metallic minerals* form a very broad category, widely distributed throughout the world and including various compounds of sulphur and nitrogen, potassium, phosphorus and many different chemicals, all of which are extremely important in modern industry. Finally there are minerals such as coal, oil and natural gas all of which are used as *sources of energy*. Again their distribution varies, but the main coal producing areas are in western Europe and the western U.S.A., and for oil, the Middle East and North America.

The distribution of these various minerals depends on the underlying geological structure. For example, non-ferrous

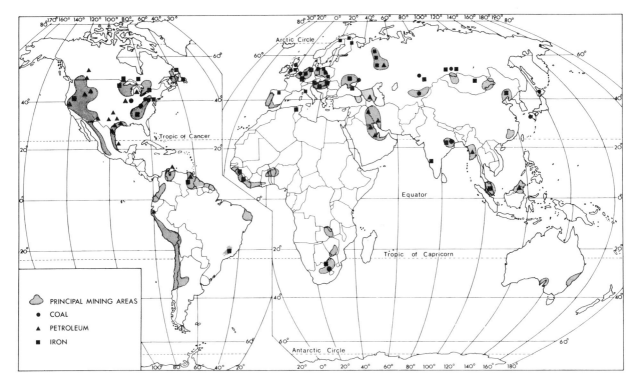

Figure 4.5
World distribution of major mining areas

minerals are associated with areas which have experienced vulcanism and mountain-building activity in the past, and coal and oil deposits are found mainly in sedimentary rocks. But whether or not a mineral is mined depends on man's ability to recognise its potential uses, to locate the mineral deposit, and devise techniques for its extraction, processing and distribution to the manufacturer or consumer. This complex combination of factors helps to explain why mining is much more restricted in its distribution than the mineral deposits themselves, and why it has developed only in recent times. Until the second half of the nineteenth century, most people in the world possessed a simple technology which made few demands on the earth's mineral resources. But since then there has been rapid progress in mineral technology; whole new industries have come into existence, such as those for chemicals and agricultural fertilisers which are based on non-ferrous minerals, and the world's use of energy has increased dramatically.

To meet the rising demand, mining has had to develop new techniques of exploration and exploitation, working deposits which were formerly regarded as too difficult or too costly. Mines are now worked on sites which would otherwise be

145

uninhabited, like the Bolivian tin mines where men work at altitudes 4600 metres above sea level, or extract oil from the seabed perched on platforms above the stormy waters of the North Sea. Many mining operations are now conducted far from major centres of population, and from the industrial areas where the minerals are refined, processed and manufactured into a wide range of goods. This is a major change from the early stages of industrial growth, when manufacturing industry developed close to the sources of minerals and power. In the nineteenth century, iron-working, for example, was closely associated with coal and ore deposits in England, the German

Gold-mining in western Montana, U.S.A. in the 1860s. This hastily-built town known as Last Chance Gulch later became the state capital under the more dignified name, Helena

Ruhr and Pennsylvania. Now it is often more economic to transport the minerals to the manufacturing centres, a movement which involves complex patterns of international trade between the mineral producing countries, widely distributed throughout the world, and the major industrial centres which are concentrated in western Europe and eastern North America.

Unlike most forms of economic activity, mining rarely lasts long in any particular locality, unless the mineral deposits are particularly extensive or difficult to extract. Occasionally new techniques make it economic to reopen old workings, but more often a mine and its associated settlement is abandoned once the mineral deposits are exhausted. For example, gold mining in the western United States in the middle of the last century resulted in the mushroom growth of many mining settlements. A typical case was Alder Gulch in Montana where gold was discovered in May 1863. By Christmas 10 000 people were living on the site in every conceivable type of dwelling, and mining operations had spread more than twenty kilometres along the main river and its tributaries. Fifteen years later Alder Gulch was almost completely deserted and it is now one of the many ghost towns found throughout the American West. Other types of mining may have less dramatic beginnings but can result in the growth of major concentrations of population within a relatively short period of time. A good example is the development of coal mining in south Wales. In 1851 the population of the Rhondda was less than 1000, but by 1911 some 152 000 people had crowded into the neighbouring valleys, with houses, pits, slag heaps and railway sidings all tightly packed together. Here the decline of coal mining has been offset to some extent by the introduction of other forms of industrial employment; but more often people must move elsewhere when mines close down. Behind them they leave not only abandoned mines and settlements, but also a wasted

Modern coal mining in northern France: a landscape dominated by towering slag-heaps, pit gear, railway sidings and miners' houses

landscape, subject to sudden subsidence with the collapse of underground workings, and scarred with tips and slagheaps of waste materials discarded after the minerals have been extracted.

In Britain alone there is estimated to be over 38 000 hectares of this derelict land, most of it in the old coal mining areas of the north and in the china clay districts of Cornwall and Staffordshire. People today view these areas with more critical eyes than their Victorian predecessors; planning controls now ensure that land is restored after mining has ceased, and the older areas of dereliction are being slowly reclaimed.

But the human problems created by mining are less easily solved. The difficulties of finding alternative employment once mining has ceased have already been mentioned, but it assumes much greater importance in underdeveloped countries where many mining operations are now concentrated. For example, the gold and diamond mines of South Africa and the copper belt of Zambia need a large labour force, mainly recruited from among native peoples. Pressure of population on land means that workers are readily attracted from rural areas, but once they are used to industrial employment and are exposed to urban values and institutions it is almost impossible for them to readjust successfully to rural life; or return to the land when threatened by redundancy or government regulations on employment. Mining is of the greatest importance to the national economies of many underdeveloped countries in Africa and South America, but the social and political problems it creates can long outlast the productivity of the mines themselves.

The future pattern of mining in the world is difficult to predict, for estimates of mineral reserves have often proved unreliable. Mineral use varies with changes in technology, and improved techniques of exploration and recovery will undoubtedly bring new resources into use—the world's oceans, for example, are largely an unknown territory as far as mineral resources are concerned. Even so, minerals are a wasting asset which cannot be renewed by natural processes; and consumption has increased so rapidly that world shortages in some minerals seem almost inevitable. In 1973, for example, many domestic consumers in the U.S.A. were confronted with local shortages of fuel oil and petrol, a situation which would have seemed inconceivable even ten years ago. The case of fuel oils, whose major reserves are located in politically sensitive areas such as the Middle East, emphasises that mineral extraction is not simply an economic problem. It involves much deeper issues, for at present the main consumers of the world's mineral resources are the major industrial nations. If the underdeveloped countries with their enormous populations were to demand an equal share of world resources known stocks of many minerals would be very quickly exhausted.

2 Secondary Activities: Manufacturing Industry

Manufacturing industry employs a much higher proportion of the working population in commercial economies than the primary activities we have considered so far, and many times the number who work as craftsmen in traditional societies. The scale of production is perhaps the most characteristic feature of modern industry, for most manufacturing processes are geared to the mass production of goods for national rather than local markets. Small workshops with less than a dozen employees are still common, but large factories with several thousand workers and international trade connections are more typical of modern manufacturing industry. Such factories are often highly specialised, producing components which may be assembled in several different stages and at different plants before the final product is completed for sale. This type of interdependence between different manufacturing processes is known as *agglomeration* or aggregation, and it is the main reason why related industries tend to cluster together—major steel users, for example, often locate their plants near steel mills. Concentration of industry leads in turn to large scale urban development, and a pattern of settlement very different from that of traditional economies where manufacturing industry is located either on sites where raw materials are available, or in the market towns and larger villages where the majority of consumers live.

The concentration of industrial activity in certain key areas occurs at regional, national and even international level, and to understand why this should be so it is necessary to examine a little more closely the factors which influence industrial location. In selecting a site on which to build a factory, an industrialist has to decide where he can obtain supplies of raw materials, power and labour, and where his finished products are to be marketed. His decision will usually be influenced most strongly by the cost of transport, which varies according to the weight and volume of the goods carried and the transport system that is available to him. Sometimes it may be cheaper for him to locate his plant near the sources of his raw materials; or perhaps the manufactured goods are more costly to move and it is therefore better to be close to his markets. Incidentally 'the market' can mean the domestic consumer, or another factory which uses his product. Finally the transport system itself is important: many goods can be carried economically by plane, but for others water, road or rail provide the cheapest forms of transport.

When large scale industrial development began two centuries ago, in the period of technological innovation known as the Industrial Revolution, many types of manufacturing industry were located near sources of raw material and power, since these are often the most expensive items to transport when communication systems are poorly developed. Early textile mills, for example, were sited on the streams which powered their machinery, and iron working was located where suitable supplies of ore and coal were close together. With modern

A Yorkshire textile mill built in the eighteenth century on the stream which provided its first source of power; a coal-fired steam-engine was added later. Beside the mill building is a row of workers' cottages and the larger house belonging to the mill owner. (*Photo Aerofilms Limited*)

systems of transport neither of these factors is of overriding importance. In metallurgical industries, some savings may be achieved by locating near mineral deposits when these contain a high proportion of waste material. Even then only the initial processing may take place near the mine, and the refined ore is transported to the manufacturing centre. Similarly only very large energy-users, like aluminium extractors, may find advantages in locating near power sources, for oil is easily moved by tanker and pipe-line, and electricity by cable.

Today, location near markets is much more likely to effect savings in transport, mainly because modern manufacturing processes favour the sort of aggregation mentioned above. In addition, large urban centres have the advantage of dense and varied systems of communication: raw materials and goods can

The Renault car assembly works in Paris, a factory situated in the city and able to benefit from its excellent system of communications and extensive pool of labour

be easily switched between air, road, rail and water transport, and good communication networks link the city with the rest of the nation and with countries abroad. For this reason, large metropolitan centres like London or New York are particularly attractive to many types of industry, although they offer other advantages too. One such advantage is the large supply of potential industrial labour, especially important for industries which require varied skills. Car assembly plants, for example, are nearly always located near large urban areas because they need a large labour force drawn from many different trades. Another advantage of larger cities is the wide range of amenities they can offer business executives. Where such factors as markets, transport and raw material costs are evenly balanced, decisions on siting plants may be influenced by such social considerations as the quality of local schools, shops and golf courses.

Industrial location today is also greatly affected by government policy. This is particularly the case in communist states like the U.S.S.R. or China where decisions on siting local factories are based on national plans for economic development prepared and executed by central government. But non-communist governments in the Western world also use a variety of devices, from preferential tariffs to differential taxation and outright subsidies to influence the location of new industries. Often these are designed to offset regional unemployment resulting from the decline of traditional industries, such as linen or shipbuilding in Northern Ireland. Sometimes they seek to offset the economic processes of aggregation by spreading employment more widely to outlying regions. In underdeveloped countries, the role of governments is particularly important in promoting industrial development as a means of diversifying the structure of the national economy, and providing non-agricultural jobs for rising populations.

The interplay of these different factors of industrial location over the past two centuries has resulted in the emergence of distinctive industrial regions in different countries. On a world basis they can be recognised by plotting the distribution of key industries such as iron and steel, machine tools, chemicals, textiles and food-processing; or by using criteria such as the proportion of a nation's work force employed in industry, or the use of energy per capita. But whatever device is used, it is quite apparent that manufacturing industry is very unevenly distributed throughout the world. The main centres are north-west Europe and the north-eastern United States. Elsewhere there are major regional centres in the U.S.S.R. and Japan, but

Figure 4.6
United Kingdom
Development Areas,
which offer a variety of
incentives to attract new
industry

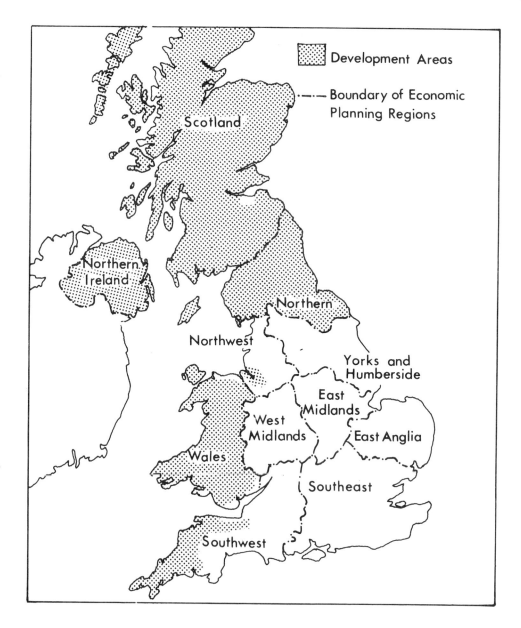

in the tropical lands industry is very thinly distributed and here as well as in the southern continents, it is mainly associated with the larger urban areas.

Europe's early lead in fostering the Industrial Revolution helps to explain its continued pre-eminence, the main industrial belt stretching from Britain in the west, through northern France, Belgium and the southern Netherlands to the Ruhr in

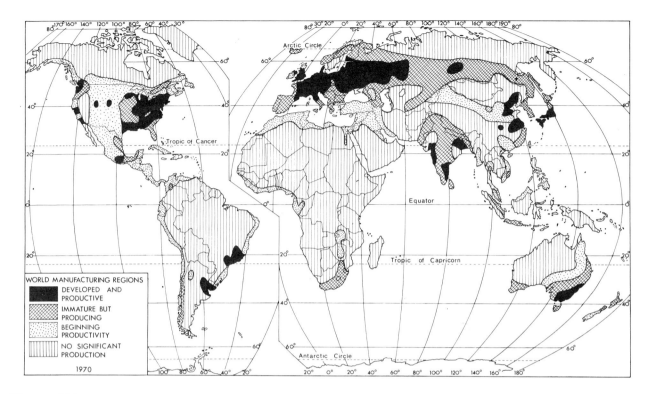

Figure 4.7
World manufacturing regions,
data 1970

Germany. This is the most concentrated and the most diverse industrial region in the world. Initially it was based on substantial resources of iron-ore and coal, and to these have been added natural gas and oil from the North Sea. In addition to its fine-mesh network of communications on land, sea, and inland waterways, it possesses major financial resources, a large workforce with a long tradition of technical skill, and an economic organisation newly revitalised through the European Economic Community with enormous markets at home and overseas.

In North America, a similar combination of human and natural resources has led to the concentration of industry along the Atlantic seaboard from Baltimore to New England, centring on the metropolitan area of New York with its fine natural harbour and extensive transportation network extending throughout the entire continent. Westward the American manufacturing belt extends to the southern shores of Lakes Erie and Michigan with heavy industry based on steel, and Chicago with its food processing plants. Outlying regions are located on the Gulf and Pacific coasts, with specialist electronic and aerospace industries which require highly skilled labour.

155

Compared with Europe and North America industrialisation came late in Russia, and with the exception of the Moscow region, markets were less important than sites of raw materials in fostering industrial growth. Thus the main centres of heavy industry are in the Ukraine, the Urals and the Kuznetsk basin of Siberia where there are major deposits of iron-ore, coal and manganese. Farther east, Japan has become one of the world's major industrial powers despite the destruction of much of its manufacturing plant during the Second World War. Industry in Japan is concentrated in three relatively small coastal areas, focusing on Tokyo–Yokohama, Nagoya and Osaka–Kobe. Virtually all its raw materials and energy requirements are imported, but skilful management and labour have ensured one of the fastest rates of economic growth in the world during the post-war period. Much of its industrial production is exported, and Japanese cars, electronic and optical equipment compete

Making watches in a Japanese factory

effectively with home produced goods in western markets. Compared with Japan, India and China have experienced only modest rates of industrial growth, and their main manufacturing areas like those of South Africa, Australia and South America tend to be restricted in area and are mainly associated with larger towns and cities.

Industrial development has created its own distinctive environment in each of the world's major industrial nations. Initially factories were built on the edge of older settlements or in the open countryside. Often they were sited along rivers which provided a supply of water and a means of disposing of effluent, and sometimes a source of power or of transport. Nearby were the workers houses, cheaply built in terraces along narrow streets which ended abruptly in the fields. But as more factories came to be built close by, the open spaces became fewer; railways competed for land with roads and housing, and the level of noise, dirt and smell increased. Gradually the new industrial towns assumed the pall of smoke and haze which has remained one of their most distinctive features.

As congestion increased the more wealthy began to move out of town, using the railway to escape to the green fields beyond, where they could build more spacious houses, semi-detached on larger plots of land. The pattern of urban development was not the same everywhere. In Scotland or Germany workers' housing was often built in tenement blocks rather than two-storey terraces, and in continental Europe the urban middle class preferred to remain near the older urban core. But in England and North America the suburb became as much a part of the late-nineteenth-century industrial town as the working class slums; and it set the pattern for future urban growth in the twentieth century. New building increasingly had to be concentrated on the urban fringe. This included workers' housing, now often provided by government; and factories which left their old cramped sites for new open locations, served by road transport and powered by electricity. Planning legislation now ensures that residential and industrial land uses are strictly segregated, and adequate space is left for services such as shops, schools and hospitals, for transport and recreation. Population densities in these new developments are planned at much lower levels than in the past, and the result is a more open settlement than the old, congested industrial town. Much more land is thus needed for urban development, and as their populations increase cities expand outward, and begin to coalesce. *Megalopolis* is the term used to describe such clusters

157

Modern industrial development on the urban fringe: cars awaiting shipment at the Ford factory at Halewood, near Liverpool

of related cities, and although it has only developed so far in one or two locations—between Washington and Boston in the United States, and on a much smaller scale, the 'Randstad' in the Netherlands—this is the ultimate settlement form produced by the increasing concentration of manufacturing industry in major industrial regions.

Life and work in industrial cities such as these is very different from the societies we have discussed so far. Home and workplace are often widely separated, involving time-consuming journeys as thousands of people crowd the transport systems at morning and evening rush hours. Through commuting, much of a man's daily life is spent away from home, while his wife stays behind to look after the house and children. Only recently has it become more common for her to work on her own account, a trend made possible by smaller families, full–time education and the expansion of female employment in service and manufacturing industries. This pattern of work creates a different set of social relationships within the family from those of traditional society where husband and wife, parents and children shared daily work on the land. Yet the family remains the most important social group at most stages in life, for except in older working class areas, relatives rarely live close by. And although neighbours may become friends, they usually lack the community of interest which in traditional society is based on similarity of work, long residence and ties of kinship.

Work in industrial society is also strictly regulated in ways unfamiliar in most other forms of economic activity. More specifically it depends on the clock, which tells people when to get up, when to catch the bus or train, when to start work and when to go home. This mechanical time is at its most demanding on the assembly line, which symbolises so much of the organisation of modern industrial society. Its speed determines the rate of production, and rules the working day of the operator. For him it is the ultimate in specialisation, because he can spend much of his life tightening the same type of bolt or

Urban leisure: These sailing boats are the *Dragon* class. Sailing is one of the fastest growing leisure activities in the British Isles, although most participants use smaller boats than these

assembling the same components, perhaps never even seeing the finished product. Modern factory work can thus be highly specialised, yet tedious and lacking in skill; highly organised yet utterly impersonal, financially rewarding yet insecure. For these reasons work is often important only for the cash the job brings in, and people live in expectation of what they can do in their leisure time. With the trend towards shorter working hours, free time increases, and the provision of leisure activities assumes the proportion of a major industry, ranging from television and radio to sporting activities, hobbies and pastimes. All these further distinguish industrial from traditional society, and leave their own distinctive imprint on the modern landscape.

3 Tertiary Activities

Modern commercial societies need a wide range of specialist services if they are to work efficiently, and the number of people who find employment in this sector has increased dramatically during the present century. Broadly speaking, tertiary activities can be grouped into four main categories. *Distribution* may be placed first, for it includes a variety of jobs which are directly related to manufacturing: transport, wholesale activities in which goods from many different manufactures are assembled in bulk in warehouses and then reorganised into smaller lots for distribution; and retailing, where goods from different wholesalers are finally sold in shops to consumers. *Finance* comes next, again associated particularly with manufacturing industry. It requires the services of a large number of specialists in accountancy and insurance as well as stockbrokers and lawyers to finance and regulate business transactions. In addition, the demand for banking and credit facilities by private borrowers rises as living standards improve. *Administration* is a third category of employment, mainly related to government service at national and local level. It now includes a wide range of occupations since governments have assumed responsibility for many social and welfare services, as well as such long established functions as defence and taxation. Finally *Personal services* may include activities as diverse as medicine and hairdressing, teaching, entertainment and journalism, but in each case the numbers employed vary with standards of living. The more money people have, the greater the demand for the sort of personal services which improve the quality of life but are not in themselves vital for basic subsistence.

The main feature that is common to these different occupations is that each provides a service for people, and employ-

A teacher with a class in Botswana, southern Africa. Teachers have a key role in modern society, especially in helping traditional communities adjust to modern eı onomies. (*Photo courtesy of Radio Times Hulton Picture Library*)

ment is thus mainly concentrated in urban centres. However, the proportion of people working in service jobs can vary considerably—some towns may have more people employed in manufacturing industry than in services, while others may specialise in this sector. Major ports, for example, like Southampton, Singapore or Capetown employ a large number of people in the distributive trades. Other towns may specialise in administration—a county town in Britain will probably have offices for the county secretary and surveyor, for planning, health and welfare, as well as local agencies for national government departments such as employment and telecommunications. A national capital likewise will house major government departments as well as the legislative and judicial bodies. In older nation states these administrative centres have usually developed in cities like London and Paris which have other major functions, but some countries have deliberately sited their capital cities away from other urban centres. Thus Washington and Brasilia, the national capitals of the U.S.A. and Brazil, have grown almost entirely through the employment generated by their administrative function.

Midtown Manhattan, New York City, dominated by the skyscrapers which house thousands of people working in tertiary employment. In this photograph the United Nations building is in the foreground. (*Photo Aerofilms Limited*)

The close relationship between tertiary employment and major centres of urban population and manufacturing industry explains why its world distribution shows a heavy concentration in western Europe and North America, with minor centres in the U.S.S.R. and Japan. Indeed in the more advanced industrial nations as much as three-fifths of the entire labour force may be employed in this tertiary sector. This represents a substantial shift in the balance of employment in these countries during the present century, for in the early 1900s a majority of the population were employed in manufacturing industry, and the proportion in service occupations was only a little above that engaged in primary activities. Today mechanisation and automation has greatly reduced the proportion employed in manufacturing industry, and tertiary employment is the fastest growing sector of the economy, especially in personal services. This can be seen in Table 4.1 below, which shows the distribution of employment by sectors in several countries. The figures for the U.S.A., for instance, show a pattern of employment typical of the most advanced industrial nations; Italy resembles that of an earlier stage of industrial development with a relatively high proportion employed in primary activities; and Egypt, with a small proportion in manufacturing industry, is more characteristic of the under-developed countries.

Table 4.1 Distribution of Employment as a percentage of total labour force (after J H Paterson, 1972)

	Primary	Secondary	Tertiary
Australia (1961)	12.2	35.8	52.0
Belgium (1963)	9.0	41.0	50.0
Egypt (1961)	36.1	11.0	32.0
West Germany (1963)	15.9	44.9	39.2
Ireland (1961)	36.1	23.6	40.3
Italy (1963)	27.3	39.0	33.7
Japan (1963)	29.7	29.7	40.6
U.S.A. (1962)	8.1	31.4	60.5

Computers are now used extensively in many sorts of tertiary activity as in this reservations centre of an airline company

In fact most underdeveloped countries appear to have a surprisingly large number of people employed in the tertiary sector, usually far more than those working in manufacturing industry. This is mainly due to the proliferation of jobs at every level of government service, which is a by-product of nationalist sentiment in the emergence of new political states; and to the greater financial rewards of jobs in commerce as opposed to the more poorly paid and less secure employment available in manufacturing industry. Expansion in the service sector helps to explain the rapid growth of the larger towns and particularly the capital cities of the underdeveloped countries, and the development of 'shanty towns', which encircle their suburbs. Here rural migrants find temporary homes, and the more fortunate among them, semi-employment as petty traders and servants. Economically this is not a healthy growth, for it is not based upon the productive sector of the urban economy; and the growing number of unemployed and underemployed form an impoverished proletariat which has considerable potential for large-scale political unrest.

4 Rich Countries, Poor Countries

Our discussion of the ways men make or earn their living has revealed something of the diversity that exists in the modern world. At one extreme, a hunter in the forests of New Guinea still practises an economy which has altered little since Palaeolithic times; and at the other, an American astronaut has all the immense resources of twentieth-century technology behind him as he begins a journey into outer space. Between these two ends of the spectrum, the majority of mankind live ordinary lives, but with very different resources and expectations. Those in the advanced countries enjoy high standards of living, the product of a technology which they themselves created; but two-thirds of mankind subsist at much lower levels, sometimes in circumstances of poverty and hunger which most Europeans and Americans find hard to conceive. The countries in which these conditions prevail are described by various terms—underdeveloped, developing, backward; collectively they are sometimes called 'The Third World'. Probably the word that gets closest to the essence of their problem is the emotive word 'backward'; for these are countries which live by tribal or traditional economies, and which have yet to absorb the technology of the advanced industrial nations although profoundly affected by their commercial structures and political machinations.

The contrast between the developed and underdeveloped

countries has been implicit in many of the topics we have examined so far. In Chapter 3 we saw that traditional economies still prevail in most parts of Asia, Africa and Latin America. Apart from tropical plantations, commercial farming is poorly developed in most of these same areas, manufacturing industry provides little employment, and between 70 and 90 per cent of the population are engaged in primary activities. These economic symptoms of underdevelopment are summarised in Figure 4.8 which shows the world distribution of income per head of population. The figures in themselves are not very reliable, especially for the underdeveloped countries; apart from deficiencies in collecting the relevant statistics, average incomes are often grossly inflated by the high incomes of the affluent few. But the map does underline the relative difference in income between the rich and poor countries: incomes in the U.S.A., the world's richest nation, are on average twice that in Britain; but incomes in Britain average between ten and fifteen times that of the world's poorest countries. The map also shows how unevenly the world's financial wealth is distributed. In fact some four-fifths of mankind live in varying

Figure 4.8
World: gross national product per capita, 1972 data. These figures are based on the aggregate production of all producers resident in a country together with net income received from abroad

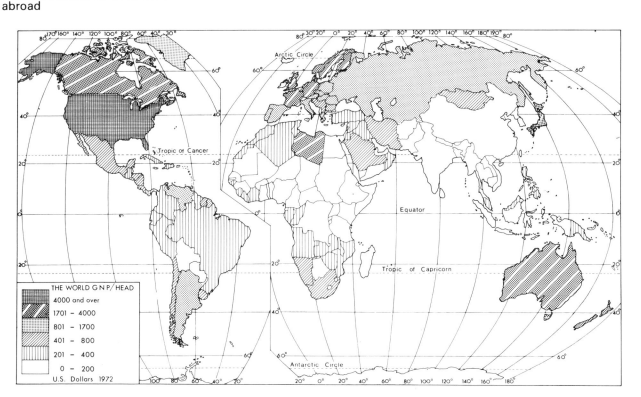

Figure 4.9
World: levels of economic development. This map combines three major criteria: gross domestic product, which is the aggregate production of all producers living in the country; the proportion of the labour force employed in agriculture and related primary occupations; and the per capita use of commercial energy. All these are accepted as among the most important indices of the level of economic development to individual countries. Data is from 1963–64

degrees of poverty, with the lowest incomes occurring in Africa and Asia; Latin America and the Middle East are slightly better off.

Income, however, is only one index of development: housing standards, literacy, life expectancy and many other social and economic variables must also be considered. And an attempt to combine several of these in a single scheme is illustrated in Figure 4.9. Here the advanced nations include the U.S.A. and Canada, Australia, New Zealand and Israel, and most European countries, accounting in all for about 16 per cent of the world's population. Czechoslovakia, East Germany, Italy and Ireland are all included in this category, although they have a higher proportion of their population in agricultural employment than the other advanced countries. The next group includes European countries such as Spain, Hungary and Poland, the Soviet Union and Japan, South Africa, and several South American countries like Venezuela which rank only slightly above the underdeveloped countries. Altogether these countries account for 15 per cent of mankind. Finally the underdeveloped countries, with 70 per cent of the

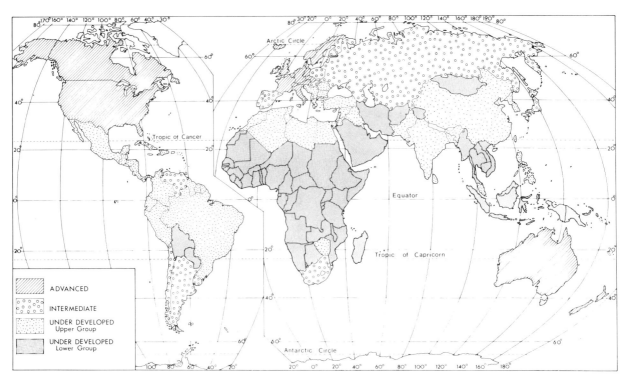

ADVANCED

INTERMEDIATE

UNDER DEVELOPED
Upper Group

UNDER DEVELOPED
Lower Group

world's population, have been divided into two groups: the slightly better off nations are mostly in South America, north Africa, Asia and south-east Europe, while the least developed are found in the remainder of Africa and in south-west and south-east Asia. In these latter areas tribal and traditional economies are most strongly entrenched.

The pattern shown on Figure 4.9 is relatively recent. Two centuries ago most countries in the world would be considered underdeveloped by modern standards. But in the intervening period the advanced nations have forged ahead, sustained by an unprecedented rate of technological development and economic growth. Meantime, the majority of mankind has moved ahead only slowly—and in some cases has scarcely changed at all. In the near future the present pattern of development is likely to become further accentuated, with the advanced nations becoming progressively richer, and the underdeveloped poorer.

To explain this we need to identify the reasons why the underdeveloped countries have experienced such slow rates of economic growth compared with the advanced nations. An earlier generation of scholars were inclined to see the influence of climate or race as accounting for the notable concentration of underdeveloped countries within the tropics and among non-white peoples; but such simple correlations can offer no valid explanation of the complex problems of economic development. Another argument is that the underdeveloped countries are far distant from the main centres of technological innovation in Europe and North America. Initially this may have been important, but for more than a century most of these countries have had close political and commercial ties with the advanced industrial nations. Today technical aid is available through many national and international agencies. The absence of mineral and energy resources is another factor which inhibited early industrial development, but today many countries of the Third World are major exporters of these commodities, and have yet to develop their own manufacturing industries. Others have argued that culture may itself be a major deterrent to economic growth, for the religious values and social traditions of many people in the Third World would lead them to reject the notion that material progress holds the key to human happiness. But the explanation which finds greatest acceptance among political leaders in the Third World is that their economic problems are a legacy of their former colonial status. Europeans, they say, exploited the resources of the Third World for the benefit of their own economies. In doing so they

167

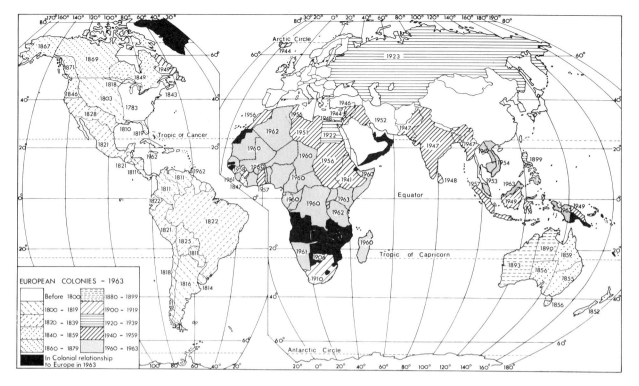

Figure 4.10
World: countries formerly held as colonies by European powers, showing the date by which each gained its independence. This map relates to 1963 when several countries in tropical Africa, the Middle East and south-east Asia were still colonial in status, as were many groups of islands in the West Indies and the Pacific Ocean. Most of these are now independent, but many are so small that they cannot be represented adequately on a map of this scale

disrupted and sometimes even destroyed native institutions, and although most underdeveloped countries have won political independence they are still economically dependent on the advanced countries. This argument of course is largely true, but European influence was by no means negative: under colonial rule new infrastructures were provided and traditional institutions altered in such a way that economic growth was at least made possible, while the colonial powers also created new economic and social systems which covered the entire world.

Obviously no single explanation can account for the present world pattern of underdevelopment; but if the causes are hard to establish, we can at least identify the problems. If the countries of the Third World are to experience economic growth they must improve their productivity, by developing a more advanced technology and creating more employment. For this they need capital, which they can attempt to raise from their own resources, or import from abroad. The latter is the traditional method, obtained by exporting raw materials for use by the industries of the advanced nations. This produces ready cash, sometimes essential for the purchase of food in the event of food shortages; but it leaves the economy of the exporting country vulnerable to fluctuations in world prices, over which it may be able to exert little control. Capital from abroad can also be obtained on a limited scale from international agencies, or as direct aid from individual nations; but the latter form of loan may have political strings attached which can compromise the independence of the receiving country.

In most instances the only effective long-term solution is for each country to concentrate on developing its own productive capacity. In many areas this is economically feasible, for the Third World contains large resources of metallic minerals, timber, oil and water power; and it has the human resources of many millions of people whose skills have yet to be fully developed. But social and political obstacles to development are formidable, and certainly far greater than those experienced by European nations at a comparable stage of growth more than a century ago. Cultural tradition, for example, can inhibit growth, both in the ways already mentioned, and in countries such as India, by religious beliefs like those which allow aged cattle to subsist on scarce resources of food. Often there is no

Modernising traditional farming. These plots on a farm in the Punjab, west Pakistan, show the contrast between crops grown with the aid of commercial fertilisers (left) and those which have been raised using traditional methods. (*F.A.O. photo*)

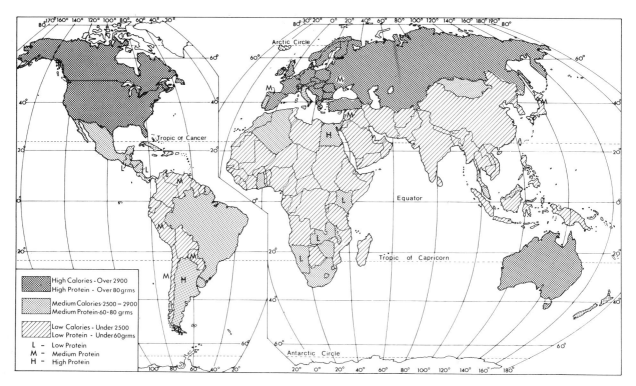

Figure 4.11
World standards of nutrition. This map underlines the regional inequalities that exist in food consumption, the most basic of all man's needs. Data 1964

indigenous class of wealthy merchants who might become industrial entrepreneurs. Social tensions may lead to political instability, as in the political *coups* which are a recurring feature of life in Latin America; while international disputes over border issues, for example, may necessitate heavy military expenditure which is only maintained at great cost to the economy, as in India and Pakistan. But undoubtedly the greatest problem facing the Third World is the growth of population which in most countries is on a scale sufficient to offset much of the economic gain achieved by greater productivity. This topic has already been considered in an earlier chapter, and in the context of economic development one can only express cautious optimism about the prospects for growth in the underdeveloped countries in the immediate future. One hopeful sign is that the rich countries are now aware of the extent of the problem and its implications for their own future well-being. They are beginning to give technical and financial assistance with fewer qualifications than in the past. International agencies are also developing and coordinating programmes of aid and development on a scale which is slowly beginning to match the real dimensions of the problem. But all of this is unlikely to reduce the gap between rich and poor nations by any significant amount for a very long time. Regional inequalities will persist, and the world pattern of development we have outlined in this chapter is unlikely to alter substantially before the end of the present century.

5 MAN, CULTURE AND SOCIETY

The technological developments of the past century and the growth of industrial economies have increasingly affected the way of life of people in every corner of the world. New systems of trade and transport link the major industrial nations with distant countries, and regional economies everywhere are affected by the twin processes of urbanisation and industrial growth. Regional patterns of livelihood are less varied now than in former times, for a world-wide commercial system imposes its own uniformities on economic behaviour, and measures success against world standards of economic development rather than of local subsistence.

Yet in contrast to the growing uniformity in economic activities, regional differences persist in other aspects of human life, maintaining a cultural diversity which is of great significance in the contemporary world. Several of these cultural activities will be examined in this chapter, beginning with the racial groupings of mankind. Strictly speaking race is a biological rather than a cultural feature, the result of genetic processes over which man himself has little direct control. Biologically, the criteria used to distinguish racial groups in man are relatively minor, but in social and political terms they have become highly significant as different racial groups have come into closer contact through migration and greater mobility in modern times. Social relations between peoples are also influenced by differences in language and religion, the former being especially important since it provides the basis for all forms of communication. But in the modern world, political boundaries which delimit national territories have become increasingly significant because governments today closely regulate the lives of their citizens and international politics directly influence the relationship between peoples throughout the world. This chapter will examine four aspects of man's cultural diversity—race, language, religion and political organisation.

1 Race

A walk along the busy streets of one of the world's great cosmopolitan cities will quickly reveal the tremendous variety of man's physical appearance. For in the crowd we will see

Caucasoid, Mongoloid, Negroid:
the variety of racial types in a New
York crowd

people of many different shapes and sizes; skin colour which
ranges from white through brown to jet black; eyes which may

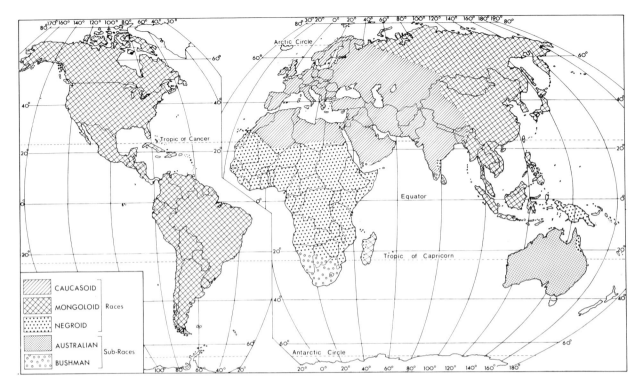

Figure 5.1
World: distribution of major racial groups

be like dark chocolate or blue as the sky; and hair which differs both in colour and in texture—from blond and straight to black and woolly. Automatically we would relate each distinctive physical type to a particular geographical area: tall, dark-skinned people with woolly hair to Africa, the pale, fair-haired types to northern Europe, and the small people with straight hair and almond-shaped eyes to China or Japan. In fact our regional identifications could be quite wrong: the 'African' may have been born in London and speak with a Cockney accent, and the 'Asian' may come from California. But our original assumption is correct in that the ancestors of both came originally from tropical Africa and eastern Asia respectively. Before the great voyages of discovery initiated by Europeans in the fifteenth and sixteenth centuries, people in the same geographical areas did tend to be of similar physical appearance; and it is only during the past two centuries that this geographical pattern has been disturbed by large-scale migrations, especially of Europeans to the Americas, Australia and south Africa, and Africans to North America.

These differences in the physical appearance of mankind are expressed in the term *race,* which is used by scientists to mean a subdivision of mankind whose members share a certain number of inherited physical characteristics. This definition relates only to physical appearance; it has nothing to do with such cultural attributes as religion, language or nationality which are often implied when people talk about race in every-day speech. Scientifically speaking, it is quite wrong to speak of the Latin race or the Japanese race. Latin is a language and Japan a modern state, and neither speech nor politics has anything to do with the colour of a man's skin or the shape of his eyes. Physical appearance and cultural behaviour are produced by very different processes: we can change our nationality or learn a new language, but even a plastic surgeon can do very little to alter the basic features of our face or body. For example, a Chinese Buddhist, born in Peking and speaking Mandarin as a child may emigrate to the U.S.A. and become an English-speaking, Protestant American citizen; but he will still retain the Mongoloid features with which he was born. It is important to emphasise the basic difference between race and culture right at the beginning of this chapter, otherwise we may make some very wrong assumptions. For example, one sometimes hears the assertion that the white races are inherently superior to the black races, since no major technological discovery was ever made by a black man. It may be true that black races have been technologically backward, but the explanation lies in the history of cultural innovation and has nothing whatsoever to do with race. Scientists may seem unduly sensitive about the correct use of the word race, but in the past the precise scientific meaning has been debased by politicians and laymen attempting to justify particular policies by reference to a concept of race which has no basis in modern science.

Race then is a purely biological phenomenon, and differences between races are established by measuring certain recognisable physical features. Those most commonly used can be divided into two groups: *skeletal features* such as the shape and size of skull, the development of brow ridges, projection of the jaws and cheek-bones, stature and body build; and *surface features*, which include the colour of skin, hair and eye, hair texture, the appearance of the lips, and certain other features such as the accumulation of fat on the thighs and buttocks. The study of blood groups and other biochemical characteristics provides further data which has yet to be fully integrated with the older methods of classifying mankind into racial groups. Skeletal features are important and easily measured indices for establishing racial categories, and have the special advantage that the body form of modern man can be compared with those

175

of his remote ancestors to establish the changes that have occurred through time. But surface features provide a more obvious means of identifying modern racial types, and one which is much less affected by differences in nutrition. Pigmentation, which affects the colour of skin, eye and hair, is one of the major variables used, but hair texture and eye form are also important. Each of these features displays an enormous range of variation between individuals, but with careful measurement distinctive categories can be recognised. Moreover, some features are inter-related: for example, hair that has a woolly texture is normally black, and it is mainly associated with black skin, a broad nose and thick lips. Racial classifications are based on the recognition of significant linkages like this, but it is important to remember that they are statistical categories. Nature does not provide ready-made divisions into which mankind may be grouped, and any racial classification is bound to be arbitrary.

In practice it is fairly easy to identify the three main racial groups—Negroid, Mongoloid and Caucasoid, for only a limited number of distinctive features are involved. Further subdivision is more difficult since it raises questions of origins which are not easily resolved. For example, the dark-skinned Australian Aborigine has some features which are Negroid in character, others which are Caucasoid. Is he to be regarded as a separate racial type—a Caucasoid who has developed Negroid features whilst isolated from others of his group in a tropical environment? Or is he the product of inbreeding between Negroids and Caucasoids? Questions like these are important in determining the sequence of racial evolution in man, and the course of his early migrations, but they are not our immediate concern. Instead it is more relevant for us to be able to identify the three major racial groups and establish their geographical distribution before the great migrations of recent times brought about the very radical changes which have already been referred to above.

Racial Groups

The *Negroid* peoples are the most distinctive of the three major groups, distinguished by dark skin which ranges from dark brown to black; dark eyes which show a similar range of colour; black hair which may be woolly or kinky in texture; noses which are broad and flat, small ears and thick everted lips. Males usually have a sparse beard and little body hair, but there is a tremendous range in stature, for the Negroids include some of the world's tallest and smallest people—the Dinka of

the upper Nile and the Pygmies of the Congo Forest. The most
characteristic Negroid features are found in people of tropical
Africa, but they extend eastward in a discontinuous band
across the Indian Ocean to the Andaman Islands and the
Malaya peninsula, New Guinea, the Fiji Islands and parts of the
Philippines.

North of the Sahara—in Africa, most of Europe and western
Asia—*Caucasoids* are the dominant racial group. Most have

light-coloured eyes and skin; hair that is generally wavy but may be straight; narrow, prominent noses, thin lips and abundant body hair and beards among the men. Like the Negroids they vary greatly in stature, weight and body form, and in western Asia some may have skins as dark as many negroids.

In eastern and northern Asia are found the third major group, the *Mongoloids*. Their skins range in colour from dark brown to light yellow, their hair is mainly straight, coarse and dark, and sparsely distributed on their bodies. The face tends to be flat in appearance, with high cheekbones and a nose which flares outwards at the nostrils. The eyes are especially distinctive, their long, slit-like appearance caused by the epicanthic fold—a skin covering which droops over the eyelid. The classic Mongoloid type is found in Siberia, Mongolia, Tibet and northern China, but Mongoloid features also predominate among the peoples of Japan and south-east Asia.

Mongoloid: a woman from Inner Mongolia. (Photo courtesy of The American Museum of Natural History)

Each of these major groups has several subdivisions. Caucasoids, for example, include the tall, fair, blue-eyed Nordic peoples, the stocky Alpine type and the small, dark-skinned Mediterranean group of southern Europe and north Africa. The Eskimo and American Indians are both members of the Mongoloid group, although the epicanthic fold is often absent among the latter; and people with many Negroid features are found in the Pacific, especially in Melanesia. However, their blood-groups differ from the African Negroids.

Most people in the world today belong to one or other of these three major groups and their various subdivisions. But in the southern hemisphere, in Africa and Australia, are found several small groups of people who do not readily fit the above categories. The Bushmen of southern Africa, for example, differ from their Negroid neighbours by having yellow or brown skin, flattish faces, Mongoloid-like eye folds, and lightly-curled hair which grows in small tufts over the scalp. Their buttocks are often heavily padded with fat in the form known

179

Bushman: a man from Namibia, south-west Africa

Australian Aborigine: a man from the Alice Springs region of central Australia

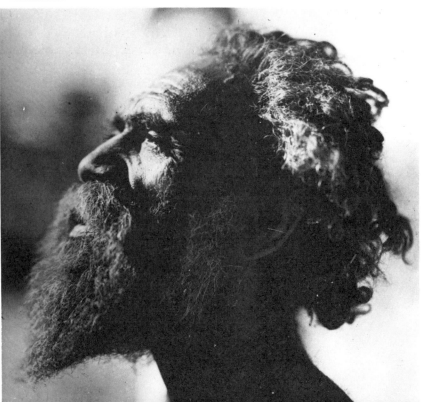

as *steatopygia*—it may act rather like the camel's hump, providing a reserve supply of food and water in the extreme conditions of the deserts in which the Bushmen now live. In Australia, the Aborigine has some skeletal features which resemble those found in early man—especially heavy brow-ridges and projecting jaws, and although their skins are brown they are more like Caucasoids in appearance than their Pacific neighbours. Geographical isolation may explain some of the features which distinguish both these groups of people, for they live at the extremities of the southern continents, far from the main migration routes of early man.

Elsewhere in the world, the major racial groups tend to merge with each other along the boundaries of their respective territories. For, biologically, mankind is a single species, *Homo sapiens,* whose members can interbreed. But if all racial groups are interfertile, how were they able to develop their distinguishing features in the first place, and why was each group predominant within a particular geographical area? Briefly, the answer is that at some stage in its evolution, the species *Homo sapiens* was separated into several groups long enough to develop certain distinctive features through normal genetic processes. These processes affect all biological organisms, and will be reviewed briefly before considering how they may have affected racial evolution in man.

Man's physical appearance is ultimately determined by the tiny particles known as genes which he inherits from his parents. Each population possesses a stock of genes which is transmitted from one generation to the next. But since each individual is the product of some 44 000 pairs of genes, the possible combinations are immense, even in a relatively small population. This is one of the reasons why individuals differ so much in their physical appearance, even though members of the same family can bear quite a strong resemblance to each other—in the shape of a nose or colour of hair, for example. In fact the physical similarities which form the basis of race in man are really an extension of these family resemblances to a much larger population—they result from the recombination of particular sets of genes within the same group over many generations. New genes are added to the existing stock by the process known as *mutation:* this can arise by individuals from outside a particular group breeding with the original members and adding to the existing stock of genes. The isolation of a community will prevent this, and as a result of inbreeding its members slowly develop certain features which distinguish them from their neighbours. The effect of this type of geographical isolation is exemplified in Darwin's classic study of the Galapagos Islands. But mutation can occur within a group through the influence of *natural selection*. This occurs because the genetic composition of certain individuals enables them to survive better than their contemporaries—they may have a stronger physique or a constitution which makes them more resistant to certain endemic diseases. As a result their genetic structure will become normal in the population, as the less well endowed individuals gradually die off—aided perhaps by sexual and social selection which favours certain individuals as marriage partners rather than others. Genetic processes can thus explain why small populations, isolated from others of their species for a long period of time, can develop certain characteristic features of their own. But what features are most likely to develop?

Here environment may supply the answer, by encouraging certain features which enable the organism to cope with its environment more efficiently. Zoologists, for example, have shown how different warm-blooded species respond to latitudinal variations in heat, light and solar radiation, and have expressed these as a series of ecological rules. Bergman's rule, for example, states that the animals of a given species are larger in colder regions and smaller in warmer ones—they also have longer hair. Allen showed that animals living in deserts and grasslands have larger extremities than those of the same or related species living in forests or on mountains. And finally Gloger noted that pigmentation is greatest in warm and humid areas.

These ecological rules provide clues which may explain some distinctive features which differentiate races of man. Bergman's rule, which applies to body form rather than stature, helps to explain the contrast between the stocky frame of the Eskimo with its thick layers of fat and the slender Pygmy. It is true that the tall Dinka of the Nile also live in a tropical climate, but they are slender in build, and the weight and volume of their bodies is less than that of the Eskimo. Similarly desert dwellers do have larger limbs, fingers and toes, and noses, than the Eskimo, enabling their bodies to keep cool by providing a large surface area of skin through which transpiration can take place. Gloger's rule also applies broadly to man in that the darkest skins are found among the Negroid peoples of tropical lands, the heavy pigmentation acting like a filter against strong ultra-violet radiation. Light coloured skins are a decided disadvantage in tropical sunlight, and although most Caucasoids can produce more pigment if necessary—we call it

The Pygmy and the Dinka: the shortest and the tallest people in the world. Both live in tropical Africa, the Pygmy from the Congo and the Dinka from the southern Nile.

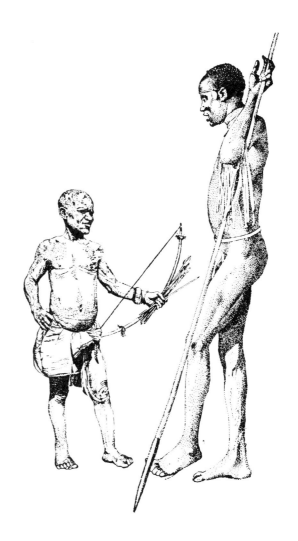

sun-tan—a very blond skin remains susceptible to sunburn, blistering, and the highly unpleasant fever known as sunstroke. Thus such Negroid features as dark skin, a slender lanky body and numerous sweat glands are all useful assets for living in a hot climate.

Conversely in cold climates there are advantages in having a stocky frame well insulated with fat to keep the body and its extremities warm. Other Mongoloid features may be explained in this way too: the shape and appearance of the face, padded with fat to prevent heat loss; the nose flattened and the cheekbones protruded to reduce the surface area of skin to a minimum; and the eyes protected by the fatty tissues of the epicanthic fold. Even the coarse straight hair and the scanty beard may have some protective value since they ensure that sweat and moisture are not trapped near the skin where they might become frozen. Genetic processes and ecological adaptation thus seem to explain some of the physical differences in mankind which are used to distinguish different racial groups. But how did they come about, and when did racial differentiation take place? To answer these questions we must look briefly at the ancestors of modern man and the environments in which they lived.

Man's Antecedents

The story of human evolution is exceedingly complex, for it is based on the interpretation of a fossil record in which there are many gaps. Recent discoveries have added greatly to our knowledge, but they have made it more difficult to provide an adequate summary since current theories are constantly being challenged by fresh evidence. However, there seems little doubt that the most dramatic events in the evolution of modern man occurred during the Pleistocene period when the distribution of the world's climatic and vegetation zones was radically altered by the spread of ice sheets on the poleward margins of the continents. Briefly, the glacial advances which took place at

Figure 5.2
Time scale of human evolution

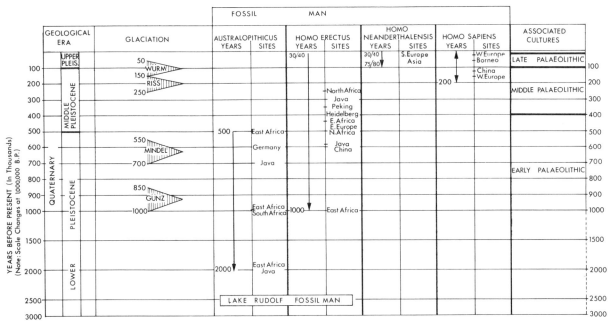

intervals during the Pleistocence, caused the tropical forest belt to shrink towards the equator, deeply affecting the way of life of all tropical mammals, including the Primates who were ancestors of modern man.

The earliest known member of the family *Hominidae* to which man belongs, has been named *Australopithecus* and has been described as resembling a man from the neck down, and an ape from the neck up! Certainly he walked upright but his skull was ape-like and his brain had less than a third the capacity of *Homo sapiens,* about the same as a modern chimpanzee. His origin remains a mystery, but he was living in Africa at least two million years ago, and similar remains have also been found in the Levant and in Java. *Australopithecus* died out about half a million years ago, but meantime he had been joined by another inhabitant of the tropics in the Old World, *Homo erectus,* who was much more man-like in appearance. He had a bigger brain, measuring 800 to 900 cubic centimetres in the earliest specimens, 1000 to 1100 in the later; a more vaulted forehead; he walked fully erect, made stone tools and had learned how to use fire. *Homo erectus* and *Australopithecus* overlapped in space and time, living in the same east African environment for at least half a million years. But biologically they belonged to different species and did not interbreed. The conventional theory is that *Homo erectus* probably evolved in Africa from an early form of *Australopithecus,* but this is being challenged by the evidence of new fossils found in the early 1970s at Lake Rudolf in northern Kenya. These have been dated at two and a quarter million years old, and if they are finally accepted as of *Homo erectus* type then they are as old as the oldest known specimen of *Australopithecus.* However, if the origins of *Homo erectus* are still unknown, there is evidence to show that he ranged much more widely than *Australopithecus.* Half a million years ago he was well established in north Africa and Java; a little later he appears in China; but so far no specimens have been found in western Asia or Europe. Between these different specimens there is little difference in body form, but from the point of racial origins Chinese *Homo erectus*—known as Sinanthropus—is of particular interest, for he had a flattish face and high cheekbones, very similar to that of the modern Mongoloid. Consequently some scholars have wondered if racial differentiation was already taking place in *Homo erectus.*

Homo erectus vanished from the earth during the latter part of the Upper Pleistocene period. He survived longest in south and central Africa, and in Java where his remains have been dated at between 30 000 and 40 000 years old. By this time modern man, *Homo Sapiens,* had appeared in most parts of the Old World. In Europe a primitive form is recorded as dating from about 250 000 years ago; in China from about 150 000 years ago; and dating from 50 000 years ago onwards he is found increasingly in Java, Borneo, Kenya and north Africa. Significantly in each of these places there are indications of racial differentiation even in the earliest specimens. Fossil *Homo sapiens* in China had some Mongoloid features, the skulls found in Java and Borneo were like modern Australoids, and the north Africans who belong to a much later date—about 10 000 B.C., were Caucasoid in appearance. Indeed the Negroids are the only major racial group not positively identified in fossil form.

It is still not clear how *Homo sapiens* was related biologically to *Homo erectus,* for many of the earlier sapiens-like fossils of the middle Pleistocene period cannot be dated with real certainty. Current theory is that *Homo sapiens* evolved from *Homo erectus* in several different locations by normal evolutionary processes, and that the modern races of man were established in this way. Again, finds at Lake Rudolf may upset this view, for some scholars believe that some of the fossils dated to two and a quarter million years ago are more like *Homo sapiens* than *Homo erectus.* If this were accepted, *Homo sapiens* would be a couple of million years older than he is thought to be on present evidence. Another problem relates to the later development of *Homo sapiens,* for about 80 000 years ago there appears another form of man, *Homo neanderthalensis,* who lived in southern Europe and Asia for between forty and fifty thousand years before he too vanished, leaving no trace in later populations. *Homo neanderthalensis* had a brain as large as *Homo sapiens,* but he was shorter, heavily built with a long, wide face, low forehead, deeply protruding jaw and large nose. His origin is uncertain. He may have developed from *Homo sapiens* as an evolutionary side-line, and disappeared either through unsuccessful competition with him or as a result of some process of hybridisation. At present no one can really explain his fate.

By the end of the Pleistocene period, the present stage of man's evolutionary progress had been completed. Before the first glaciation, several genera and species of man-like Primates were living in the tropical lands of the Old World, but when the last glaciation ended only one species, *Homo sapiens,* had survived; and he was now to be found in every part of the world. That he had survived at all where others failed must be due to two main reasons. Firstly, his ecological adaptation to changing environments must have been more efficient: certainly evolution proceeded more rapidly in Europe, west Asia and China during the Pleistocene period than it did in the tropical lands of Africa or south-east Asia. Although the ancestors of *Homo sapiens* lived in the tropics, probably in Africa, they had moved north to the Eurasian land masses during the latter half of the Pleistocene period. Here physical adaptation to later climatic changes must have resulted in the racial differences we recognise today, although in no instance did this proceed so far as to form different biological species. Secondly, the survival of *Homo sapiens* was assured by cultural means, in his ability to make and use tools and weapons, and to communicate his experience to others of his species through language. Earlier hominidae had developed some of these skills: *Australopithecus* used stones as implements, and *Homo erectus* fashioned tools; but the larger brain of *Homo sapiens* indicates how much further he had progressed in the development of culture. With new weapons, the possession of fire and clothing, he could now live almost anywhere on earth, and further physical adaptation was unnecessary.

At present we can only speculate about the movements which took man to the different continents by the end of the Pleistocene period. From the African tropics the main zone of movement during the last glaciation must have lain to the

Figure 5.3
Old world: distribution of sites where fossils of early man have been found

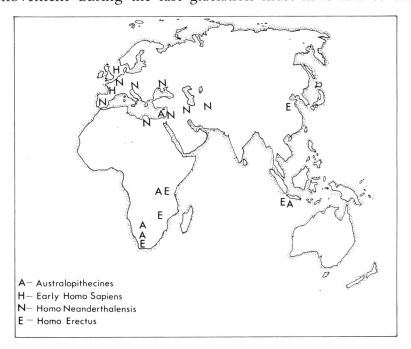

A — Australopithecines
H — Early Homo Sapiens
N — Homo Neanderthalensis
E — Homo Erectus

south of the Tertiary mountains of south-west Asia and the Afrasian deserts, which at that time would have enjoyed a more genial climate. Along this zone people moved eastward, some to central and northern China and Mongolia where they were eventually overtaken by changing climate, and isolated for sufficiently long to develop some distinctive features by mutation and natural selection.

This seems the most likely explanation for the development of the Mongoloid features which represent adaptation to extreme cold. Some were already present in Sinanthropus, the earliest Chinese example of *Homo erectus*; and they are fully represented in the first known examples of *Homo sapiens* who form the post-glacial populations of central Asia, from Siberia to north-western China. From this eastern homeland, members of this Mongoloid group travelled north-east to the Bering Strait, crossing to North America probably about 35 000 years ago. Within a few thousand years they had occupied the New World, from Alaska to Tierra del Fuego. Movement towards the south came later, but by the end of the first millennium B.C. south-east Asia, Indonesia and the Philippines were predominantly Mongoloid. Formerly the Malay archipelago had been occupied by Australoid peoples, who also formed the indigenous population of New Guinea and Australia. Crossbreeding between them and the Mongoloids produced a hybrid group which formed the later populations of Polynesia and Micronesia in the Pacific. Isolated groups of Australoid type are also found in northern Japan, where they are known as the Ainu; and in southern India, indicating that this particular group was once much more widely distributed. This gives some support to the view that they may have evolved from *Homo erectus,* to whom they bear some resemblance, notably in their pronounced brow ridges, and receding forehead and chin.

At the opposite end of the Old World, on the desert margins of north Africa, are found the earliest people of Caucasoid type. They seem to have spread north-westward towards Europe and east to northern India about the same time as Neolithic cultures were slowly diffused from south-west Asia. In north-west India their descendants are dark skinned, but in Europe they developed the white skin which reaches its most extreme form in the blond-haired blue-eyed Nordic type.

Much less is known about the origin of the third major group, the Negroids. Tropical Africa would appear to be their homeland, but the Pygmy form is also found across the Indian Ocean, in the Andaman Islands and the Malay peninsula, and

Figure 5.4
Old world: early migrations. The movements are highly generalised, but they show the direction of migration which brought Negroids, Caucasoids and Mongoloids into areas occupied by Negritoids, Bushmanoids and Australoids

there is no agreed theory which explains this distribution. In Africa the normal–sized Negroid may have developed in the Savanna belt, possibly in the western Sudan. Certainly their present distribution throughout western and southern Africa has occurred within historic times. In the south, for example, tribes such as the Zulu and the Matabele were moving into former Bushman territory about the same time as Dutch settlers from the Cape were moving north. And by then some of their number were also being carried across the Atlantic by slave traders to establish the Negroid groups of the New World.

This was the first of the intercontinental migrations which caused a major change in the racial distribution of mankind in the course of the eighteenth and nineteenth centuries. Caucasoids, for example, are now found in every part of the world, from the tundra to the tropics, and there are almost as many Negroid peoples in North America as in tropical Africa.

189

As a result of this mixing of peoples from different stock one might expect racial differences to diminish steadily through intermarriage. In fact this is not the case, for the more mobile man has become in modern times, the more rigid are the social and political barriers he has erected to maintain racial differences. Indeed it could be said that social distance rather than geographical distance is the main reason for the continued existence of racial differentiation in man.

The explanation for this is largely historical, and it depends to a considerable extent on the circumstances in which racial groups have been brought into contact. For although the contacts have arisen in various ways—through exploration, and trade, colonisation or military conquest—the group possessing a superior technology has normally assumed a dominant position. In this way, what begins as technological superiority is later expressed in purely racial terms; and once established the notion of racial superiority is likely to persist, acting as a very powerful barrier against the mating of 'inferior' peoples with those of the 'superior' group. This sequence of events is well illustrated in the history of European expansion overseas, for their superior weapons and technology ensured their initial dominance over the less advanced societies in many parts of Africa and the Americas, and to a lesser extent in Asia. By the end of the nineteenth century, most of these areas were ruled by Europeans, and the superiority of the Caucasoids seemed unquestionable. In the words of a nineteenth-century author:

The Caucasians have in all ages been the rulers; and it requires no prophet's eye to see that they are destined to conquer and hold every foot of the globe . . . Dark-skinned races, history attests, are only fit for military governments—the superior races ought to be kept free from all adulterations, otherwise the world will retrograde, instead of advancing in civilisation.

Obviously this author would be greatly aggrieved by the disappearance of the great colonial empires of his day, and their replacement by so many new independent states, especially in Africa.

Yet Caucasoids do not have a monopoly of racial prejudice: the Chinese in south-east Asia experience considerable hostility from the non-Mongoloid peoples of Malaysia and Indonesia; and the antipathy between Negro and Arab in Africa is a further example of long-standing racial tension. But many of the world's most intransigent racial problems today were precipitated by European colonisation, mainly because European migration was so extensive, and its initial technological advantage so great and far-reaching in its effect. For example, European ships were responsible for bringing Negroes from Africa to North America early in the seventeenth century; and European markets sustained both the slave trade and the economy of the southern plantations well into the nineteenth century. Slavery in America was abolished in 1863, but Negroes continued to suffer various forms of discrimination, and they are still among the nation's lowest-paid workers. During the present century many have migrated from the rural areas of the southern states to cities in the north-east, the mid-west and California, but although this has brought them into more direct contact with white Americans there is very little inter-marriage and only a limited amount of social mixing. Within the cities residential segregation divides black communities from white, and inter-racial tension sometimes erupts in communal violence, such as occurred in Los Angeles and Detroit in 1967.

In the U.S.A. racial segregation is no longer sanctioned by law, but in South Africa relations between the four main racial groups—White, Bantu (Negroid), Asian and Coloured—are closely regulated. The term *apartheid* is used to describe the principle of separate development, by which each racial group is strictly segregated from the others, and is required to develop its own social, economic and political institutions under the guidance of the state. Apartheid is really an attempt on the part of government to reverse a trend by which the different racial groups were coming to live and work more closely together within the same urban areas, as part of the normal processes of urban growth and industrialisation. The South African government believes that ultimately this could debase the traditional values and cultures of both black and white, and that the best solution is to establish separate states—Bantustans—within the Union, in which black Africans can live their own lives and be responsible for their own affairs. Apartheid represents one solution to the problems of a plural society, but it finds little support among neighbouring governments in tropical Africa. Certainly it has done little to ease the tensions between the different racial groups, and for this reason southern Africa is one part of the world where inter-racial conflict continues to be a serious threat to political stability.

2 Language

Language is so much a part of normal life that we tend to take it for granted—until we lose the power of speech through illness, or visit a foreign country and find that we cannot make ourselves understood. Only then do we realise how inadequate are gestures and facial expressions as a substitute for language. We may be able to point to the food we want to buy in a shop, but without a common language it is extremely difficult to express our thoughts and feelings or share ideas with other people. Other mammals have this difficulty: they may have quite a range of vocal sounds, but can only communicate on a very limited scale—like the dog's bark which signals danger. Human language, in contrast, is a much more elaborate and flexible system of vocal sounds which can be used to express ideas as well as immediate needs, and can relate past experiences as easily as present events. Language enables men to cooperate and interact with each other, and to transmit knowledge from one generation to the next. This type of exchange is essential for the growth of culture. For that reason language has been called 'the vehicle of culture', since it provides the means of communication on which all civilisation is based.

No one knows exactly how and when language originated. The early hominids could have survived quite easily without it, as their primate relatives have continued to do; but the growth of culture which began in Palaeolithic times could not have occurred without verbal communication. Palaeolithic man must have been able to talk to other members of his group. Some scholars believe that the facility for language may be innate in man, an essential part of the biological equipment of *Homo sapiens*. Others think it was a skill which had to be acquired through learning, that language began through the association of specific sounds and gestures. Of course speech-like sounds fall very short of coherent conversation, for language uses sounds to form meaningful words, and groups the words in sentences to convey abstract thoughts. In fact before language could develop in the form known today man had to achieve a very complex mental feat, breaking down his pattern of thought into its constituent parts. For example, as we watch a car travelling along a road the total scene is transmitted through our eyes to our brain without any conscious effort. But if we have to describe what we see to a blind person we have to analyse the scene very carefully, and consciously identify everything we see in front of us, using different words to describe the car, the driver, the road and the individual features of the landscape. Language therefore is much more than a range of vocal sounds: it involves a whole series of highly complicated mental patterns and processes whose inter-relationships are still not fully understood.

All known languages are organised in much the same way. Firstly, they use only a certain number of sounds, far fewer than the range which can be produced by the human voice. These sounds are called *phonemes,* and they are the basic units around which language is built. Different languages may use different phonemes: the glottal stop of German or the 'clicks' used by Bushmen are unfamiliar in English, and English speakers have considerable difficulty adjusting to the phonemes used in Chinese or even in French. Secondly, all languages group their phonemes to form words—each of which is a sound or sounds with specific meanings. Finally, words are combined into still larger units which we call sentences. Here the words are grouped according to definite grammatical rules which makes their meaning clear to the listener.

These three structural features are basic in any language, but obviously they can be combined in so many different ways that innumerable variations are possible. In fact it is estimated that there are nearly three thousand different languages spoken in the world today, but in earlier times there may have been more than twice that number, when people were less mobile and many communities had few external contacts. Under these circumstances languages tend to be highly localised, and may be spoken by relatively few people. But with the increased mobility and migrations of the past few centuries many of the smaller language groups have disappeared, to be replaced by one of the major European languages spoken by merchants and colonists. Sometimes the colonial powers were directly responsible for promoting their own language, but more often younger people simply found it useful to learn the language spoken by the people who could provide new jobs and a higher standard of living. In this way many local languages have declined, as is the case with Manx and Cornish in Britain, or Irish before its revival during the present century.

Often change in language occurs as a result of migration or conquest, with the dominant group imposing its language upon the indigenous population. Latin provides one of the best documented examples of this process. It was first spoken in the area around Rome and spread steadily through Italy and around the Mediterranean basin with the expansion of the Roman Empire. By the early centuries of the Christian era it was the principal language of Europe west of the Rhine and the Danube, replacing most existing languages. With the fall of Rome, Latin began to lose its former importance, for the merchants, soldiers and civil servants who were responsible for its initial expansion no longer travelled the roads of Europe. Local idioms and patterns of speech began to transform standard Latin into a series of local dialects, of which the most

Figure 5.5
The Roman Empire: the
maximum extent of the
territory in which Latin
was the official language

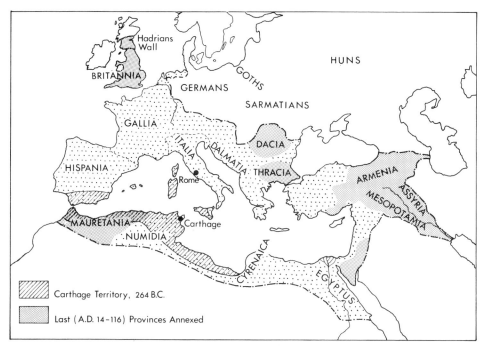

Carthage Territory, 264 B.C.

Last (A.D. 14–116) Provinces Annexed

important were associated with the more powerful states of the early Middle Ages, such as France, or merchant cities like Florence in Italy. Italian, French, Spanish and Portuguese were all derived from Latin in this way, thus bearing a strong family resemblance to each other—they are known as the Romance languages—while differing considerably in their vocabulary and grammar. Meantime Latin itself became a dead language, no longer spoken by ordinary people. But it did outlast the Roman Empire by more than a thousand years, mainly because its use by the Roman Catholic Church ensured that it was spoken and read by clerics and scholars throughout Europe. Until quite recently knowledge of Latin was considered the hallmark of the educated man, and only in the 1960s has its primacy in church liturgy been effectively challenged.

Understanding the ways in which languages change helps scholars to identify the oldest language among a particular group, and even to reconstruct languages which are no longer spoken. We have just seen this illustrated in the relationship between Latin and its modern descendants, the Romance languages. Another important ancestral language is Indo-European. Unspoken for many centuries, its existence is suggested by marked similarities found in languages as far apart as Iceland, Ireland and central India. Modern branches of this language in Europe include the Romance group—French,

Spanish, Portuguese and Italian; Germanic, the term which covers the languages of the Scandinavian countries as well as German and English; Celtic; Greek; Illyrian which is spoken in Albania; and the Balto-Slavonic group, spoken in eastern Europe from Lithuania and Poland to Russia, Czechoslovakia, Serbia and Bulgaria. Further east the Indo-Iranian branch of the same family includes modern Persian and Kurdish, as well as Bengali, Hindi and other languages of northern India. It is thought that the common ancestor of these different languages was spoken by a people who lived in western Eurasia about 2000 B.C. Some think their original homeland may have been to the north of the Baltic Sea, others that it was located in west-central Europe, north of the Alps. What is certain is that members of this language group began to migrate from their homeland during the second millennium B.C. spreading so widely that their language diverged into many modern forms, now spoken by more than one thousand million people.

Establishing relationships such as these provides one means of classifying the immense variety of languages spoken in the modern world, by grouping them according to their descent from a common ancestor. In this way it is possible to recognise

Figure 5.6
World: major linguistic families

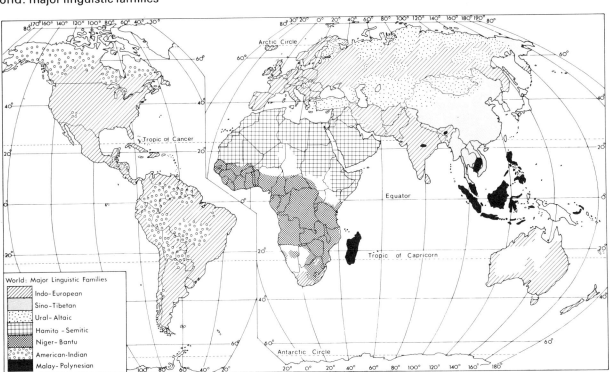

World: Major Linguistic Families
- Indo-European
- Sino-Tibetan
- Ural-Altaic
- Hamito-Semitic
- Niger-Bantu
- American-Indian
- Malay-Polynesian

195

the following major linguistic families in addition to Indo-European: Sino–Tibetan, spoken in eastern Asia; Ural–Altaic in central and northern Asia; Hamito–Semitic in northern Africa and south-west Asia; Bantu in Africa south of the Sahara; the American Indian language; and Malay–Polynesian which extends westward to include the island of Madagascar. Linguistic relationships of this sort are important to the geographer since they can provide clues about culture contact and migrations between different parts of the world in early times. They are especially valuable when linguistic evidence can be used in conjunction with archaeological or ethnographic data to check existing theories. Sometimes, of course, linguistic studies raise problems which cannot be easily resolved. Basque is one such case. Today it is spoken by half a million people living in northern Spain and south-west France, but it appears to be unrelated to any other known language and its origin remains uncertain.

For many practical purposes it is more important to know the distribution of languages that are actually spoken in the world today: an Irish speaker may be interested to know that his language is related to Iranian, but he will find this historical information of little use if he wants to buy a meal in Nastrabad! If he speaks English he is more likely to be understood, for it has become one of the world's truly international languages, spreading steadily with the growth of British trade and political influence during the eighteenth and nineteenth centuries, and receiving a further stimulus from American expansion after the Second World War. Numerically, fewer people speak English than Chinese—one estimate is 350 million for English compared with 600 million for Chinese. Next in order come Spanish, Hindi, Russian, Arabic, Japanese, Indonesian, Portuguese, German, Bengali, French, Italian and Urdu. Each of these is spoken by more than 50 million people and together they include some 60 per cent of the world's population. At the other end of the scale are more than five hundred languages each spoken by less than half a million people. The majority of these are found in the tropical lands, in Africa, southern Asia and parts of middle and south America where contact with Europeans came late and many communities lived in relative isolation. In contrast to these are languages like English, Spanish and Portuguese, all of which are dominant over extensive territories as a result of their colonial experience. Chinese, however, is spoken over a much more restricted area despite its numerical predominance, for the Chinese have not been active colonists until quite recent times.

196

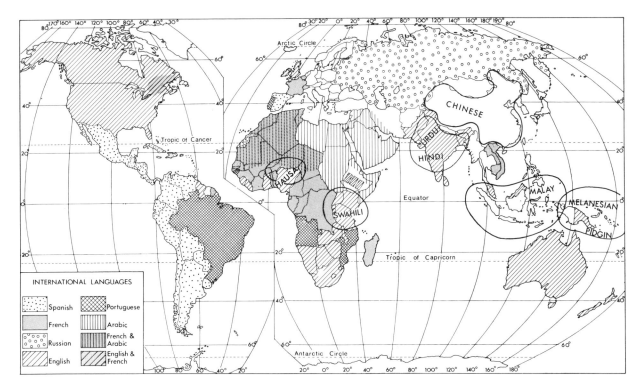

Figure 5.7
World: major international
languages spoken today

One point needs to be stressed when examining the distribution of languages spoken in the modern world. No language area is homogeneous in the sense that everyone living within its boundary speaks that language alone. Some may not even understand it properly—as in the case of Chinese whose many local dialects differ markedly from the Kuo Yü Mandarin Chinese, the national language of the state. Official languages —which are those shown in Figure 5.7—are simply those taught in schools and used in government. They are written and spoken according to definite rules of pronunciation, meaning and grammar which are recorded in standard works of reference, like dictionaries. The language of everyday speech may be quite different—local dialects, which are regional in character, may differ in many respects from the official language, as a Glaswegian or a Cockney soon finds when he comes into contact with a government official.

In fact most official languages originated as the dialect of a region which achieved political dominance over a larger territory. French is a good example. It began as the dialect spoken in the Ile-de-France, one of several in the area we now know as

197

France. The other Romance dialects were Provençal in the south, Norman, Burgundian, and the dialects of Aquitaine, together with Basque in the south-west and the Celtic language of Brittany. French only became the official language of the state as the political influence of the court at Paris was slowly extended during mediaeval times. A great burst of creative writing by dramatists, essayists and poets during the seventeenth century aided its further growth and the development of a standard form. By the mid nineteenth century French had replaced all other Romance dialects throughout the country, and only Basque and Breton remained in daily use. In both cases the language has acted as a rallying-point for political movements seeking regional autonomy, especially in the case of Brittany, and the survival of the language is regarded as crucial for the preservation of the regional culture. A similar

Figure 5.8
France: the growth of French as an official language

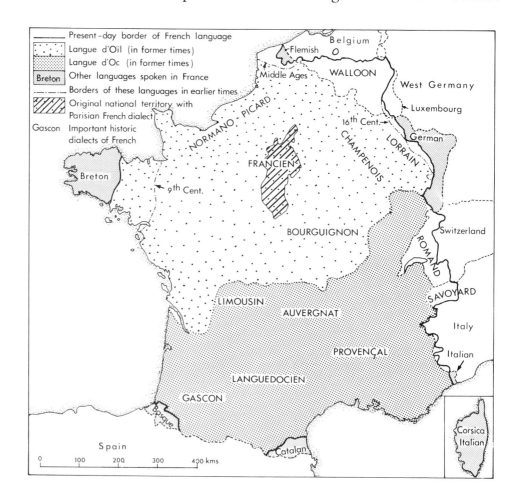

stand is taken by Welsh nationalists against the spread of English, while the cause of Irish nationalism in the late nineteenth century was itself closely linked with the movement for the revival of the language.

In fact language and politics often became deeply intertwined, especially where several groups, each speaking a different language, are associated in the growth of a particular state. Each group may promote its own language for recognition as an official language of the state, and failure may lead the promoters to feel that their cultural identity is at risk. This is especially the case with former colonial territories, anxious to assert their sovereignty by dispensing with the language of their former rulers yet faced with the difficulty of choosing an official language from among several alternatives spoken by different tribal groups. Ceylon and Kenya are two examples of states which have suffered from internal dissension over the language problem, but it is one which also affects much older countries than these. French-Canadians, for example, fought a long political battle to achieve equal status for their language alongside English, spoken by the majority of Canadian citizens outside the province of Quebec; while in Europe, domestic politics in Belgium have been dominated for many years by bitter disputes between French and Flemish speakers.

National pride accounts for recent, slight increases in the number of official languages recognised at international level, but the general trend is for more and more people to speak one of the major world languages like English, French or Spanish. Numerically Russian and Chinese are also extremely important, but since neither of these two countries was a major colonial power in the last century their languages are less widely distributed beyond their immediate national territories. Certainly the dominance of the great international languages is likely to increase as the world becomes more interdependent in trade and politics. Easy communication and mutual comprehension between individuals and states becomes a top priority, especially in an age when nuclear warfare could result in the total annihilation of mankind.

3 Religion

One of the main functions of religious belief and practice is to enable man to come to terms with the forces in life which he can neither understand nor control—especially those like earthquakes and thunderstorms which threaten his very existence, or death itself which forces him to think about the purpose and meaning of his life on earth. Through religion man tries to communicate with the wider universe he perceives beyond his own limited horizon, just as through language he communicates with his fellow men. This supernatural element is strongly emphasised in most of the world's religions, although it is discounted increasingly in an age in which scientific reason proclaims that everything in nature has a rational explanation. Consequently, for modern man, religion is more inclined to represent ideals and values of an ethical nature, although it differs from purely secular ideologies like communism in retaining its belief in a God or gods.

Because religion provides man with a conceptual framework for living his life on earth, it influences many other aspects of his culture. Some religions, for example, have explicit rules about family life: Islam allows men to have several wives, whereas Christianity holds firmly to the idea of monogamy; some sects forbid their adherents to marry members of other religious groups; Hindus are not permitted to marry outside their own particular caste, a social convention which creates a very rigid society, since people tend to live and work with others belonging to the same caste. Political power may also be vested in rulers whose authority is derived from their position in the religious hierarchy. The most extreme form of this concept is the god–king, a supreme ruler like the Egyptian Pharaoh who was both God and man. Alternatively, Church and State may be combined into a single system as in Tibet where the Dalai Lama was both head of the religious hierarchy and of the state. More often, organised religion simply enjoys a fairly close relationship with the secular government, lending its support to the state in return for special privileges. In Europe, for example, such a relationship existed between the Roman Catholic Church and the Holy Roman Empire of the Hapsburg dynasty, and it continues with the Anglican Church in England. Increasing secularisation has tended to loosen such ties during the present century, although in many countries a particular church may become closely identified with individual political parties; this is the case in the Netherlands, Italy and West Germany. Political dissension in the modern world is rarely created by disputes between different religious groups, but where the group is a minority and feels its existence is threatened then religion can become a highly emotive political issue. Cyprus, Ceylon, Israel and Ireland are all countries affected by bitter communal strife in recent years. For example, in 1947 when Britain left India, the subcontinent was divided into two states, India and Pakistan, largely on the basis of religious differences between Hindu and Muslim.

Economic activities may also be influenced by religious beliefs and practices. For example, Jews and Muslims both consider the pig to be unclean and unsuitable for human consumption, while in India, the Hindu veneration of the cow means that cattle are neither slaughtered nor eaten. The Christian church has also had its food taboos, like the Lenten fast or the prohibition on eating meat one day in the week. This particular rule had important consequences for the economic development of north-western Europe in early mediaeval times, since it stimulated the herring fisheries of the Baltic Sea upon which the early trade of such wealthy mercantile cities as Amsterdam and Hamburg was based. About the same period the Christian church also took a firm stand against charging interest on the loan of money, with the result that Jews, who were not bound by such rules, assumed a leading role in international finance and formed wealthy communities in many European cities. Organised religion has much less influence on modern industrial economies, but the seasonal rhythm of work in factory and business is still based on the holy-days, or holidays, prescribed by the church in earlier days.

Like other human activities, religious worship is often associated with particular places, and it is this relationship, together with the spatial distribution and organisation of different religious groups which most concerns the geographer. Many religions, for example, are very closely related to the environment in which they originated, and they reflect this in their literature. Some of the stories and parables in the Christian Bible are difficult to understand without some knowledge of the geography of the eastern Mediterranean. Of course Christian belief and ethics are not tied to any particular region: they are universal in their application, although some concepts may have to be adjusted to local circumstances. The idea that Hell is an unpleasant destination would be difficult to get across to an Eskimo if the missionary used conventional imagery, since his listener might feel that a very hot place represented his idea of heaven!

Unlike Christianity, many religions cannot be transplanted successfully, for their gods are linked with particular places —like Mount Olympus the home of the Greek god Zeus. To worship or to obtain the gods' blessing, the believer had to come in person. Other places may become holy through their association with a revered spiritual leader or prophet. Very often they became places of pilgrimage, where the faithful went to pray or to meditate, to ask for favours or gain merit. Christianity has many holy cities like Jerusalem, Bethlehem,

Rome or Santiago de Compostela in north-west Spain, one of the great centres of mediaeval pilgrimage. Many European pilgrimages began to decline during the fifteenth and sixteenth centuries, but in other parts of the world pilgrims still vie with tourists in their journeys to different holy places. All practising Muslims try to visit Mecca at least once in their lifetime, and Hindus still travel to Benares to bathe in the holy waters of the Ganges. Not surprisingly, cities that attract pilgrims are usually important trade centres, with merchants and pilgrims thriving in a mutually profitable relationship.

In the holy city, religion becomes visible in the landscape, but a more widespread visible expression of religious faith is the church or temple, a building set aside by the local community exclusively for religious purposes. For the Christian, the church is the House of God in which people assemble for worship; but many religions do not need large or elaborate buildings, simply a shrine in the corner of a house or village—or an open space where people come for public worship.

Mecca, the holy city of the Muslim world. This photograph shows the great central shrine visited by thousands of pilgrims each year. (*Photo Aerofilms Limited*)

Where separate buildings are necessary they are usually architecturally distinctive—like the towers and spires of Christian churches, or the minarets of the Muslim mosques. Both proclaim their faith even in alien environments: there is no more appropriate symbol of the Anglican community in Calcutta than the great Victorian gothic cathedral; or the mosques of Muslims in London. Cemeteries also proclaim religious belief in a visual way, since most societies dispose of their dead according to practices prescribed by their beliefs. In western Europe, for example, the great stone tombs known as megaliths still stand as memorials to the dead of Neolithic times, several thousand years after they were first erected. Throughout the world, the neat headstones and crosses of Christian cemeteries testify to the widespread activity of missionaries from European countries especially during the last century.

Hindu pilgrims line the banks of the Ganges during the Kumbh Mela festival at Hardwar, north of Delhi, India

Most religions have some form of territorial organisation to maintain contact between their adherents and allocate the areas served by individual priests. Among the Christian denominations, the Roman Catholic Church and the Mormons are the most highly organised in this respect, dividing the entire world into dioceses and parishes. Other Christian churches have a rather looser form of spatial organisation, especially those like the Baptists and Quakers who tend to allow individual congregations to manage their own affairs. Muslims, Hindus and Buddhists have no formal parochial organisation, but communities maintain contact through the training of priests and monks, the preaching of itinerant holy men, and by pilgrimage to specific holy places. At the other extreme are religions which are entirely local in character, based on individual tribes and communities and with little or no formal territorial organisation.

The distinction between local religions and those which are universal in character provides one method of classifying religious belief on a world-wide basis. Local religions are those with relatively few adherents, which relate fairly strictly to a particular locality and make no claim to being world-wide in their application or consciously to seek converts to their particular beliefs. Many local religions are animistic in the sense that their gods are the spirits of particular mountains or forests, whose worship is relevant only to the people who live within a specific territory. Several of the world's major religions began in this way, shedding earlier animistic beliefs as their theology became more sophisticated. Hinduism is a modern example of an ethnic religion, associated with a particular social system through the institution of caste, and like all ethnic religions capable of only limited extension since it does not engage in active missionary work.

Universal religions, in contrast, are considered by their adherents to be applicable to all mankind and they deliberately aim to achieve world-wide acceptance. They are also exclusive in the sense that each considers itself to be the only true religion, a conviction which has sustained their growth often from quite small beginnings. Christianity and Islam, in particular, have expanded most rapidly through organised missionary activity, but the scale of their work and the difficulty of maintaining contact between widely scattered communities has often led to local schisms, such as the split between the Roman Catholic and Greek Orthodox communions in the Christian churches. Often the universal religions have an ethnic character derived from the areas in which they originated: Islam for example is pre-eminently associated with the Arab world, and Christianity with Europe, for Europeans were mainly responsible for spreading the Christian faith through their colonial enterprises between the sixteenth and nineteenth centuries.

It is difficult to estimate the number of people belonging to any one religious faith, for few countries collect data on religion as part of their population census. Even if they do, the figures may not be reliable; many people in modern societies for example, may state that they are Christians although they have no affiliation with any church. So the figures given in the table below are only really useful in comparing the approximate strengths of the world's major religions.

Table 5.1: World Religions (Figures in millions)

	Religion		Adherents
Local religions:	Tribal		150
	Judaism		13
	Shinto		35
	Vietnamese & Korean		36
	Chinese		540
	Hinduism		400
	Total:		1 174
Universal religions:	Buddhism		230
	Christianity		
		Roman Catholic	530
		Protestant	260
		Orthodox	107
		Total:	897
	Islam		420
	Total:		1 547
Others	Total:		269

Notice that the total figure for local religions is not much smaller than that of the universal group. This is largely due to the inclusion of 'Chinese religions', a term which is meant to include both Confucianism and the very large number of animistic and other beliefs held in traditional Chinese society. Like all religions these are proscribed by the Communist Party, and there is no way in which the true number of adherents can be established. Very likely the figure given in the table is grossly overestimated. A further point to note is the group termed 'tribal religions'; this is simply an amalgamation of thousands of local religious beliefs and practices, many of which are animistic. Among the universal religions, Christianity has the largest number of adherents, with the Roman Catholic Church the largest single denomination. Islam comes next and Buddhism third, although figures for the latter are very uncertain because of the difficulty of estimating the number of practising Buddhists in modern China.

The world distribution of the major religions underlines the contrast between universal religions like Christianity with its world-wide extent, and the more compact territories associated with local religions such as Hinduism (Figure 5.9). Of course the distributions shown are highly simplified, for few religions are exclusive to any particular area—Britain, for example, is shown as a Christian country, but in fact it contains many adherents of other religions and a very high proportion of its population is atheist. The distributions shown also relate very much to the twentieth century. A hundred years earlier the pattern of world religions would have been much more complex, with many more parts of the world included in the category of local religions, especially in South America, Australia and many parts of Africa now nominally Christian. In fact the spread of Christianity to its present extent has occurred

Figure 5.9
World: major religions

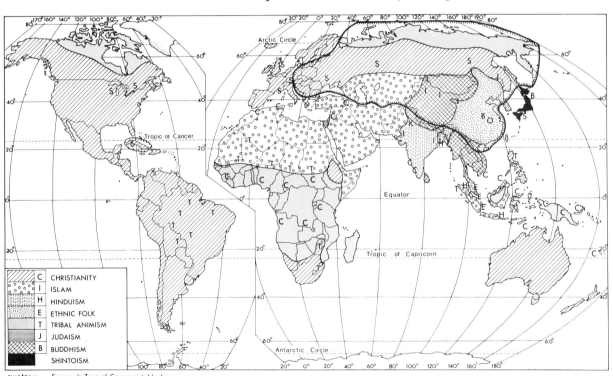

	C	CHRISTIANITY
	I	ISLAM
	H	HINDUISM
	E	ETHNIC FOLK
	T	TRIBAL ANIMISM
	J	JUDAISM
	B	BUDDHISM
		SHINTOISM

Surrounds Zone of Communist Ideology
Other Minority Elements: K Sikhism, O Taoism, S Secularism.

206

only within the past few centuries, for before the discovery of America it was largely confined to Europe and the Mediterranean lands. Each European colonial power helped to disseminate its own particular branch of the Christian faith, so that Central and South America became Roman Catholic through the missionary activities of Spain and Portugal, whereas North America, southern Africa and Australasia became mainly Protestant since they were largely settled from northern Europe.

South of the Mediterranean, in north Africa and south-western Asia, the Christian realm is bounded by Islam with which it waged a long and bitter conflict in mediaeval times. Islam owes its origin to the prophet Mohammed who began his mission in the early seventh century A.D., combining elements of Judaic and Christian doctrines and ethics in his theology with Arab tradition and custom. Mohammed was born in Mecca, and the spread of Islam was mainly associated with the routes followed by the caravan traders and nomadic tribes of the Afrasian deserts. At the height of its expansion Islam penetrated far into the Balkan lands of Europe and the Iberian Peninsula. Indeed by the fifteenth century it was the most widely distributed religion in the world, extending far beyond the arid lands of south-west Asia to the Bay of Bengal, the Malay peninsula and Indonesia where it was brought by Arab traders.

Beyond the islands of south-east Asia, Islam made little impact upon the indigenous Asian religions of Hinduism and Buddhism. The former is one of the world's most distinctive local religions which developed sometime towards the end of the second millennium B.C. through the fusion of two different cultures: one associated with the Aryan peoples moving south into the valley of the Indus, and the other with the native Dravidian people of the Indian peninsula. At one time Hinduism extended further east into south-east Asia, but today it is pre-eminently an Indian religion, which exerts a very strong influence on Indian life and culture.

Buddhism likewise began in India where its founder, Gautama was born in the foothills of Nepal some time in the late sixth century B.C. The code of ethics he taught placed special emphasis on meditation, and Buddhism is essentially monastic in its organisation. Buddhism made few converts in India: but one branch did spread widely in south-east Asia, in Burma, Thailand, Laos and Cambodia, as well as Ceylon; while another branch was diffused along the trade routes of inner Asia to Tibet, Mongolia and northern China. Here it came into contact with Confucianism, which became the state religion of

Buddha: this fifty-three foot-high bronze statue is in a temple at Nara, near Osaka in Japan. (*Photo © 1976 by Orion Press, Tokyo*)

China during the second century A.D. Confucianism, like Buddhism, was based on a code of ethics which was highly tolerant of other religious beliefs and practices, so that pre–communist China had a complex pattern of religious affiliation.

A similar complexity persists to the present day in Africa, for this has retained many local religions, associated with different tribal groups and communities. This is also the case in the sparsely populated tundra and boreal forest areas of North America and Eurasia, which, like Africa and the tropical forests of the Amazon Basin in South America, were among the last areas to establish permanent links with European colonists.

One final point to be noted about the distribution of the world's major religions is their common origin in the Old World, for most were closely associated with the area of ancient civilisation commonly called the Fertile Crescent. At its western end, near the Mediterranean, arose Judaism and Christianity, with Islam a little further south; to the east developed Hinduism and Buddhism. The explanation for this pattern seems to lie in the expanding trade which linked the early

Figure 5.10
Eurasia: the core areas in which the world's major religions had their origins

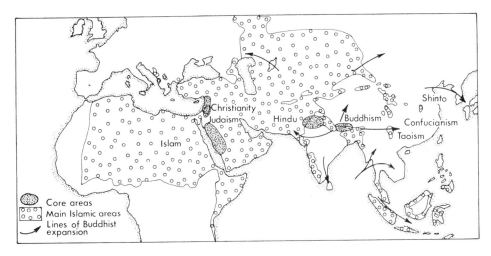

centres of cultural growth focussing on the great alluvial valleys of the Nile, Tigris-Euphrates and Indus. This area was a major cross-roads of the ancient world, a link between different cultures and environments which led to the exchange of ideas as well as goods. But along with the stimulus towards new religious thought and experience conflict might also arise, a tendency which is perpetuated in the same area by the present strife between Arab Muslim and Israeli Jew. In this particular

The continuing confrontation between Jew and Muslim is exemplified by this Israeli woman sergeant instructing girls of the youth army in the use of guns

case religion is only one of several factors leading to armed conflict, and in general in the modern world it is most unusual for religious differences to lead to open warfare. But in earlier times this was not the case. Religious differences have often led to the most brutal wars, such as those between Christians and Muslims at the time of the Crusades, or between Roman Catholics and Protestants in Europe during the sixteenth and seventeenth centuries. With the separation of Church and State in modern times, and increasing secularisation, the holy war is now a thing of the past. Instead moral justification for conflict is now sought through political ideologies like fascism, communism or socialism, each of which is promoted with a conviction and zeal similar to that used by missionaries preaching religious faiths.

4 States and Nations

In the preceding section we saw that religion helps man to come to terms with the unknown elements in his environment and to develop moral values which influence his relationships with his fellow-men. Politics represent another aspect of man's social relationships, for it is through government that standards of group behaviour are established and enforced, conflicts resolved and decisions made about future activities. Societies differ considerably in the way in which political authority and power are allocated and policy implemented, and these aspects of political organisation are studied by several branches of the social sciences. All political systems have also a territory over which they exercise jurisdiction, and it is this spatial aspect of political organisation with which the geographer is primarily concerned. This section will examine how the idea of political territory has evolved from its simple beginnings in tribal societies to the complex organisation of the modern state and it will conclude with a brief examination of the relationships between states as revealed in the political map of the present-day world.

Territory and the Growth of States

A sense of territory seems to be as innate in man as it is in many other animals. For us it is represented in the idea of *my* desk, *my* garden or *my* street; an area which we may own or rent or at most share with others of 'our own sort', people we know and recognise. For early man, the idea of territory was similar: it was the preserve of the group to which he belonged, the living space in which he had his home and whose resources provided him with food, water and other requirements. The size of his territory varied with the numbers in his group, the type of economy practised and the resources of the area. Thus hunters and food-gatherers like the pygmy might have a territory covering perhaps fifty square kilometres of tropical forest, whereas nomadic herdsmen might range over several hundred square kilometres of seasonal pasture. Tribal societies like these rarely have elaborate systems of political authority and power, but their territories have the same spatial attributes as much more complex political systems—that is, a core area where homes are located, an area whose resources are used for the support of the economy, and boundaries beyond which the group rarely moves except when its population becomes too big or its own resources are depleted. When this happens and the group moves beyond its traditional boundaries it may trespass on the territory of a neighouring group, and possibly endanger their chances of survival. Competition for living space is normal in all forms of organic life: in man as with other animals it results in the types of behaviour we recognise as aggressive and defensive, and it can lead to open warfare—the most extreme form of organised aggression. In fact political organisation often begins with the need to defend territorial boundaries, for this requires that someone be given authority to direct peoples' resources and energy for their mutual protection.

Larger population groupings and more varied economic activities inevitably require more complex political structures and more sophisticated methods of territorial organisation. Historically this seems to have occurred with the growth of cities in south-west Asia during Neolithic times. The need to conserve land and water resources in a semi-arid climate led to a close political association between the city and the surrounding land which helped to sustain it; and as some cities grew in size and wealth, competition meant that the weaker settlements were gradually absorbed by their more powerful neighbours. Urban growth made it necessary to devise new political institutions to organise the developing economy of the city and its region, and to protect its citizens, their goods and property from external attack. The city-state is the name given to the form of political organisation most widely adopted—it was found throughout the Fertile Crescent in Neolithic times, in northern China, and later in central America. It remained a basic form of territorial organisation among the Greeks, although they carefully separated religious from secular power, abandoning the concept of the god-king which had been an important element in the structure of political authority in the earlier city states. Even the Roman Empire can be seen as an extension of this type of political organisation, for at the very height of its power the Empire remained closely identified with the city of Rome.

The idea of the city-state did not long survive the collapse of the Roman Empire, except in Italy where it achieved a new form during the Middle Ages in such famous trading cities as Florence and Venice. In modern Italy, the tiny state of San Marino in the northern Apennines survives as an example of this ancient form of political organisation. But elsewhere in Europe, the decline of urban life during the second half of the first millennium A.D. meant that political territory was more loosely organised, and its extent at any time depended on the military power and authority of individual kings and rulers. However, in the course of the Middle Ages there developed a new political concept, expressed by the term *nationalism*. This can best be described as a sense of common cultural heritage which becomes identified politically with a particular state and territory. The concept of 'The English Nation', for example, can be seen developing slowly in the tenth and eleventh centuries; in France it came later and in Germany and Italy it did not achieve political recognition until the last century. But once established, a sense of national identity tends to persist because it is based on such enduring cultural attributes as history, custom and language. Indeed nationalism may long outlast the state which fostered its growth in the first instance. In Britain, for example, Wales and Scotland have long been joined with England in the United Kingdom; but Welsh and Scottish nationalism survives, and in recent years has even gained enough political momentum to demand a greater degree of local autonomy in government. At a broader level, nationalism transcends the social and economic issues of contemporary politics; it appeals to deeply-rooted beliefs and sentiments, and for that reason politicians are most inclined to appeal to 'national pride' and 'national spirit' when the state is threatened by external attack or internal dissension.

The nation-state gradually became the main form of territorial government in Europe during the seventeenth and eighteenth centuries, and with it came changes in political institutions. Most important perhaps was the decline in the power of the sovereign, as absolute rule was replaced by constitutional government with its emphasis on the rights and obligations of individual citizens. As Europeans extended their power and influence in the course of the eighteenth and nineteenth centuries these ideas took root in other countries, though initially

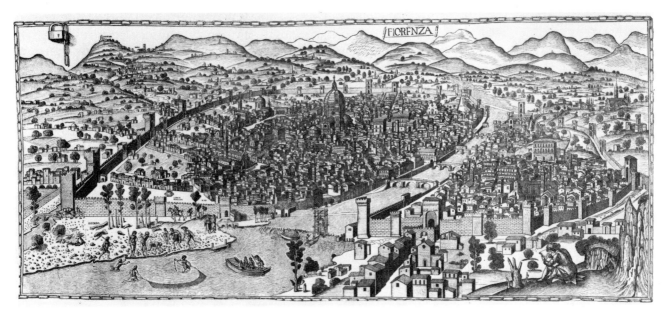

The mediaeval city state: Florence, about 1490

they were suppressed by the paternalistic rule of colonial governments. But after the Second World War most European countries lacked the resources and the will to perpetuate the old colonial systems in Africa and Asia. Within twenty years the world political map had been greatly altered, with newly independent countries accepting the nation state as their model for government.

The Nation State

Throughout the world, the modern nation state has certain distinguishing features. It occupies a specific territory with clearly defined boundaries; its citizens are subject to a common law; and its government is responsible for finance, security, welfare, and the conduct of diplomatic relations with other states. Geographically a state consists of the political territory administered by its government, and a capital city from which government business is transacted. Often, the capital was originally the commercial centre of a rich agricultural region whose rulers gradually extended their political authority over an ever increasing area. Both London and Paris developed in this way, becoming the largest cities as well as the capitals of Britain and France respectively. In Ireland, Dublin developed in much the same way, but with the important difference that it was the capital of a colonial territory. Its growth during the present century resembles that experienced by many other

213

newly independent countries in Africa, Asia and America whose capital cities have grown rapidly as a result of the many new jobs provided in government administration and services, and in business. Sometimes the capital is not the largest city in a state, nor is it necessarily situated in the richest or economically the most developed part of the country. Washington, for example, is smaller than New York, Canberra than either Sydney or Melbourne, and Brasilia is an entirely new city situated in a remote part of Brazil far from Rio de Janeiro, the largest city. In each of these former colonies the

Figure 5.11
The nation-state: the growth of the nation-state in France from its beginnings in the Ile-de-France around Paris

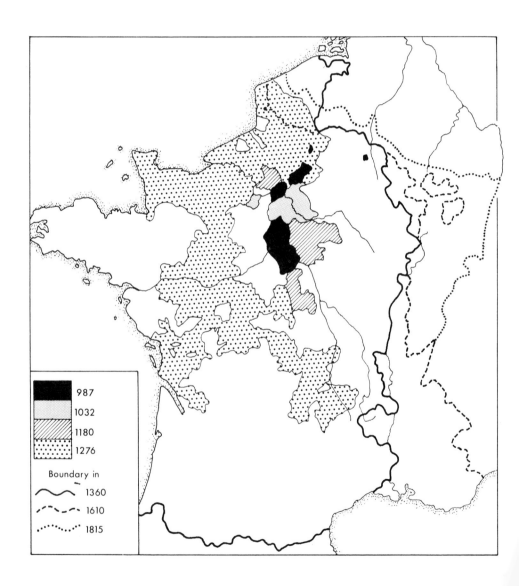

987
1032
1180
1276

Boundary in

1360
1610
1815

biggest cities are located on the coasts where the settlers first landed, and their initial growth was based on trade with the mother country. Later they became the terminal points for national road and rail systems and their commercial dominance was assured. With independence, political rivalries between the different parts of the country made it desirable to select a completely neutral site for a capital city, and Washington, Canberra and Brasilia are all located in places where no settlement had existed previously.

The accurate delineation of boundaries is a further feature of the modern state, for population growth and technological development result in increased competition for natural resources and the precise delimitation of national territory becomes extremely important. These considerations were less significant for early man, and the limits of his territories tended to be broad tracts of uninhabited land—mountain ranges, extensive boglands or deserts. On a world scale such natural frontiers continue to act as major political divides between adjacent states. For example, several international boundaries meet in the Alps and the Himalayas, the Sahara desert, and the great tropical forests of central Africa and South America.

Natural features, however, do have major limitations when used as boundaries between modern states. Rivers, for example, are readily visible on the ground, but they have a tendency to shift their courses, with the result that one state may gain territory at the expense of its neighbour. In fact many international boundaries do follow rivers, but they are a continuing source of friction with many problems arising over the use of water for irrigation, power and navigation, and over pollution. Many of these difficulties arise from the fact that rivers tend to be a natural focus for settlement, and the people who live along the banks have many common interests which may be disrupted by divided political allegiance.

To avoid some of these problems in more recently settled lands, surveyors sometimes devised artificial boundaries based on lines of latitude and longitude. The most celebrated example is the 49th parallel in North America which forms the international boundary between the U.S.A. and Canada. This method of boundary delineation works quite well where the land is sparsely populated, and there are good relations between the neighbouring states. It is much less satisfactory when used as a compromise over disputed territory in a populated area, as in the boundaries negotiated to end the wars in Korea and Vietnam during the past twenty-five years.

The artificial boundaries established in recent times tend to

Figure 5.12
The U.S.-Canadian boundary
which follows the 49th parallel

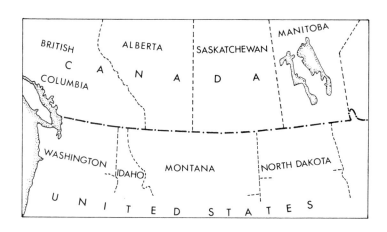

be straight and precise in their direction compared with the apparently aimless wandering of others which have evolved over long periods of time. Compare, for example, the international boundary between the U.S.A. and Canada as it crosses the prairies of the mid-west with that between the Irish Republic and Northern Ireland. The former is a surveyor's line, determined by a treaty in 1846; the latter follows townland boundaries, some of which may have marked the limits of land belonging to different groups of families in the first millennium A.D. Even today it is usually difficult to identify the Irish border on the ground, unless one is a local farmer, a situation which is quite different in many other countries whose national boundaries may be clearly marked by barbed-wire, observation towers and mine-fields. In extreme cases, as in Berlin, a high wall marks the boundary between neighbouring states, although this is insignificant in its scale and extent compared with the great wall of China, built in the third century B.C. and close to 2500 kilometres in length.

The identification and siting of international boundaries is often a source of friction between neighbouring states. Since mediaeval times in Europe it has been a major cause of open warfare, with every major conflict ending in a long period of political negotiations as diplomats try to settle their boundaries yet again. Today this is no longer confined to the land, for as man begins to explore the oceans for new sources of food and raw materials, competition is renewed between states for a share in the world's last great untapped resource. The so-called 'cod war' of the 1970s between Britain and Iceland is a dispute of this kind, concerned with the major issue of how far a state may claim jurisdiction over the seas that surround its shores. Similarly the discovery of oil beneath the North Sea and in

Figure 5.13
The hierarchy of local government in south-west England

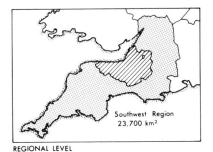

REGIONAL LEVEL

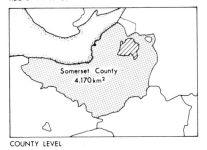

COUNTY LEVEL

DISTRICT LEVEL

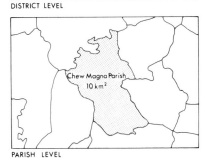

PARISH LEVEL

other parts of the world raises a whole series of questions concerned with the ownership of the seabed and its mineral wealth.

Boundary delineation is not simply an international problem, for all states divide their territories into different units for internal administration, usually with some degree of local autonomy for particular functions such as welfare, education and housing. In Britain, the county has long been the major unit of local government. In the Netherlands similar functions are split between the provinces and the municipalities, and in the U.S.A. there is a more complex hierarchy ranging from the Federal government down to the state, the county and the township. Besides these, the country may be divided into other areas for various specialist functions, for example, judicial districts, hospital boards, income tax areas and economic development authorities, all forming a highly complex system of internal administration and political decision-making. Often the existing units are based on historic divisions which have little relevance to modern conditions, and from time to time the central government decides to reform the administrative structure. In Ireland, for example, units such as the townland and the barony have long been abandoned for most administrative purposes, while in Britain and Northern Ireland a complete reorganisation of local government was effected during the early 1970s.

Within its territory, every nation state exercises total sovereignty, but to survive as an independent entity it requires the support of its citizens and their consent to be governed. Normally this is achieved through the institutions and processes of government which are designed to achieve a compromise between conflicting interests, for few countries are entirely homogeneous in the political composition and attitudes of their inhabitants. Regional and sectional interests, for example, may run counter to the policies pursued by the government at national level. A remote region may feel it is receiving insufficient government help in establishing industries, or farmers may consider that beef prices are much too low. Ideological differences may create further divisions, reflected by the existence of separate political parties. In democratic societies these differences are expressed through parliamentary debate and citizens are given the opportunity of expressing their views on the policies of different political parties through periodic elections.

However, many states do face serious problems in achieving a consensus, with the result that the stability of the state may itself be threatened. This situation can arise in several ways. Firstly, a minority group may seek unification with a neighbouring state with which it shares a common nationality. This was the case in Poland, Czechoslovakia and Alsace after the First World War, when German minorities were created following boundary adjustments—indeed their existence contributed to the events which led to German expansion in the late 1930s and the outbreak of the Second World War. Secondly, minorities may be created through the division of tribal territories between several colonial powers. Following independence they may seek reunification with members of the same tribe in neighbouring states, a movement which has led to open conflict in former colonial areas, in the former Belgian Congo for example and in Nigeria. Thirdly, the state may consist of several distinct groups, identified by nationality, race, religion or language, who nonetheless agree to sink their differences in a common allegiance to the one government. A good example of this type of plural society is Malaya, where the indigenous population forms just over half the total, the remainder being Chinese and Indians, most of whom came as labourers to work in the former British colony. Such states may become stable political entities, like Switzerland, but their politicians must

The ethnic complexity of Singapore reflected in its architecture and riverboats

always be wary of offending the susceptibilities of one or other group.

The World Political Map

In the world today there are about two hundred nation states which differ enormously in area, population, natural resources, their level of economic development, military power and political prestige. At one end of the scale is tiny San Marino in Italy, with a population of 17 000 and an area of 98 square kilometres; at the other is China with more than 750 million people, or the U.S.S.R. which covers 22·3 million square kilometres. But despite this great range in scale, each of these countries shares one common feature: each is an independent sovereign state.

Between them, such states cover some 80 per cent of the world's land area. The remaining areas are politically dependent on some other country, colonies like British Honduras or trusteeships under international law, like South-West Africa. Forty years ago, the world political map would have appeared very different, with much of Africa and southern Asia classified as dependent territories, mostly under the colonial rule of European powers like Britain and France. But a century earlier, the map would have been different again—with South America under colonial rule and much of tropical Africa simply divided into tribal territories.

The rise of the nation state as the predominant form of territorial government is thus very much a twentieth-century phenomenon and its spread is a by-product of increasing European influence on world affairs over the last few centuries. Yet the nation state itself is by no means a stable entity— the recent history of Europe shows many changes in the number and extent of individual countries within a comparatively short time. For example, modern states like Ireland, Finland, Poland, Czechoslovakia and Yugoslavia did not exist before the First World War; and others, including Austria, Denmark, France, Germany and Italy have all experienced boundary changes during the same period. Indeed territorial change is endemic to most political systems. Sometimes it arises for purely political reasons—a struggle for power between rival ruling dynasties like the Bourbons and Hapsburgs in Europe, or conflicting political ideologies, as in Vietnam or Korea. More often the motive for expansion is economic—the need for more land to support a growing population, access to mineral resources or the protection of trade routes. All these

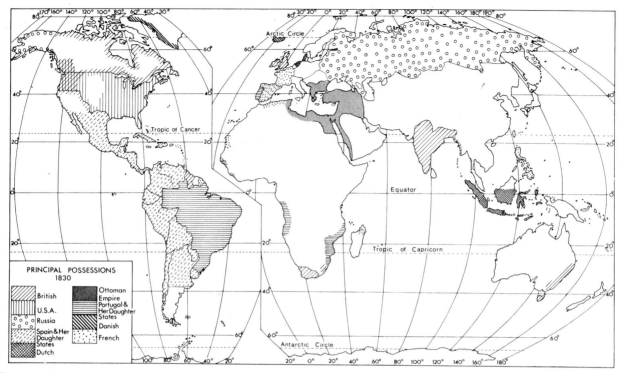

Figure 5.14
World: political divisions in 1830

motives were involved in European colonial expansion during the nineteenth century, in Japan's military conquests in southeast Asia during the Second World War, and in Germany's two attempts at European dominance during the present century. In the latter case the catchword *lebensraum*, literally 'living space', expressed the feeling that a powerful state like Germany needed more land and resources to accommodate a growing population. As justification, it was asserted that states were like organisms, expanding as they grew towards maturity and contracting as their power waned. This analogy had obvious attractions for a relatively young nation state such as Germany was at the beginning of the twentieth century, but organisms are very different types of systems from nation states, and the model was a dangerous over-simplification of the complex processes involved in the development of a modern country.

The break-up of the old colonial empires after the Second World War led to a greatly increased number of nation-states throughout the world, but this fragmentation of the political map into many independent countries seems to run counter to

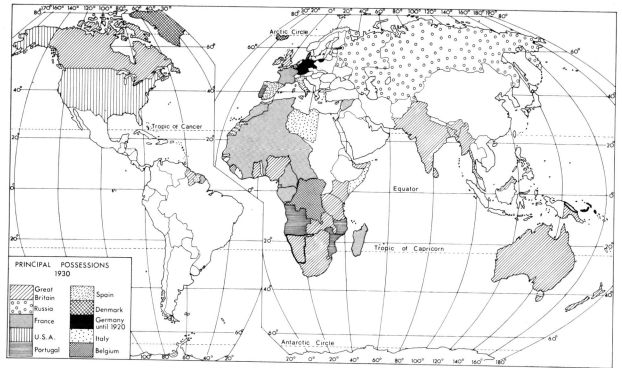

Figure 5.15
World: political divisions in 1930

Legend:

PRINCIPAL POSSESSIONS
1930

- Great Britain
- Russia
- France
- U.S.A.
- Portugal
- Spain
- Denmark
- Germany until 1920
- Italy
- Belgium

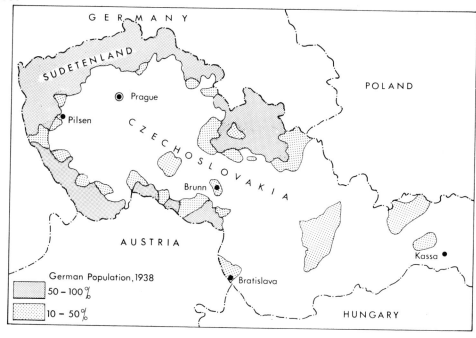

Figure 5.16
The German minority in Czechoslovakia in 1938. The desire to reunite them with the mother country was one of the causes of the Second World War

German Population, 1938

- 50 – 100 %
- 10 – 50 %

another marked trend in modern life—the growing interdependence which has come with industrial development and technological innovation. In fact this has had a major influence on world political organisation, for overlying the fine-grained pattern of independent states are a whole new series of larger political groupings and specialist international agencies. Some of these are based on a common heritage, like the British Commonwealth; others on the solidarity of shared political ideologies, such as the ties that link the Communist countries of eastern Europe and the U.S.S.R., and differentiate them sharply from the capitalist states of Western Europe and the United States of America. Military alliances such as NATO, SEATO and the Warsaw Pact reinforce these political groupings and extend the political influence of the great powers over many smaller states. Other major groupings are designed to bring economic advantages to member states, like the European Economic Community which includes not only the nine major European partners but also extends trading benefits and privileges to several overseas countries which were formerly colonies of the European powers concerned.

Figure 5.17
World: Western strategic alliances. Those shown are: the North Atlantic Treaty Organisation (NATO); the Central Treaty Organisation (CENTO); and the South-East Asia Treaty Organisation (SEATO). Data, 1973

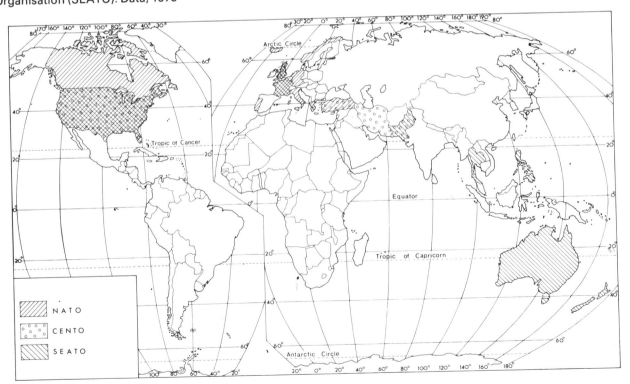

Figure 5.18
Supra-nationalism in Europe: The European Economic Community

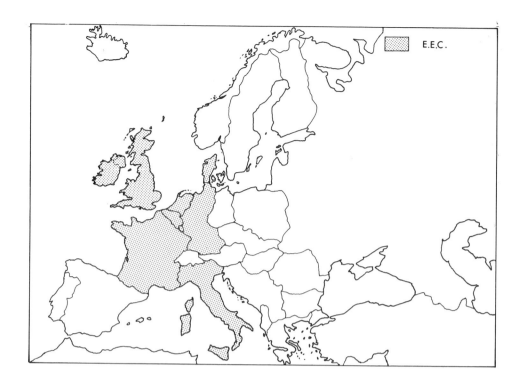

In addition, a whole series of international agencies is maintained by the United Nations Organisation, founded at the conclusion of the Second World War to provide an international forum within which member states could resolve their differences without resorting to war. Too often, the national rivalries and conflicting interests of the great powers have meant that the U.N. has been unable to live up to the political ideals and aspirations of its founders, but through agencies like UNESCO (United Nations Educational, Scientific and Cultural Organisation), F.A.O. (Food and Agricultural Organisation), and W.H.O. (World Health Organisation) it has brought immense economic and social benefits to many parts of the world, especially among the underdeveloped countries. Indeed the development of these truly international agencies is probably the most important political achievement of the twentieth century, providing the institutional means of overcoming the deeply-rooted cultural divisions which otherwise affect the whole of mankind. (See map Figure 5.19, page 224).

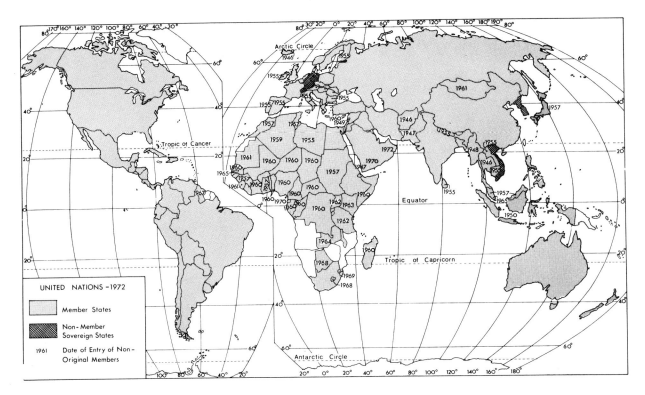

Figure 5.19
World: membership of the United
Nations in 1972. Each year the list
of members increases as the
remaining European colonies
become independent states.
Today very few sovereign states
remain outside the organisation

6

SETTLEMENT AND COMMUNICATIONS

Settlements and the communications systems which link them together are the most widely distributed and the most important of the many features created by human activity on the face of the earth. As used by geographers, the term *settlement* refers to single buildings or groups of buildings, together with such related features as roads, building lots and open spaces used as parks or gardens. It includes structures of many different shapes, sizes and functions, and it may refer to a solitary dwelling in the countryside or to a city of several million people. No matter how big or complex the individual building may be, it is derived ultimately from the very simple structure erected by early man as shelter against the elements and protection against predators, including members of his own species. For unlike many forms of organic life man is not well endowed with natural insulation, nor has he adequate teeth or claws to

A shelter made by the Bushmen of the Kalahari Desert in Namibia. It is simply constructed with a framework of light branches loosely thatched with grass. (*BBC copyright photograph*)

Occasionally man uses natural shelters as dwelling places. This photo shows a very rare contemporary example—a cave used by members of the Tasaday tribe of the southern Philippines. This is the communal living area for the group. The cave floor is covered with tree bark, and a pile of wood for burning stands beside the fire. Opening off this are smaller caves used by individual families. (*Photo by Helmut R. Schulze, Camera Press*)

defend himself when attacked. Instead he uses fire and clothing, and builds shelters to protect himself, his family and their possessions against the extremes of heat and cold, of wind, rain and snow, and against other animals. Many of the earliest shelters were little more than windbreaks, designed to protect the fire as much as man himself, for once extinguished, fire was difficult to rekindle. Often they were temporary structures, abandoned when the family moved on to a new hunting ground or cleared a fresh plot for cultivation. Sometimes, however, migratory people devised quite ingenious mobile homes, like the tepee of the Plains Indians of North America, or the yurt of the Kazak herders of central Asia.

In the study of settlement, geographers are concerned with five main aspects—morphology, pattern, distribution, function and size; and we will define these first before going on to

The tepee of the Plains Indians of North America was made of soft buffalo hide placed over a frame of spruce or pine poles. The flaps at the top form a smoke hole which can be closed when it is wet or windy. (*Photo courtesy of The American Museum of Natural History*)

examine rural and urban settlements in more detail. In this context, *morphology* refers to the spatial arrangement of individual buildings within a particular settlement. It consists of three main elements: the buildings, the plots on which they stand, and the network of lanes and streets whose layout helps to determine the morphological appearance of the settlement itself. While the geographer may concentrate on the ground plan of the settlement, he is also concerned with the vertical dimension—the architectural form of individual buildings. This he studies for two reasons. Firstly, the different floors in a building may be used for different purposes—a city skyscraper, for example, may have shops on the ground-floor, offices in the middle and residential flats at the top. Secondly, the architectural style and materials used in building are important in interpreting the cultural heritage of the area in which the settlement is located.

227

Settlement morphology: a Meo hill village near Chiengmai, northern Thailand. Here the houses are grouped in a haphazard way, apparently without any formal plan. There are no 'streets'—simply open spaces between the different houses and pathways linking houses and garden plots. To the left of the photograph clearings have been made in the forest for crops of rice, maize and beans

The second term, *pattern*, refers to the way in which distinctive forms of settlement are distributed within a particular area. In rural districts, for example, the settlement pattern may be *dispersed*, meaning that it is composed of farmsteads which are separated from each other by distances of say half a kilometre or more. Alternatively the farmsteads may cluster together along a road or around a church or market place, forming a pattern which is said to be *nucleated*. Pattern may also be used when referring to distinctive layouts of housing, roads or land use within a city—thus a suburban pattern implies a residential area in a city composed of individual family houses each with its own garden.

Use of the term *distribution* often implies both density and limits of settlement. The former is really an index of the intensity of land use, high densities in rural areas indicating productive farmland, and in towns and cities crowded residential areas. The latter distinguishes areas in which settlement is found from those which are uninhabited, because they are too steep for building, too exposed or damp, or are avoided for other reasons. In fact the limits of settlement are usually set by

Nucleated settlement: Bourmont, near Ressons-sur-Natz in northern France. This is a typical settlement in an area where villages predominate. (*Photo Cambridge University Collection: copyright reserved*)

man's technical capacity, his economic needs and aspirations at any given point in time. Thus areas devoid of settlement in one period may be inhabited later, following innovations in building technology or the introduction of new methods of farming. In Ireland, for example, much hill land was settled and cultivated in the early nineteenth century when population was at its height, and later abandoned as population fell in the years after the Great Famine.

By studying morphology, pattern and distribution, the geographer can describe the settlement in an area; but to explain why certain forms of settlement are adopted and particular sites chosen he needs to know how the inhabitants make a living and the way in which they organise their social life within a particular environment. These considerations are included in the term *function*, the fourth aspect in settlement studies. Economic and social organisation in turn are affected by the technological capacity and cultural heritage of the

Settlement limits, illustrated in the Tanat Valley in north Wales where steep slopes in an upland area set limits to cultivation and consequently, to settlement. (*Photo Aerofilms Limited*)

inhabitants of the area, and by the physical characteristics of the local environment. For example, people who use power–driven machinery in farming and the car for transport are likely to have settlements which differ in form and pattern from those who work with hand tools and travel on foot—compare the dispersed farmsteads of Nebraska in North America with the villages of central India. The architecture too is different, the wooden frame buildings of North America representing a very different cultural tradition from the mud houses of Maharashtra.

The physical environment also influences settlement, directly affecting the choice of site through topography, water supplies and the distribution of marshland; and indirectly through variations in soil fertility, the availability of mineral resources and of forests, all of which influence the location of economic activity. Once geographers placed great emphasis on the role of such environmental features in determining the form and pattern of settlement, but now it is generally accepted that technology and economy are more important. For even the most hostile environment will not prevent development if man has the necessary capital, machinery and power, and he considers that the economic gain will outweigh the expenditure. Thus the need for oil brings settlement to deserts which

Settlement in a hostile environment: the 'main street' of Molodyozhnaya, the Soviet observatory and base in the Antarctic

would otherwise be uninhabited, and men live in the icy wastes of Antarctica for scientific and military reasons.

The fifth and final aspect in settlement studies is *size*, which may be measured according to the area covered by the settlement, or more usually, in terms of its population. Thus at one end of the scale is the isolated farmhouse inhabited by only one or two people; at the other a city, extending over several hundred square kilometres and with its population numbering millions. Broadly speaking, major differences in settlement size depend on functions: settlements based on farming, for example, are usually small, their size limited by the productivity of the surrounding land. In contrast a large city provides a great variety of jobs for its inhabitants, and its size really depends on the prevailing state of the national economy, modified by local circumstances. In practice the distinction between rural and urban is blurred in modern industrial societies, but it is still a convenient way to classify settlement on a world scale, and it is the method followed in this chapter.

1 Rural Settlement

Most people who live in rural settlements are engaged in farming, but there are usually a number who work in other jobs—shopkeepers, postmen, teachers, clergy, doctors, road maintenance men or quarry-workers. Indeed some rural settlements may have no connection with farming at all although

231

they are located in the countryside—like small mining settlements or factory villages. Generally speaking the proportion of farmers is lowest in modern industrial societies, where a greater number of alternative jobs is available to country dwellers, and use of the car makes it easier for people to work in the city and live in the countryside. In these circumstances, the term 'rural settlement' simply means settlements located in the countryside which are smaller than towns; but in most parts of the world its use implies communities whose livelihood is based on farming. Such communities may live in farmsteads which are either grouped in clusters or stand apart from their neighbours. In practice this distinction between dispersed and nucleated settlement is rarely rigid: both forms of settlement may be found within the same area at the same time, and one may succeed the other in response to economic or social change. But no matter which settlement form predominates, the basic unit is the house itself, and this is the one with which we begin.

The Dwelling House

Primarily the house is built as a family home, but it may also act as an office, workshop or store. These different functions influence the design of the house, especially the size, number and arrangement of the different rooms. For example, the family for whom the house is built may consist simply of parents and children as it normally does in our own society. Indeed the size of the modern house is so geared to this family unit that it can feel very overcrowded if grandparents or other relatives have to be accommodated as well. Our modern houses have no special room for the old people, like the bed–outshot or *calliagh,* traditional in north-west Ireland, which projected out from the kitchen near the hearth, and was

Figure 6.1
The bed-outshot or *Calliagh* (shaded in the drawing) found in traditional houses in north and west Ireland

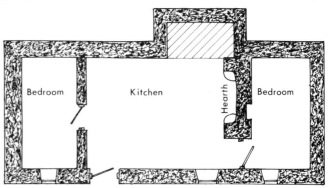

House with bed-outshot in kitchen: Co. Mayo, Ireland

Longhouse of the Dyaks of western Sarawak, inhabited by a group of related families. This photograph shows the long verandah which is communal open space, the door to the right leads into the living areas used by individual families. Like most traditional homes in south-east Asia, this house is built of wood raised off the ground on piles

just big enough to contain a bed. In other societies, houses may have to be very much bigger, for they are designed to be lived in by several related families. Such communal houses occur among tribal societies in south-east Asia, tropical America and British Columbia, accommodating more than a hundred people in some instances. Large groups might also live together in a very different type of social situation where a wealthy family might have a very large number of servants, as well as friends and relatives in the same house. The mansions belonging to European nobility especially during the eighteenth and nineteenth centuries are good examples of this type, often providing a stark contrast with the houses of their farm tenants as, for example, in Ireland.

Besides providing a home for the family, the rural dwelling often sheltered livestock and produce as well. In western Europe, the so-called 'byre-dwelling' was common along the Atlantic coastlands from Scotland to Portugal, the family living at one end of a long rectangular house and the cattle at the other. Many houses were also adapted for use by craftsmen such as weavers or cobblers, while in towns merchants might have their shop and stores on the ground floor, family apartments on the next storey and apprentices and servants living in the attic.

Man has shown great ingenuity in designing structures adapted to these basic needs. Most often the different functions

Figure 6.2
The byre-dwelling, a disused house at Binghamstown, Co. Mayo where the cows were tethered facing the gable wall to the right of the plan

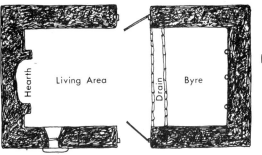

House in Co. Mayo, Ireland

are accommodated within a single-storey building, partitioned into several rooms each used for a different purpose—just as the modern bungalow has its kitchen, lounge, bathroom and bedrooms. Once the family and farm animals shared the same single room but with improvements in living standards the livestock were separated from the living quarters, first by a partition wall, and later moved to an entirely separate building. This sequence is well illustrated in the development of the byre dwelling in Ireland, Wales and Scotland, and in the traditional farmhouses of the north-eastern Netherlands and adjacent districts in Germany. Today farmsteads in industrial societies have usually a large number of specialist buildings grouped round the dwelling. An alternative method of containing different functions within the same building was to erect a structure of more than one storey. Among houses of this sort are the pile or stilt houses which are especially characteristic of south-east Asia. Many are built out into a lake or on the edge of the sea, but on land the space beneath the house is used as a store and livestock shelter. More elaborate are the farmhouses of many countries in southern Europe, where wine is kept in a basement, the family lives on the ground floor or first floor and the crops are stored on a second storey.

Houses also differ in the shape of their ground plan as well as in elevation, the most important distinction being between those which are circular or oval, and those which are rectangular or square. Round houses are relatively uncommon today. Probably the best known example—and one of the most ingenious, is the Eskimo igloo: elsewhere round houses are found mainly in tropical Africa and to a lesser extent in India. Formerly they were more widely distributed—in Europe during prehistoric and early historic times, and in Ireland they were probably the most common form during the first millennium A.D., occurring both as timber-frame dwellings and as stone-built *clocháns*. But the round house has one major disadvantage: its diameter is limited by the length of the available

Pile dwellings in Cambodia, built on a framework of bamboo poles with bamboo thatch and walls of bamboo matting. (*Photo Frederick Ayer from Photo Researchers, Inc.*)

A round house with mud walls and a thatch roof, common in many parts of tropical Africa. This one is in Chad in north central Africa. (*Photo courtesy of The American Museum of Natural History*)

timbers used in its roofing, or by the stresses involved in constructing a roof of stone or ice. Because of this the round house cannot be easily extended unlike a rectangular building where additional rooms can simply be added to side walls or gables.

Round houses were common in Ireland from the early Iron Age until the end of the first millennium A.D. This is the reconstruction of one excavated at Carrigillihy in Co. Cork. (*Photo courtesy M. J. O'Kelly, University College, Cork*)

Building technology and the materials used in construction represent yet another influence on house design, and help to accentuate the regional diversity caused by differences in economy and society. Generally people prefer to use local materials to save the effort and cost of transport, and their buildings thus reflect the resources of the local environment. On a world basis, timber is the material most frequently used in house construction, for it is the most widely accessible, relatively easy to work with simple tools, and highly flexible in the way it can be used. Different timbers of course all have their strengths and limitations. Coniferous trees are generally lighter, with straighter trunks than most deciduous hardwoods. Very often the whole trunk is used in building, one being laid horizontally on top of another to form the walls. Log cabins made in this way are typical of the coniferous forest belts of northern Eurasia and North America. In contrast, deciduous trees like oak are usually sawn into planks and beams which are used to construct a framework for the walls and roof. The walls are then clad with planks or wattle-and-daub; or bricks are used to fill the spaces around the frame, and the roof covered with thatch or tiles. This type of frame-house is especially common in western and central Europe where deciduous forests were once widely distributed.

When timber is scarce, many other materials may be used in its place. In the tropics, tough savanna grasses are widely used

236

A Canadian log-house in the Yukon, built early in the present century. Corrugated iron now partially covers the original shingles on the roof. The axles in the foreground are from a wagon used for hauling wood to fire the boilers of the riverboats which carried men and materials during the gold rush

An oak frame-house: Milstead Manor, Kent

in central Africa, but mud is probably the most widely used substitute—sometimes mixed with straw or dung and built directly as a wall or fashioned into bricks to be dried in the sun or baked in kilns. Stone is also used, but only if other materials are unavailable or unsuitable, for it is heavy to handle and difficult to fashion into desired shapes. Exceptions are the softer sedimentary rocks like certain limestones and sandstones, widely used in the Mediterranean lands of Europe when forest resources became depleted.

The use of local materials meant that areas with strongly contrasting environments often had marked regional styles in buildings. In England, for example, the low stone-built houses of the Cotswolds were succeeded northwards by the timber-frame houses of the west Midlands and the solid limestone buildings of the Pennines. Once established, regional styles persisted as long as rural craftsmen continued to use traditional methods and materials. The development of new systems of

Houses built of mud in Aleppo, Syria. (*Photo E. Boubat from Photo Researchers, Inc.*)

238

Rendered walls, tile roof and metal frame windows became the accepted mode of building in many parts of Britain during the 1930s

transport has led to changes in recent years, for mass–produced materials like brick and cement block, corrugated iron and asbestos sheeting can now be manufactured cheaply and easily transported; and they are often easier and quicker to use, and more durable than local products. In addition, building designs are also based increasingly on urban styles, so that regional variety in house types is slowly being replaced by mass uniformity.

Villages and Hamlets

In most parts of the world, the single dwelling standing in isolation from its neighbours is comparatively rare: most people, now and in the past, live in settlements where the houses are grouped in clusters of varying size. The words 'village' and 'hamlet' are often used to describe such clusters, but geographers have no agreed definition of these two terms. In practice 'hamlet' is used for settlements which are smaller than a village in size, and with a very limited range of service functions.

Archaeological evidence shows that in earlier times clustered settlement was far more common than it is even today, and

239

that in many areas dispersed farmsteads are a relatively recent development. In fact group settlement has many advantages over isolated dwellings, not least because in many types of economic activity people can more easily pool their experiences, technical skills and labour if they live together in the same place. In Ireland, for example, where the clustered form of settlement known as the *clachan* was common until the last century, land was held jointly by the families living in the cluster. Work was carefully coordinated, each family sharing in many different tasks throughout the year — winning turf, making hay, cutting corn and gathering potatoes. Implements were often shared, especially more expensive items like the plough; and each farmer might contribute an animal to the ploughteam. This same type of cooperative work was also found in many other societies: in the *manorial villages* of mediaeval Europe where farmers laboured under the direction of the landlord or his servants; and in modern communities like

An Irish clachan, Doornane, Co. Kilkenny. (*Photo Cambridge University Collection: copyright reserved*)

the *collective farms* of the Soviet Union or the *kibbutzim* of Israel. In each of these examples, economic cooperation is accompanied by nucleated settlements, but this is not absolutely necessary: as long as people can communicate easily with each other there is no reason for them to live together simply to coordinate their work. This is certainly true in modern farming, where the car and the telephone enable neighbours to work together while living at a distance from each other. In other words the need to cooperate in work does not necessarily require that people should live together in clusters, although in many circumstances there are good reasons why they should do so.

The need for defence was a further encouragement to group living in earlier times. Often the predators were animals, like the carnivores of the African savannas which prey upon domestic animals. The *kraal* is a settlement form adopted to meet this particular threat, the houses being built in a circle around a central brushwood enclosure in which cattle, sheep and goats are penned overnight. Beyond the houses an outer ring-fence guards the perimeter. The *ring-fort* in Ireland, a form of settlement common throughout the first millennium A.D., is thought to have had a similar function, its circular enclosure protecting the cattle at night from the attacks of wolves and cattle rustlers! For men are often the main predators against whom defence is necessary. It was for this reason that the walled settlement grouped around a castle was common in many parts of mediaeval Europe; and why farm families are often resettled from dispersed dwellings into compact settlements during political emergencies, such as the communist guerrilla campaigns in Malaya in the 1950s or more recently in

Model of a Zulu kraal, southern Africa. Notice the brushwood fence round the perimeter and the pen for cattle at the centre of the enclosure. (*Photo courtesy of The American Museum of Natural History*)

241

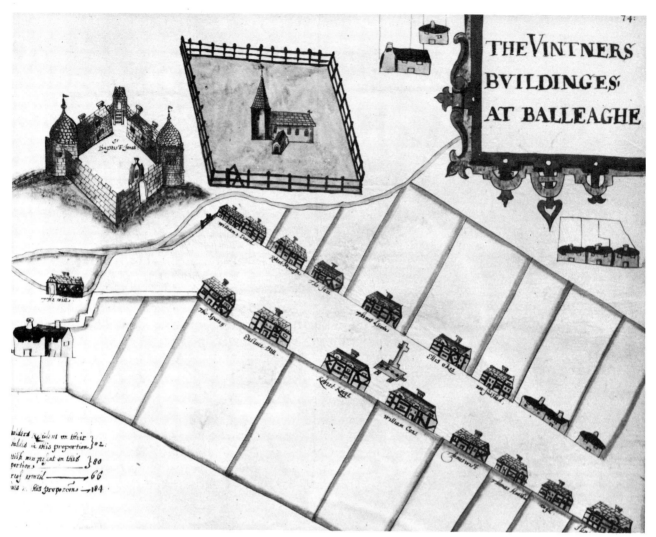

THE VINTNERS BVILDINGES AT BALLEAGHE

A planned village of the Ulster Plantation: Bellaghy, Co. Londonderry as it appeared in 1622. The village street is broad and straight, flanked by timber-frame houses with the landlord's house built inside a defended courtyard or 'bawn'. Notice the church, the market cross and the stocks in the middle of the street

Vietnam. But defence is rarely of major significance in promoting group settlement unless people are under grave and continuous threat. An example from seventeenth-century Ireland illustrates this point, for colonists in the Ulster Plantations were required by the government to live in villages as a protection against the 'meer Irish'. But soon after the initial colonisation, a government inspector complained that they were living 'scattered up and down upon their proportions', that is in dwellings built on their own farms.

Sometimes the way in which society itself is organised is a

major reason for living in groups, especially where the extended family or kindred are of major significance. For example, the kin rather than the individual family may own the land; often they act as a cooperative unit, besides helping with rearing children and looking after the sick and elderly. In Ireland, for example, the clachan was normally the home of close relatives, for kindred held land on joint leases, and sons built their houses near their fathers' on marriage. Indeed the clachan was often named after the kin group that lived in it, for example, Blaneystown or Walshestown. Yet kindred can operate as a social group, maintaining close family ties when settlement is dispersed, as happens in rural Ireland or Wales today.

Group-living in clustered settlement offers many advantages, but no single factor is of over-riding importance. That is probably why settlement in many countries has shown a marked tendency to change from nucleated to dispersed, and sometimes back again according to changing circumstances. In Ireland the change from the clachan to the isolated farmstead occurred mainly in the period after the Great Famine. Some clachans disappeared as a result of declining population which left only a single dwelling still inhabited among the ruins of a once large community. Sometimes the change resulted from deliberate planning by landlord and government trying to replace the former common fields with individual farms in an attempt to make farming more viable. In Europe as a whole the advent of enclosure, and the new methods of farming—new crops, new breeds of livestock and improved implements—all

Figure 6.3
Planned settlement, Cloonkeen, Co. Mayo. In this example a government agency, the Congested Districts Board, changed the pattern of settlement from nucleated to dispersed as part of a scheme of land consolidation, to create compact holdings from many scattered plots. It built new farmhouses, each on its own land, and encouraged farmers to leave their old homes in the clachan. The two different shadings represent land held by two typical farmers before and after the consolidation carried out in 1909

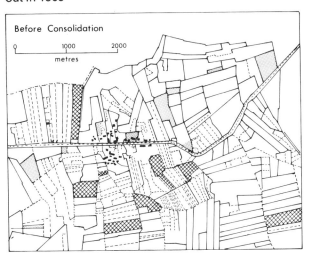

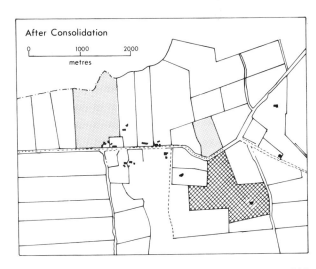

led to the break up of farm villages and their replacement by individual farmsteads during the late eighteenth and nineteenth centuries. Present economic conditions which favour the large farm unit, continue this trend today. Most villages have declining populations, with fewer farmers and farmworkers, while the local craftsmen who once made the tools, implements and household goods needed by the community have long since disappeared. Only in areas near the larger towns and cities have villages increased their population by providing homes for commuters; and in seaside districts by attracting holidaymakers as seasonal residents.

Morphology

Rural settlements are highly varied in their morphology, and the classification given below is only one of several which have been devised to distinguish the more common types. This type of classification applies only to morphological appearance—it has nothing to do with origin or function. Settlements may be morphologically similar, like the Bulgarian village and the Irish *clachan*, but the reasons why a particular form was adopted may be quite different in each of the countries concerned. As a general rule, settlement morphology can only be interpreted

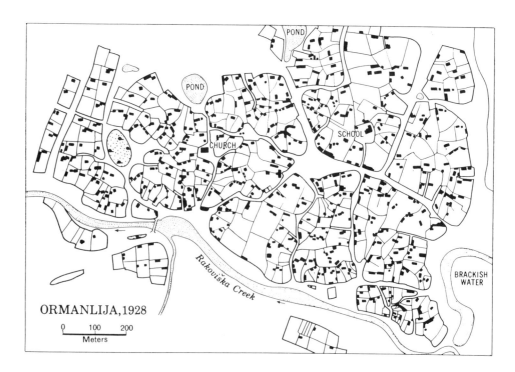

Figure 6.4
Amorphous settlement, represented here by Ormanlija, a village in Bulgaria as it was in 1928

with reference to the economic and social history of the country being studied.

Table 6.1 Forms of Nucleated Settlement

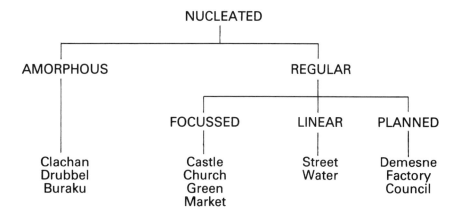

```
                        NUCLEATED
                            |
        ┌───────────────────┴───────────────────┐
    AMORPHOUS                                 REGULAR
        |                           ┌────────────┼────────────┐
        |                       FOCUSSED      LINEAR       PLANNED
        |                           |            |            |
    Clachan                      Castle        Street      Demesne
    Drubbel                      Church        Water       Factory
    Buraku                       Green                     Council
                                 Market
```

Probably the most widespread form of nucleated settlement is that which lacks any definite core or focal point, the individual buildings sited in a haphazard way with little reference to each other. Amorphous clusters like this were once found along the Atlantic coasts of western Europe, from north-west Spain to Scotland, and in western Germany where they are known by the term *drubbel*. Much further afield, the *buraku* settlement of Japan is often similar in form. Such settlements vary enormously in size from five or six dwellings up to several hundred. But they share several common features: all are farm settlements; few have any shops or other services; and most are, or were, associated with a system of common fields rather than individually worked farms. This is a simple type of settlement, its haphazard appearance showing no attempt at formal planning, and in most of the areas in which it is found it appears to be a primary form of settlement. Indeed some of the earliest prehistoric settlements appear to have a similar lack of plan. But this does not mean that all amorphous settlements are of great antiquity. Indeed the converse may be true—the Irish clachan has prehistoric antecedents, but many date back only to the great period of population increase at the end of the eighteenth century.

Regular settlements are usually more recent in origin, their formal plan implying a greater degree of economic and social organisation. This applies in particular to those settlements which have either a church or castle as a focal point, for here the organising authority is explicitly recognised in the plan of the settlement. Both these forms are common throughout

Focussed settlement: Regensburg in Switzerland where the castle forms the focal point. (*Photo Aerofilms Limited*)

Focussed settlement: the village green lies at the centre of Finchingfield in Essex

Europe, and many date back to mediaeval times. An earlier type of settlement is the so-called 'green village' in which houses are grouped around a central open space which may contain a pond and perhaps a church or school. The green may be of any shape—rectangular, square, round or triangular, and its original function was probably to provide grazing for livestock driven into the village at night for safety. Later it often acted as a common on which markets and fairs were held. The green village is common in England and in central Europe where a distinctive form is the *rundling* in which farmsteads are grouped around a roughly circular common, rather like the Bantu *kraal*. A variation of this form is the almond-shaped *angerdorf*, which is thought to have been introduced by German colonists to lands east of the Elbe about 1000 A.D. (Figure 6.5).

A second major type of regular settlement is the linear village in which houses line both sides of a single street. This form occurs widely in east and south Asia, and in western Europe. German geographers, who have been pioneers in the study of rural settlement, consider that in their country linear settlements were introduced as planned villages in early mediaeval times, and they recognise two forms: the *strassendorf* (literally, street village) found in the lowlands, and the *waldhufendorf* (forest village) which is associated with woodland clearance in upland areas. In low-lying, marshy areas of north-west Germany and the Netherlands another type of linear settlement is found in which rivers and canals take the place of the road as a means of communication and base line for land colonisation. Here the houses are built on the higher, firmer ground along the river banks, and farms stretch inland as long narrow strips. A similar form of settlement was also adopted by French colonists in North America, along the St Lawrence River in Quebec and the Mississippi in Louisiana. Again the river provided the main means of communication, and properties granted to the original settlers stretched inland, often for many miles. Initially settlement was dispersed, but equal rights of inheritance among sons led to increasing subdivision: the farms became long narrow strips—'long lots' is the American term —and as new homesteads were built the settlement assumed a linear form.

Most of the preceding settlement types have evolved slowly through time, but the final group were consciously planned before any development took place, sometimes on formal geometric patterns. This settlement type has a long history, in Europe dating back to the Roman colonisation. More recent examples have usually been planned by an individual de-

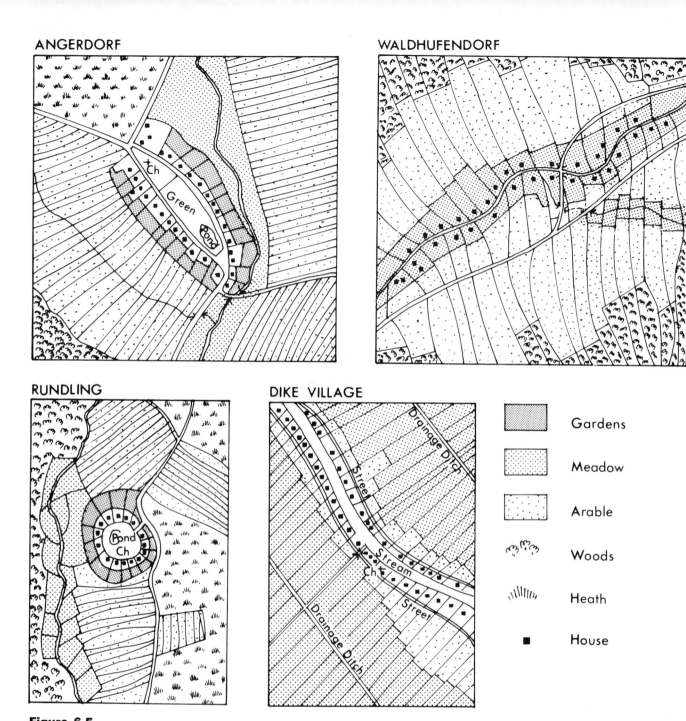

Figure 6.5
Focussed and linear settlements, represented by plans of the *Rundling* and *Angerdorf,* and the *Waldhufendorf* and *Dike* villages respectively

A typical Strassendorf or street village: Beragh, Co. Tyrone, Northern Ireland. (*Photo Aerofilms Limited*)

veloper, sometimes employing the professional services of an architect or surveyor. Demesne villages, built by landlords to provide houses for their workers are familiar examples of this type built in the eighteenth and early nineteenth centuries in many parts of the British Isles. Often they were planned to enhance the layout of an adjoining mansion and its park, and had public buildings such as a church, market house and almshouse erected by the landlord himself. Sometimes the state has been the planning authority, stipulating the location and design of the settlement but leaving the development to designated agents. In Ireland, the settlements built during the Plantation of Ulster in the early seventeenth century are examples of this sort, while modern Israel provides further illustrations of new rural settlements planned by the state as part of the colonisation of newly occupied territory. Finally the state itself

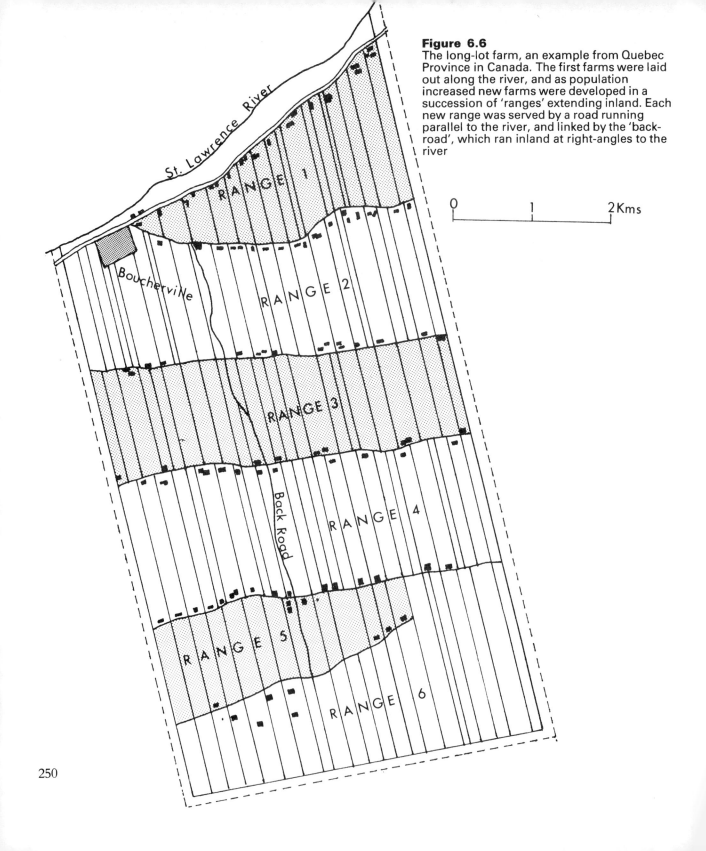

Figure 6.6
The long-lot farm, an example from Quebec Province in Canada. The first farms were laid out along the river, and as population increased new farms were developed in a succession of 'ranges' extending inland. Each new range was served by a road running parallel to the river, and linked by the 'back-road', which ran inland at right-angles to the river

St. Lawrence River

Boucherville

RANGE 1

RANGE 2

RANGE 3

Back Road

RANGE 4

RANGE 5

RANGE 6

0   1   2 Kms

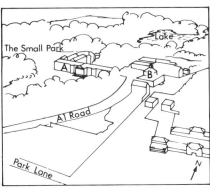

Demesne village: Hillsborough, Co. Down. Developed by the Hill family, it became the centre of their large estates in Down towards the end of the eighteenth century when the new mansion (A) and courthouse (B) were completed. More recently the mansion was the official residence of the Governor of Northern Ireland. (*Photo Aerofilms Limited*)

has also assumed responsibility for providing housing for lower paid workers, and throughout Britain and Ireland the council estate has become an increasingly familiar type of planned settlement in rural areas.

Pattern

The distribution of settlement in any area, its density and limits, depends upon the resources available to man in the process of making a living. Likewise the form and pattern of local settlement reflects how man organises his social and economic activities, adjusting to the character of his immediate

A cattle station in Australia's
Northern Territory

environment and his own cultural traditions. In this way the
African kraal is an efficient form of settlement for a society in
which the extended family normally lives and works together,
and whose economy is based on livestock rearing in an environment in which there are many predators. Similarly, the
isolated cattle station in Australia acts as both home and
workplace for a family and its employees who live in a marginal environment, raising large numbers of livestock for sale to
distant markets.

However, it is rare for economies to remain unaltered over
long periods of time, or for societies to remain unaffected by
external contacts. Both are subject to change, and settlements
respond, increasing in density, expanding their limits and
adding new forms; or conversely, declining, contracting and
abandoning former sites. In periods of change it rarely happens
that older settlements are completely swept away. Some survive as relict features, their sites marked by ruined castles or

A deserted village, Ballyduagh, Co. Tipperary. Apart from its mediaeval church—in the bushes, centre—little is known about the history of this site which was discovered through aerial survey. (*Photo Cambridge University Collection: copyright reserved*)

houses. Other settlements may be modified to meet the new circumstances like the mediaeval village which becomes a commuter suburb. In many areas rural settlement has been added to constantly over long periods of time: in southern Europe some villages occupy foundations built in Roman times; in England many date back to the Anglo-Saxon invasion, and a village may include houses built by the local council in the 1970s, as well as a twelfth-century church and Elizabethan cottages. All of these older forms are included in the contemporary pattern of settlement because they represent an investment—in buildings, roads and farms—which few rural communities can afford to discard. Instead the new must be accommodated within the old, and rational decisions on the best place to locate a new house or align a road, have to take account of the buildings, boundaries and rights of way which are already there (Figure 6.7). In this way the past exerts a very strong influence on the present, a point which must be remembered constantly in interpreting patterns of rural settlement.

Rural settlement patterns thus tend to show considerable

253

Figure 6.7
Great Waltham in Essex, a village
where a council housing estate of
the early 1950s (**B**) and more
recent development (**C**) have
been grafted onto a mediaeval
core (**A**)

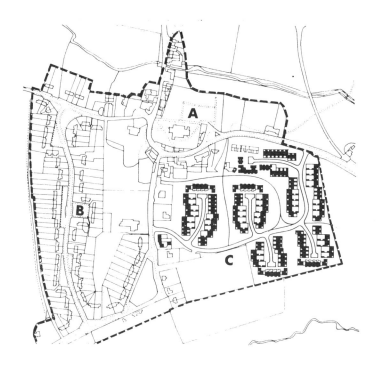

The chequerboard pattern of
roads and fields provides a rigid
framework for rural settlement in
Foard County, Texas, U.S.A. The
system of land planning used
here is explained in Figure 6.8
although in fact most of Texas
was not included in the Federal
Land Survey. Note the
windbreaks between the fields

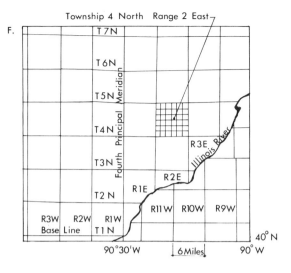

Figure 6.8
U.S.A. Federal Land Survey: the basic principles are illustrated in this set of four diagrams from west central Illinois. Surveyors first established a base-line (running east-west), and a 'principal' meridian (running north-south). The intersection of these co-ordinates provided the regular grid from which the land was divided into square blocks. In descending order of size, these blocks were called Townships (6 miles across), Sections (1 mile), and Quarter Sections ($\frac{1}{2}$ mile). The official term for the Township was 'Township and Range', indicating the method used to locate townships on small-scale maps. Thus the Township shown in the diagram is referred to as T (township) 4 N (north) R (range) 2 E (east). This system of land division was used on land acquired by the Federal Government after it was established, that is the lands north of the Ohio River and west of the Mississippi

variety in long settled lands. Where the pattern is more uniform it is likely that the area has been subject to little economic or social change over a long period. Alternatively it may have been recently colonised. For example, settlement patterns in much of tropical Africa and South America must have been remarkably stable for many centuries before the coming of European settlers. Conversely the regular pattern of dispersed farmsteads in the mid–west and west of the U.S.A. represents a very recent phase of land colonisation and one which was based on government survey and lease. Its remarkable chequer–board appearance is derived from the principle adopted by the surveyors, of using a six square mile (15·53 sq. kilometres) area as the basic unit of survey. This was then subdivided into townships, sections and quarter sections, each with their appropriate roads and farmsteads.

2 Urban Settlement

Towns and cities differ from villages and hamlets in their size of population and the area they cover, but above all, in the work their inhabitants do. For towns began as places where

255

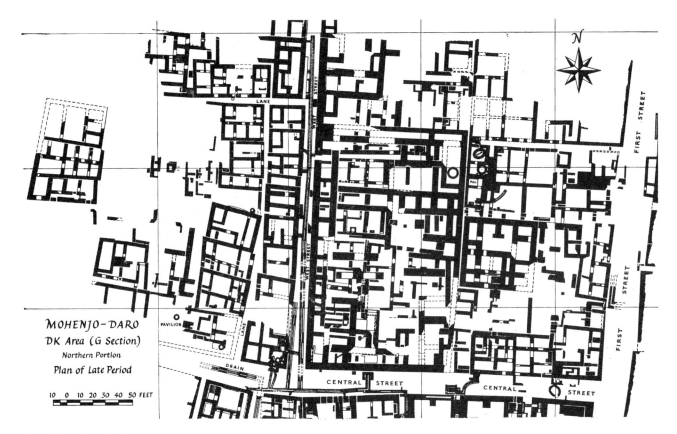

MOHENJO-DARO
DK Area (G Section)
Northern Portion
Plan of Late Period

10 0 10 20 30 40 50 FEET

Neolithic city: Mohenjo-daro, a
planned city on the Indus River
which was already a large urban
community by the end of the third
millennium B.C.

people came to trade goods, and this service function has
remained the mainstay of urban economies down to modern
times. Archaeological sources indicate that the earliest towns
developed during the Neolithic period, when trade was stimulated by improved methods of food production and technological innovation. By the second millennium B.C., settlements
that were truly urban had appeared throughout the Fertile
Crescent, from the Nile to the Indus; a little later they developed in China, and in the New World—in Yucatan, Mexico
and Peru, during the first millennium A.D.

Under the Romans, Europe experienced a great era of town
building during the first few centuries A.D., but with the
collapse of the Empire, trade declined and many urban settlements were abandoned. Further east, trade contacts between
the Mediterranean and Indian oceans were maintained by Arab
merchants and seamen, and small urban centres continued to
flourish. But in Europe, the revival of urban life did not take
place until towards the end of the ninth century, beginning in

256

Mediaeval city: Antwerp as it appeared in 1567, a flourishing sea port and one of the most important commercial cities of north western Europe

Italy, and extending northwards as trade expanded in the Baltic and the narrow seas between Britain and the Continent. Thus the major cities of medieval Europe were all located on major trade routes: Venice, Genoa, Florence and Milan in northern Italy; Bruges, Antwerp and London, and the Hansa towns of the Baltic Seas.

The mediaeval city in Europe was essentially a trading centre, its leaders wealthy merchants; but with the rise of the nation state a new type of city began to appear—the capital, seat of the royal court and of the bureaucrats who served it. Soon the capital city became very much larger than other urban centres: towards the end of the sixteenth century cities rarely exceeded 50 000 people, but London had a population of 250 000 and Paris 180 000. Two centuries later London had 800 000 and Paris 670 000; and both had become the main commercial cities as well as political capitals of their respective countries.

During the nineteenth century, a further function was added to many towns and cities in Europe—manufacturing industry. Towns had always engaged in some manufacturing activity, much of it craftwork in metals, textiles and leather and often as a by-product of normal trade. But the nineteenth century saw the development of manufacturing on an unprecedented scale, much of it concentrated in large factories employing hundreds

Baroque city: Versailles, a former royal hunting park, to which Louis XIV moved his Palace to escape from the congested streets of late seventeenth-century Paris. The new settlement was designed to enhance the dignity of the royal court, with broad streets radiating from the Palace as its focal point. Notice the extensive pleasure grounds which complete the sense of royal pomp and grandeur

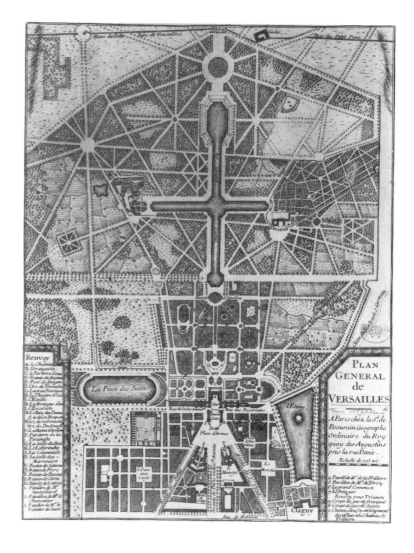

of workers. The fastest growing towns were on or near the coalfields which provided power for industry, or the ports where raw materials were imported for processing; but most towns and cities shared in the general economic growth. For besides the new jobs in factories there was a steady increase in service employment, in the retail and wholesale trades which sold the goods produced by manufacturing industry, as well as in banking, insurance and transport. New systems of transport, based on the railway and the steamship, spread the effects of the Industrial Revolution even more rapidly, and ports expanded rapidly in India, China and south-east Asia, in the

Industrial city: Glasgow, wreathed in the smog created by the heavy industries which made it one of Britain's major industrial centres in the nineteenth century. (*Photo Aerofilms Limited*)

Americas and later in Australia as well as in Europe. By the end of the century, Europeans in particular had become city-dwellers. This can be seen in the figures for England and Wales, given below.

Table 6.2 Percentage of population in England and Wales living in towns, 1800–1890.

Towns over (population)	1800	1850	1890
10 000	21·30	39·45	61·73
20 000	16·94	35·00	53·58
100 000	9·73	22·58	31·82

Today the trend is towards even larger concentrations of population in large cities. Expansion in service employment with rising standards of living is partly responsible, but many types of manufacturing industry also seek locations near large cities where the bulk of their customers are found—with the advent of electric power and road transport they no longer need to be sited near the sources of raw materials and power.

259

Transport too has enabled the modern city to increase rapidly in size, for the electric train, the bus and the private car all encourage large-scale commuting over ever increasing distances from the city.

Urban Morphology

These characteristic phases in the development of urban life are closely reflected in the spatial pattern of its streets and buildings. For most towns grow in a fairly haphazard fashion, adding new districts in periods of growth, designed according to the economic needs and social conventions of the time. Each historic phase of growth has its own distinctive pattern of development, and provided these can be identified, it is possible to reconstruct the history of many towns and cities by studying their plans and walking through their streets. Of course some towns have been planned from the very beginning, the most common form being the regular gridiron in which building lots are delimited by streets which cross at right angles. Towns like these can be as old as the Neolithic city of Harappa in the Indus valley; built in classical times like Pompeii; planned in the twelfth century like the *bastides* of France and Wales which were established during military colonisation; or developed during the nineteenth century like Seattle or San Francisco. No other city form has such a long history, or is so widely distributed.

Sometimes in Europe, the regular street pattern of the Roman town survives at the core of a modern city, but more often the nucleus is composed of the narrow, winding streets and alleys which belonged to the mediaeval town. It was usually a compact settlement, encircled by walls which inhibited its growth, and heavily congested with traffic on market days as farmers carted in their produce for sale in the market place. Very often this lay at the centre of the town, with the market house, the church and the guild halls of merchants and craftsmen grouped nearby.

By the mid sixteenth century further expansion was made possible by removing the old defensive walls, now made obsolete by the widespread use of gunpowder. Initially these were replaced by new defences—great broad ramparts and ditches often planned to elaborate star-shaped designs which gave defending troops maximum protection and fire power. When these became outmoded in their turn, they provided a line around the city which was often used to build a ring road and parks. Internally the city was also made more spacious by new planned developments in which the cramped tenements and narrow lanes of mediaeval times were swept away. In their place were built broad streets suitable for wheeled vehicles, laid out in regular, geometric shapes—squares, circles and crescents. The increased wealth was invested in new buildings, classical in their design and grander in scale than most of their

Chichester: the layout of the Roman town is clearly seen in the north-south and east-west crossing of the main streets, and in the alignment of mediaeval city walls, built on Roman foundations. The original grid pattern of minor streets has not survived, mainly because of property developments undertaken by various religious institutions in the Middle Ages. (*Crown Copyright reserved*)

Carcassonne in south France. A perfectly preserved mediaeval town standing on a site first made defensible in Roman times. The towers of church and castle rise above the irregular streets and tightly packed houses to the right of the old town, and later suburban development creeps around the hillock, still protected by two encircling walls. (*Photo Aerofilms Limited*)

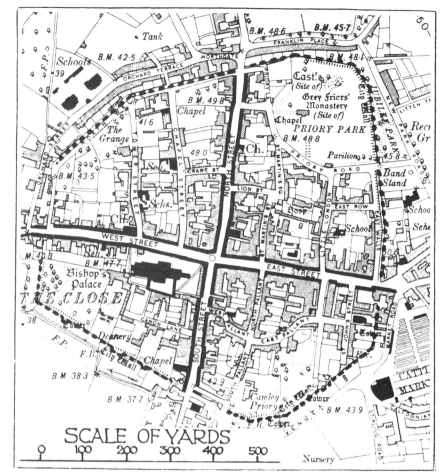

262

predecessors. Mediaeval man lavished attention on his churches; Renaissance merchants on secular buildings—on houses, commercial premises and government offices. This is especially evident in capital cities where urban architecture and design served to enhance the dignity and power of the state. In Washington, for example, the architect L'Enfant devised a series of radial avenues which focussed on three major public buildings: The Capitol, the Supreme Court, and the White House, symbolising the three essential elements of the Federal Government. In Paris a similar grand design was executed in a massive rebuilding programme undertaken in the mid nineteenth century.

Figure 6.9
Washington D.C: showing the
central area designed by l'Enfant

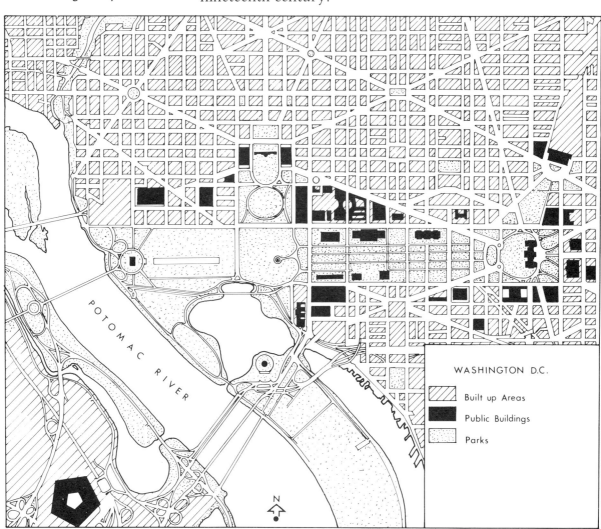

WASHINGTON D.C.

Built up Areas

Public Buildings

Parks

The orderliness and wealth of the eighteenth-century city distinguishes it from the hasty and often haphazard accretion of the nineteenth century, and from the many new settlements created by industrial growth. Visually the most prominent new features were the factories whose tall chimneys spewed smoke endlessly into the sky, and the rows of workers' houses, built in regular brick terraces along narrow streets. Downtown, new shops, banks and town halls were built, often to grandiose designs which symbolised the growing civic pride of the middle class businessman; and railway stations inaugurated a new era of urban transport and architecture. Initially only the well-to-do could afford to move out of town, building villas which were scaled-down replicas of the mansions of country gentlemen. But as the century wore on, more people came to use the fast and relatively cheap transport provided by the railway, and new suburbs spread steadily around main and branch line stations.

Naarden in north Holland is one of the finest examples of Renaissance fortification: it was designed according to the military designs of Marshall Vauban in the late seventeenth century, and was intended to form part of the defences of Amsterdam. (*Photo KLM Aerocarto, The Hague*)

Preston in Lancashire, a typical industrial city of the nineteenth century with its factory chimneys and regular, narrow streets of terraced houses. (*Photo Aerofilms Limited*)

Real suburban growth, however, belongs to the twentieth century and the advent of the private car as a form of mass transport. Early in the century the electric tramcar and the corporation bus encouraged speculative builders to develop land that lay some distance from the railway. After the Second World War the pace of development quickened as urban authorities began to build public housing on this cheaper land which lay at the city's outer fringe. Some of this housing is in high-rise flats, but otherwise it differs little from the estates built by private developers: roads are often laid out in complex serpentine patterns which baffle the visitor, shops and services are relatively few and there is often little cohesion or form to the plan.

Most suburbs are purely residential, housing workers from the inner city. But factory development is also beginning to appear in many suburban areas too, for modern industry requires extensive sites for storage and parking; and land is cheaper in the suburbs. Down-town, the city skyline is also changing, increasingly dominated by immense towering office blocks in which an increasing number of urban dwellers find employment. Fast vertical transport by lift makes such buildings practical while the modern city itself depends on the transport systems which move great numbers of people in and out of the city each day to their homes in the suburbs.

The Central Business District: Times Square, New York, with its endless traffic, commercial advertisements and towering office blocks

Urban land use

Overlying the network of streets and buildings which give the city its morphological pattern are a series of functional zones which can be distinguished in most modern cities. The central business district (often shortened to C.B.D.), is easily identified by the multiple stores, specialist shops, hotels, municipal and government offices, banks and a multitude of national and international companies all of which have their offices here. Each of these activities consciously seeks city centre locations for various reasons: multiple stores because they are most accessible to the biggest number of potential customers, business firms because they can make use of a wide range of services, besides being accessible to clients and customers. But

The zone of transition: decaying tenements in the Gorbals area of Glasgow, now largely cleared and redeveloped

only big firms can afford the high rates and rents of the city centre: the others find accommodation elsewhere. Sometimes the C.B.D. is itself divided into sectors. In New York, for example, the major shops, hotels and theatres are in mid-town Manhattan, while the business area is located in Wall Street in the south of the island. In London, the corresponding sections are the West End and the City, and Westminster where government departments are situated near the Houses of Parliament. Usually buildings in the C.B.D. are comparatively new, unless they are of special historical significance; for the C.B.D. is the sector of the city in which redevelopment occurs most rapidly, buildings being altered and replaced according to the needs, wealth and prestige of their owners or property developers.

Beyond the C.B.D. is a zone of mixed land uses; older factories and warehouses intermixed with older residential terraces and tracts of derelict land. This has been called 'the zone of transition', a phrase which aptly describes its changing functions as new development pushes in at the edge of the C.B.D., and once substantial housing deteriorates into slum property. Here live the city's poor, immigrants from the country, and racial and ethnic groups who are denied entry to better residential districts—the Loop in Chicago or Harlem in New York are examples of Black ghettoes found in this zone.

On its outer fringes, the zone of transition is succeeded by working-class housing, typically the terrace houses built in uniform rows by nineteenth-century speculators. Much of this property may also be in process of renewal by local authorities, with new housing built at much lower densities than in the past and with more public open spaces. Beyond are the middle class suburbs, and an outer commuter zone, where settlement consists of scattered nodes and ribbons along the major roads and railways.

Suburbia: semi-detached houses built to standard designs by speculative builders just before the First World War at Watford on the outskirts of London

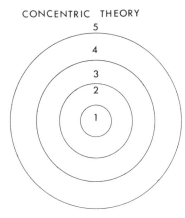

CONCENTRIC THEORY

Figure 6.10
The Concentric Zone theory of urban structure

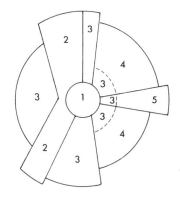

SECTOR THEORY

1 Central Business District
2 Wholesale Light Manufacturing
3 Low-class Residential
4 Medium-class Residential
5 High-class Residential

Figure 6.11
The Sector theory of urban structure

This 'concentric zone' pattern of urban land use was first recognised by a Chicago sociologist, E. W. Burgess, in the 1920s. He considered that it resulted from growth occurring at the centre, and pushing outwards, rather like ripples extending outwards when a stone is thrown into a pond. Behind the crest of development comes a trough where property is affected by the normal processes of ageing and decay before pressure for redevelopment begins again.

Of course this pattern does not fit all cities. In some, the concentric zones are interrupted by wedges of similar land use, extending from city centre to suburb—perhaps a sector that is entirely industrial, or one devoted exclusively to middle class housing, as in Belfast's Malone Road district. This 'sector theory' of urban growth was suggested by another American scholar, Homer Hoyt, who considered that the type of development found near the city centre early in its growth could persist as the city expanded outwards. Hence an industrial quarter might well extend outwards from the C.B.D. right to the edge of the modern city, forming a very different growth pattern from that envisaged in Burgess' concentric zones. Walter Firey added a further comment on the sector theory by noting that growth might also be affected by the character of the land into which the city was expanding. For example, high quality farmland will be sold for development at prices which only the wealthy can afford, and hence it is most unlikely to be bought for industry or public authority housing.

These theories help to increase our understanding of the spatial patterns which can be readily identified in many western cities. They are most applicable to the cities of North America, which have less complex morphological and land use structures than those of Europe and Asia. For the cities of the Old World have an urban history that spans many centuries, and are themselves the product of very different cultural traditions. Asian cities, for example, tend to have a much denser pattern of building than those of Europe, and they lack the clearly defined street plan and distinctive commercial core which has characterised the European city from classical times. Instead the city may be divided into residential quarters, each inhabited by separate groups such as the merchants, craftsmen and labourers. In India, these residential divisions may be further accentuated by caste, which continues to have a powerful influence, even in new housing areas.

Over the past few centuries, European influences have altered these indigenous patterns, sometimes by developing entirely new towns on European lines, more often by grafting

African city: a typical section of the native quarter in central Lagos shows houses packed together without reference to any systematic street plan. (*Photo Aerofilms Limited*)

new commercial cores and European residential areas onto existing settlements. Often the results are quite striking. In west Africa for example, the formal plan of the European sectors contrasts sharply with the amorphous structure of the African town. This resembles an interlocking system of overgrown villages in which there is no recognisable pattern in the layout of streets, and houses, workshops and markets are mixed together indiscriminately.

European cities also differ in many respects from those of North America. American and English city dwellers prefer to live in single-family houses, each with its own garden, but continental Europeans and the Scots are more likely to live in apartments, with the wealthiest people living in the city centres rather than in the suburbs. This residential pattern is also found in the cities of Latin America, where the poorest housing is usually found in 'shanty towns', built by rural immigrants at the edge of the city. Unable to afford even the cheapest

European city: a section of the thirteenth district of Paris, showing old and new apartment blocks. These are the common form of residential development in many European cities, in contrast to the single-family house and garden which is favoured in Britain

accommodation in permanent dwellings they appropriate vacant land on which to build homes from packing cases, petrol cans or corrugated iron. Settlements like these are found in many of the world's underdeveloped countries, where the rate of population growth far exceeds the capacity of governments to provide low-cost public housing.

Shanty town on the outskirts of São Paulo in Brazil. A stark reminder of the poverty that exists on the fringe of the modern city in many parts of the world. (*Photo John Moss/Colorfic!*)

The problem of housing people with low incomes is common to cities in all parts of the world, but there are two further consequences of modern urban growth which affect western cities in particular: city centre congestion and the continuing expansion of the suburbs. The first is the inevitable outcome of the concentration of employment and major services within the C.B.D. This was logical and efficient as long as people travelled on foot or were brought to the centre by train or tram, and when business had to be conducted between individuals face to face. Today the situation is very different. Far more people work in city centres than ever before and many now want to travel by private car; hence streets planned in the age of the horse-drawn carriage can no longer cope with the vastly increased volumes of traffic. Consequently, the city centre has become less efficient as a place in which to conduct many forms of business. Fortunately, the variety of telecommunications now available means that city centre locations are less essential for many firms, and these, along with hotels and department stores are now moving to the suburbs. Here there is less traffic, easier access to new urban and national motorway systems, and relatively cheap land on which to build and provide parking

Urban traffic: the fine pattern of broad streets designed for Paris by Haussmann a century ago can no longer cope with the million people who commute daily to the central business district

Suburban growth: Clearview, Long Island, New York. Most of the people who live here commute daily to New York City. (*Photo Aerofilms Limited*)

spaces. But suburban growth also creates problems. The new residential districts have lower population densities, spread more widely and are less cohesive than the old, while their widely spaced service centres and poor public transport create difficulties for those without a car, especially the poor, the elderly and the infirm. Moreover, constant expansion pushes the countryside ever further from the city with a consequent loss of farmland and sometimes of open spaces which the townsman can use for recreation.

For these reasons continued urban expansion is seen as a mixed blessing, especially in the more crowded countries of western Europe. Planners have increasingly sought new ways of controlling growth in order to improve the quality of the urban environment and at the same time ensure the conservation of rural areas at the edge of the city. In Britain, the method most widely used since 1947 has been to designate 'green belts' around the larger cities, within which new development is very strictly controlled. Growth is then encouraged either in existing towns situated some distance away, or in completely new towns. Wherever this policy has been applied—first in the London region, later in north-east England, central Scotland, and most recently in Northern Ireland—the new towns have achieved a fair degree of success. Most have grown quite rapidly, attracting people and industry and creating a new and attractive urban environment. But they have not succeeded in relieving population pressures and congestion in the older cities to any significant extent. Indeed they have sometimes added to existing problems, for by constricting growth, the green belts

Figure 6.12
The London Region: the green belt and new towns

THE LONDON REGION

Bletchley
Letchworth
Luton
Stevenage
BISHOPS STORTFORD
Witham
Aylesbury
Welwyn
Hemel Hempstead
Harlow
CHELMSFORD
HIGH WYCOMBE
WATFORD
Thames R.
Basildon
SOUTHEND
Canvey Island
READING
ROCHESTER
Bracknell
Tadley
Camberley
Frimley
Basingstoke
GUILDFORD
MAIDSTONE
Edenbridge
Crawley

HASTINGS

■ Central Area

□ Contiguous Built up Area

▨ Green Belt or Wooded Areas

-·-·- Greater London Conurbation Boundary 1961 Population 8.182,550

——— The London Planning Region Boundary 1961 Population 12.465,941

● The Eight London New Towns

○ Expanding Towns

◍ Other Major Centres

——— Main Roads

+-+-+ Railways

0 10 20 30 40 50 kms

have helped to increase the value of urban land and made it all the more difficult for public authorities to buy land for the renewal of older working-class housing.

Other solutions to the problems of urban growth are now being examined by city and regional planners, and it may well be that the city of the future will have quite a different morphology to the one we know today. Some of the experimental forms proposed are illustrated in Figure 6.13. First, the *core-city*—originally advocated by architects like the American, Frank Loyd Wright—is designed to achieve very high residential densities by housing people in immensely tall skyscraper blocks which would also include shops and offices. A much more human scale is envisaged in the second example, the *radial city*, where growth is encouraged along radial transport routes with open spaces left between. This plan is being followed in Copenhagen, and it is very similar to the pattern of urban development which followed the expansion of the railways in nineteenth-century Britain. A third type adopts a *linear* form, similar to that used as the plan for the new towns of Cumberland in central Scotland and Craigavon in Northern Ireland.

Figure 6.13
Planned forms of urban growth

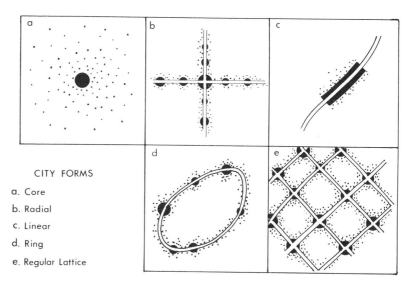

CITY FORMS

a. Core

b. Radial

c. Linear

d. Ring

e. Regular Lattice

Figure 6.14
Linear city: the plan for Craigavon, Co. Armagh, which is designed to link two existing towns, Portadown and Lurgan, and develop a new city centre

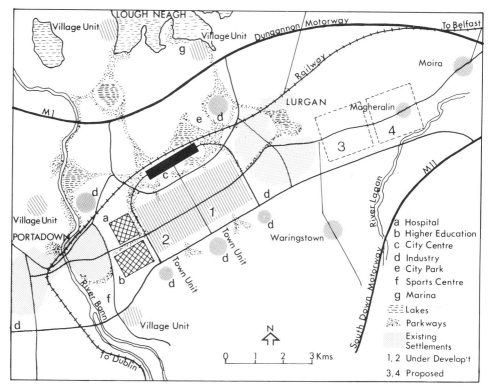

a Hospital
b Higher Education
c City Centre
d Industry
e City Park
f Sports Centre
g Marina
≡≡≡ Lakes
Parkways
Existing Settlements
1, 2 Under Develop't
3, 4 Proposed

Here a central spine road links the existing towns of Lurgan and Portadown, a new city centre is to be built along the spine and on either side are located industrial estates and residential areas. Future growth can take place simply by adding new sectors at either end of the spine. The fourth example, the *ring-city*, already exists in embryo in the Randstad of the Netherlands—the arc of cities which stretches from Rotterdam in the south to the Hague and Amsterdam. It is rather like a doughnut in shape with service centres strung out along the ring, each expanding outwards whilst the centre of the ring is retained as open space. Finally the *regular lattice* town has its service centres dispersed throughout the urban area, with low density housing and plenty of public open space. Designed for the high personal mobility associated with the private car this city form resembles Los Angeles except that it has no C.B.D. Amongst all the forms illustrated it is the one furthest removed from the European ideal of what a city should be.

Patterns of Urban Settlement

From urban morphology and land use we now turn to a broader consideration of the spatial relationships between settlements and the principles which may influence their location. For although the distribution of urban settlements in most countries appears at first glance to be entirely random one feature is immediately apparent: small settlements are more numerous than large ones; or put another way, there are more villages than towns, and more towns than cities. Furthermore, villages are sited at closer intervals than towns, and towns are more closely spaced than cities. If we try to test this simple observation by actual measurement we will find that there is in fact a fairly precise and regular relationship between the size of urban settlements and their spatial relationships.

If we measure size first we will find that urban settlements can be ranked according to the size of their population, and that there is a regular ratio between the size of population in each rank of settlement and that of the largest city. In other words, a city which ranks second in size will have half the population of the largest city, a fourth rank city will have one-quarter and so on. This ratio is called the *rank-size* rule, and as can be seen in Figure 6.15 it works in practice—at least for many of the developed countries. What is the explanation? The answer is to be found in the structure of commercial services provided by towns and cities of different sizes. Each service needs a minimum number of customers if it is to operate economically: and the term used to indicate this is *threshold*. Goods and services that are bought or used frequently—like grocery stores or newsagents, are said to have low thresholds; others used less frequently, such as jewellers or solicitors have high thresholds.

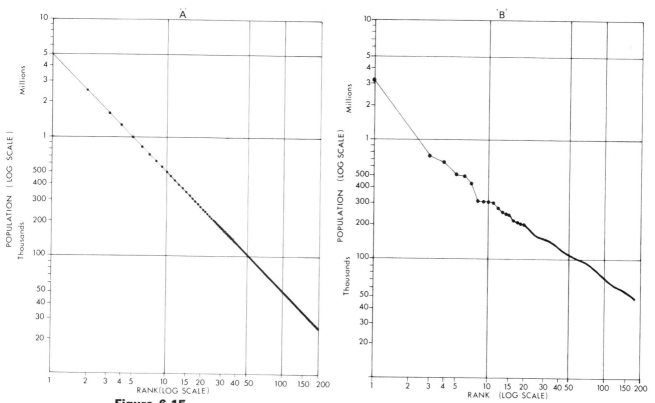

Figure 6.15
Diagram A shows the regular profile postulated by the Rank-size rule when the urban centres in an area are ranked according to the size of their populations. Diagram B shows an actual profile, that of the urban centres of England and Wales according to the 1961 census. This profile is less steep than the theoretical one, it shows more breaks, and the largest city, London, is much larger in population than the Rule would indicate. It would be larger still if the population of the built-up area was indicated, instead of that for the smaller area covered by the administrative County of London which has been used here

Low threshold services can operate with far fewer potential customers than those with high thresholds; people will probably visit their newsagent every day, but they will consult a solicitor perhaps once in five years. Hence low threshold services will be more numerous than those with high thresholds.

If this is applied to urban settlements it follows that small settlements will only have services with low thresholds, and that high threshold services will be confined to larger settlements. The smaller settlements are then said to be *low order* centres, the larger *high order* centres. Figure 6.16 illustrates this point, indicating the types of services which may be found in settlements of different size. The fact that services are arranged in a hierarchy of this sort helps to explain why low order

277

Figure 6.16
Functions appropriate to different
categories of service centres

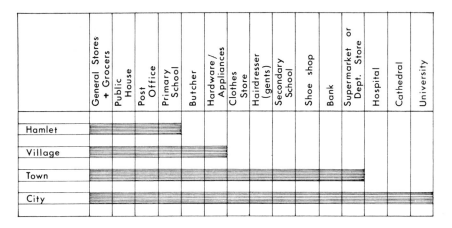

centres are more numerous than high order centres—why in England there is only one city as big as London but many towns the size of Litchfield or Littlehampton.

The ranking of service centres also explains the regularity which can be distinguished in the spacing of villages and towns. A German scholar, Walter Christaller, was the first to explore this relationship in what later became a classic study of towns in southern Germany. He discovered that low order centres were located at distances of seven kilometres from each other; those of the next order were twelve kilometres apart, for he estimated that they needed three times the population of the lower order centres to support their more specialised services. Table 6.3 shows how this principle could be further applied up the urban hierarchy.

Table 6.3 The urban hierarchy in southern Germany (after Christaller)

Settlement Order	Distance apart (km)	Population	Market area (km²)	Population
Hamlet	7	800	45	2 700
Township Centre	12	1 500	135	8 100
County Town	21	3 500	400	24 000
District City	36	9 000	1 200	75 000
Small State Capital	62	27 000	3 600	225 000
Provincial Capital	108	90 000	10 800	675 000
Regional Capital	186	300 000	32 400	2 025 000

In their distribution, he noted that the centres assumed a regular lattice-like pattern based on the area served by each centre which he decided resembled a hexagon in shape. This held true for each order of service centre from the smallest to

Figure 6.17
Christaller's theory of the spatial arrangement of service centres

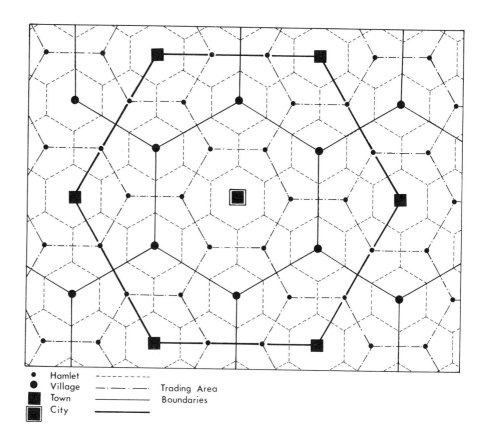

- ● Hamlet   ---------
- ● Village   —·—·—·—   Trading Area
- ■ Town   ———————   Boundaries
- ▣ City   ———————

the largest, and the result was an overlapping pattern of market areas like that illustrated in Figure 6.17.

Christaller's *Theory of Central Places* provides a ready explanation of urban settlement patterns in areas such as southern Germany where the rural population is evenly distributed and good transport facilities give equal means of access to the service centres. This means that it is most applicable to the mid-west of the U.S.A. and the prairie provinces of Canada, or to newly colonised lands like the Ijsselmeer polders in the Netherlands, where new settlements were planned on similar principles. But in many places population is unevenly distributed, for topographical or other reasons; and communication systems may be poorly developed. These anomalies will distort the pattern of central places, but they do not invalidate the theory. Like all geographical models—including the Rank-size rule, it is intended to simplify the conditions that exist in the real world, so that spatial relationships can be more readily understood.

Figure 6.18
Ijsselmeer polders,
Netherlands: the
structure plan of the
north-eastern polder with
its minor service centres
located in a radial pattern
around Emmeloord the
major centre. Urk, the
village in the south-west
corner, was formerly an
island inhabited by
fishermen and is still a
fishing community

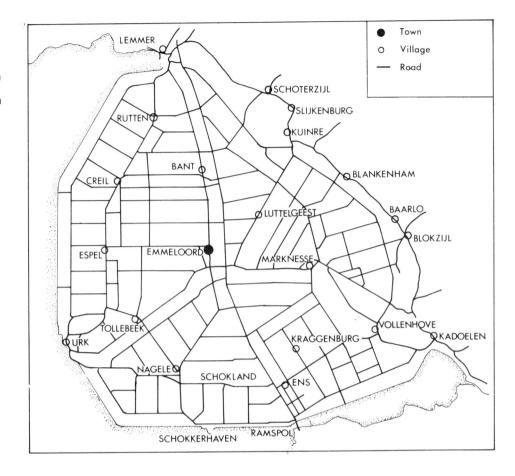

In fact many urban centres are engaged in specialised activities which have nothing to do with their normal service function. For example, localised power or mineral resources may well encourage the growth of specialised manufacturing towns—like the iron and steel towns of the Ruhr coalfield, the woollen towns of Yorkshire, or the pottery towns around Stoke-on-Trent. Similarly major transport routes encourage urban development, especially where goods must be transferred from one type of transport to another—at road and railway junctions or at the head of sea and river navigation. These are called 'break-of-bulk' points, and they are often convenient centres for certain types of manufacturing industry as well as for wholesale distribution. The local advantages offered by particular sites are thus extremely important in stimulating urban growth and their influence must be considered in any analysis of urban settlement patterns.

The World's Cities

The distribution of the world's major cities shows that they are concentrated in six regional clusters: north-west Europe, roughly centred on a line running from Liverpool through south-east England and the Netherlands to the Ruhr in Germany; north-eastern North America, where the term *megalopolis* has been used to describe the corridor of urban settlement stretching from Boston to Washington D.C.; the Pacific coast of North America focussing on southern California; the area around the mouth of the River Plate in South America; central and southern Japan; and south-east Australia. In all these areas with the exception of Japan, urban growth is a direct result of European colonisation, and throughout the world, the modern city in its form and function is very much a product of the European urban tradition. Between them these areas contain most of the world's urban dwellers. In England and Wales the urban population is as high as 80 per cent of the total; in Australia, West Germany, the U.S.A., Canada, Denmark and Japan it is only slightly less. But in the underdeveloped countries the proportion is very much less; in fact in

Figure 6.19
World cities with more than a million inhabitants. Over a hundred 'million' cities are included in this map

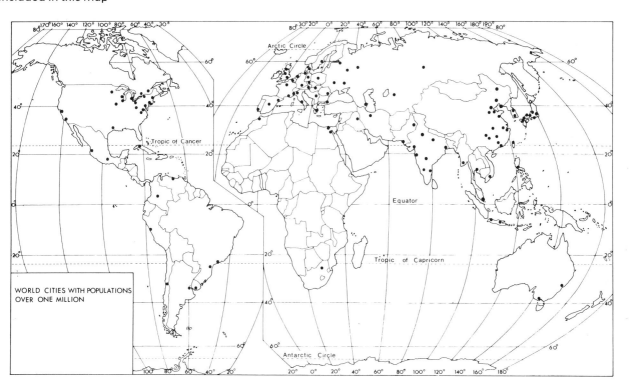

WORLD CITIES WITH POPULATIONS OVER ONE MILLION

the world as a whole only one-quarter of the total population can be classified as urban dwellers.

This pattern is likely to change in the not too distant future. Already the really big cities—those with populations in excess of 1 million, are increasing in number, and their distribution is changing. In 1850, for example, Paris and London alone topped the 1 million mark; by 1900 there were eleven 'million' cities, six of them in Europe; by 1955 the number had increased to sixty-nine, and by the late 1960s there were more than eighty. Moreover the most recent additions are in the under-developed countries, where the growth of urban population is now much faster than in the older industrial countries. Projected population growths for two cities illustrate this contrast between the developed and under-developed countries. At present, New York has about 14 million people, and Calcutta 7 million; if present trends continue, New York could have 30 million people by 2010, but Calcutta's population might be between 36 and 66 million, depending upon the projection chosen.

Figure 6.20
The world's urban population: the percentage of national populations classified as urban by each country, 1970 data

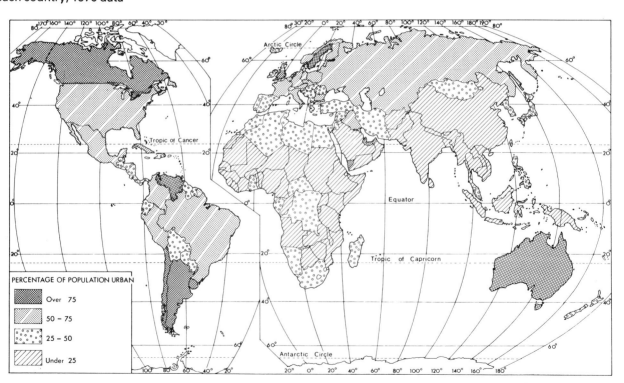

282

Of course such enormous concentrations of population may never arise, but even a modest increase in urban population can create grave problems for the economies of the under-developed countries. We have already seen that the rate of growth of modern cities strains the resources and organisational capacities even of advanced nations. In the under-developed countries the problems are very much greater, for already there is a large and impoverished population in every large city, without housing, adequate food and even such essential services as water and sewerage. In this situation, the projected increase of population in the under-developed countries is likely to create even more formidable problems. Even the more conservative estimates of population growth suggest that half the world's population will be living in urban areas by the year 2000, with 45 per cent in cities of more than 1 million people.

3 Transport and Communications

Large cities of the type just described could not exist without modern systems of transport and communication. Their existence depends upon cars, trucks, buses and railways, ships and aircraft for the movement of people and goods, and upon the information spread by post and telecommunications, radio, newspapers and television. Indeed we are so used to a high degree of personal mobility and instant world-wide communications that it is difficult to realise that all this has developed only within the past two generations. For all but a fraction of the time man has been on earth travel has been slow and costly, trade limited in volume and extent; and people could spend their entire lives in ignorance of the world beyond their immediate neighbourhood or parish. Yet despite these limitations, man has always been willing to travel, and has spent a great deal of time and energy devising new ways of transporting himself and his goods. Often the motive for travel is simple curiosity, but from the earliest times the main reason has been trade. Here the role of transport is to overcome regional differences in the distribution of resources: some places are better endowed than others—they have better timber, more minerals or yield better crops; or their people are more skilful in the manufacture of certain goods. Trade compensates for these inequalities by moving goods and/or people between areas of production and consumption.

For long periods, trade movements took place over comparatively short distances and needed very little organisation. Yet even prehistoric man engaged in quite extensive trade. In Neolithic times, for example, amber from the Baltic was traded in the Mediterranean and stone axes quarried on Tievebulliagh mountain in County Antrim were carried east as far as Denmark. But the wholesale movement of goods on a world-wide basis has developed only in modern times, with the invention of new methods of transport using inanimate sources of energy. Today there is virtually no technological limitation on man's ability to move anything he chooses from one place to another across the earth's surface; and even now he is at the beginning of travel in outer space.

Modern transport has thus become a major industry in its own right serving the industrial economies of the world and influencing life in every region. World culture patterns are also affected by the rapid movement of people and ideas. In a previous chapter we saw how Christianity spread with improvements in sea transport from the sixteenth century. Similarly English became an international language through the trade connections established by English merchants and seamen; and its even greater use today has been aided by air travel, in which American and British airlines have played a prominent role.

Fast transport and communications have also affected the political relations between states, both in military terms with the development of intercontinental missiles and orbiting satellites, and in diplomacy where international events can be reported in every country of the world as they actually take place. Instant warfare and instant diplomacy require quite different institutions for the resolution of conflict and conduct of international relations than in the days when weeks and even months might elapse before news of the outcome of battles might reach a capital city—for example, it took nearly a month for Philip II of Spain to learn of the defeat of his Armada in the English Channel in 1588.

Few aspects of life have thus remained unaffected by the changes in space relationships brought about by improvements in transport and communications especially during the present century. Distances have shrunk as the time taken in travel has lessened; and international relations take on a new meaning as more people and ever increasing volumes of goods enter world-wide circulation. Because transport influences every topic we have examined in this book it is appropriate to conclude by seeing how the revolution in transport came about, and the spatial networks for trade and travel which man has created throughout the modern world.

1 Man's Means of Transport

1.1 River Craft and Ocean Ships From the earliest times man found that long distance journeys were made most easily by water. Rivers often provide the easiest routeways through dense forests; their currents carry along primitive floats and rafts with little effort—and they also provide a ready supply of fresh food for men in transit. Certainly river-borne trade was a major stimulus in the growth of civilisation in the Fertile Crescent, and here too were developed some of the earliest known centres of maritime trade—around the Mediterranean and Arabian Seas, the Indian Ocean, and the China Seas. Each of these regions produced distinctive vessels: the skin floats of Mesopotamia; the reed-boats of the Nile—made famous in the Atlantic crossing of Thor Heyerdhal's *Ra* in 1970: and the outrigger canoes of the Pacific. Later they developed sea-going vessels, often of considerable size. Again these showed great regional variety in design and construction, reflecting differences in the materials available for building the hull, as well as adaptations to local conditions of shore, tide and wind. The last was especially important, for although oars and paddles were the earliest methods of propulsion, man also used the wind to

Ra, the reed-boat sailed across the Atlantic by Thor Heyerdhal

drive his vessels on rivers and at sea. His greatest problem was that the wind often blew from the direction towards which he wished to travel, and until the invention of the fore-and-aft sail, he could make no progress against it—the earliest sails could only be used for running before the wind. Consequently the development of trade routes by sea depended entirely on the prevailing direction of local wind systems; and the earliest used were those which showed a high degree of regularity in direction, like the Monsoons of the Indian Ocean or the trade winds of the Atlantic.

Sea voyages of great length and endurance were undertaken by many early seamen. Chinese junks, Polynesian canoes, Irish curraghs and Viking longships all made crossings of the world's major oceans in early historic times. But the great period of ocean travel began in the late fifteenth century, when major innovations in ship design and in navigation encouraged European seamen to venture ever further afield, until they had finally circumnavigated the world. Improvements in the sailing ship reached their peak in the mid nineteenth century in the famous clipper ships, built for the China tea trade, some of which achieved remarkable speeds making a six hundred and fifty kilometre run in a single day. But by then the iron-built steamship was already well established, and by the end of the century sailing ships had virtually disappeared except from coastal waters. The steamship had several major advantages. It was not dependent on the vagaries of wind and tidal current, but

Clipper ships: this contemporary illustration shows the *Taeping* and the *Ariel,* two famous ships which raced each other from Foochow in China to London in the summer of 1866. The voyage took ninety-seven days, and the two ships docked within twenty minutes of each other

Supertanker: the *British Argosy*, a tanker of 100 000 tons d.w. docking with a cargo of crude oil from Kuwait at the BP terminal on Milford Haven, south Wales

could run at a constant speed and to a fixed sailing schedule. It was also faster than the sailing ship: by 1890 the Atlantic crossing took only seven and a half days, compared with three months when the *Mayflower* carried the Pilgrim Fathers in 1620. The new iron ships could be built much bigger than the old wooden merchantmen—the biggest clipper ship was about 2000 megagrams; modern supertankers often exceed 200 000 megagrams.

With the coming of the steamship, the number of vessels in trade increased enormously—world tonnage now exceeds 132 million megagrams gross. Cargoes could now be carried in bulk, in ships specially designed for specific materials, like ore carriers, oil tankers and container vessels. Specialisation is also necessary in ports, with sophisticated equipment needed to handle different cargoes. Consequently much of the world's shipping trade is concentrated on a relatively small number of major ports in each country, with the largest in the developed countries, like Rotterdam or New York.

1.2 Cars, Trains and Planes Until the nineteenth century, land transport was primitive compared with the ocean ship and the river barge, and still depended on muscles for its motive power. Originally man himself was the carrier, his only vehicle the sledge and *travois*—a simple drag-frame such as that used by the Plains Indians of North America. In much of eastern Asia and the Americas, human porterage was virtually the only means of land transport until the coming of Europeans; but in the Old World domesticated animals like the ox, horse, ass and mule were all used in transport, either as pack animals or to haul wheeled vehicles. The wheel was undoubtedly the most important invention. It was first used in chariots sometime during the late fourth millennium B.C., and later in the form of carts and waggons. With the development of suitable harness and shoes for horses it helped to extend the range and capacity of land transport.

Without adequate roads, vehicles could only move slowly and with great difficulty: indeed freight was usually transferred to waterways at the earliest possible moment. Road building does extend back to prehistoric time—it seems to have been first developed by the Persians late in the first millennium B.C. But the great road builders of early times were the Romans and the Chinese at opposite ends of the Old World, and the Incas in the New World. In each of these areas road systems were systematically planned and constructed; but their straight alignments ignored topography and made them less suitable for wheeled vehicles—indeed the latter were unknown in the New World. The collapse of the Roman Empire led to the decline of road building in Europe, and until the eighteenth century roads were little more than tracks, often impassable during the winter months. Modern road building dates back only to the early years of the nineteenth century, when two Scottish engineers, Thomas Telford and John McAdam, introduced new methods of construction designed to improve drainage and reduce dust and mud.

Meantime the problem of improving inland transport was tackled in a new way—by digging canals. In England many schemes linking the main rivers and coastal ports with the new industrial centres were completed during the last quarter of the eighteenth century and early nineteenth century; but by the 1840s the canal was superseded by a completely new form of transport, the railway. This proved to be the most significant innovation in land transport since the invention of the wheeled vehicle, for simultaneously it increased the speed of land transport and reduced its cost. In England the first railway line opened in 1825, and by the middle of the century rail networks were spreading quickly both in Europe and North America.

In the early years of the present century two further innovations revolutionised transport. First, came the motor vehicle, which unlike the steam locomotive, needed no special track to run on: instead it used the existing road system. Moreover it provided a personal form of transport, giving the individual freedom to move where he wanted and when he liked. As manufacturing costs were steadily reduced, using methods pioneered by Henry Ford in the 1920s, the car and the truck spread rapidly in North America and western Europe; and by the end of the Second World War it was in use throughout the world.

The second innovation of the twentieth century was the aeroplane. It used a new medium which gave it a greater range and far greater potential than any other form of transport, for the air has no physical barriers like those encountered on land or sea. Instead its main hazards are caused by weather conditions for take-off and landing, by the topography surrounding airports, and the congestion of air space over the world's major cities. Otherwise aircraft provide the fastest and most flexible form of transport so far devised by man. Built to handle loads of different sizes they can be designed to land on tarmac or water, on pocket airstrips in the Amazon jungle or major runways at Kennedy Airport.

Together the car and the plane completed a series of major innovations in little more than a century. Between 1820 and 1920 there appeared the steam propelled ship, railway locomotives, motor vehicles, bicycles, electric tramcars and planes; and within the past few years, orbiting satellites and space vehicles bring the list up to date. These inventions, all using new sources of energy based on coal, petroleum and gas—have combined to shorten the time taken in travel. Until well into the nineteenth century, the average speed of long distance travel was no more than 16 km/h; jet passengers now travel at more than 1000 km/h, and astronauts hurtle through space at speeds of more than 29 000 km/h.

With these developments, space relations on earth have altered dramatically while other forms of communication have likewise helped to lessen the effects of distance. For between 1876 and 1923 were invented in quick succession the telephone, wireless telegraph, radio and television, all of which now make verbal communication possible on a world-wide basis by means of orbiting earth satellites.

2 Transport Networks

Most forms of transport need to operate on or from some sort of prepared routeway. The locomotive runs on rails, the barge sails along a canal, the cart trundles along a road. Even where no definite route need be followed, by the ship at sea or by aircraft, navigation aids are necessary for safe passages, and terminals for the transfer of passengers and handling of goods. Each form of transport thus has its own route network, defined by the points it connects, and normally arranged in a hierarchy of main and tributary routes as in the road classifications used by engineers. The location of the terminal points guides the selection of individual routes, and their line depends upon the character and volume of the traffic they carry, and the topographical nature of the area through which they run.

Generally trade is the main motive for the development of a route network, but strategic and political considerations may also be important, enabling military personnel or administrators to move quickly between different areas. Most route networks evolve slowly through time in response to changing needs for transport, but others are developed as a result of systematic planning. Specific examples include railways, motorways and air and sea terminals, all of which require substantial capital sums for their development and maintenance. For this reason major transport and communication networks are often constructed and operated by governments who have the primary responsibility for ensuring the economic development, welfare and political integrity of their national territories.

Figure 6.21
U.S.A.: the interstate highway system

2.1 Inland Waterways and Ocean Trade Routes Rivers like the Nile and the Tigris-Euphrates in Mesopotamia formed the earliest transport networks, providing natural routes for trade between towns. Other great river systems used at different times are the Seine, Rhone and Rhine in Europe, all of which became important during the mediaeval period; in Asia the Yangtse-kiang provides a great east-west corridor penetrating far inland from the Yellow Sea—ocean-going ships can sail as far as Hankow, over 1000 kilometres from the coast; and in the New World, the Amazon, Mississippi-Missouri and St Lawrence were all used by Europeans in exploration and land colonisation. All these great river systems had the natural advantages of wide and relatively deep channels for much of their length, few shallows or rapids, and an even flow of water. Other rivers are less suitable: those in tropical lands, for example, may become quite shallow in the dry season, while some, like the Congo or the Zambesi, may have waterfalls or other obstructions near their mouths. Equally significant for the commercial importance of a river system is its direction of flow in relation to the movement of goods and people. In North America, for example, the main traffic flows are from east to west, a pattern which helps to explain the continuing significance of the St Lawrence, which is now connected to the Great Lakes by an artificial channel. In contrast, the Mississippi-Missouri system flows from north to south against the main trade movements, and consequently it is now much less important than a century ago when it provided the easiest means of transport between the American mid-west and west. Its importance was ended by the building of the trans-continental railroads which provided fast and direct transport from coast to coast, for in general, inland waterways will only retain their commercial significance in competition with land transport if they provide a cheap and direct link between major industrial centres. This explains why the Rhine is one of the busiest systems in the world since it connects the great industrial area of the Ruhr with Rotterdam.

Sometimes rivers flow in the wrong direction for trade, or have physical obstacles which make navigation difficult. In these circumstances man has sometimes built artificial waterways, and the Romans were probably the first people to do so on any scale. However, the first comprehensive canal network was developed in England during the late eighteenth and early nineteenth centuries, to link the new industrial centres of the Midlands with ports like London and Liverpool. Their high capital cost was justified by the need to move bulky raw

Figure 6.22
England and Wales: the inland waterway system in 1858

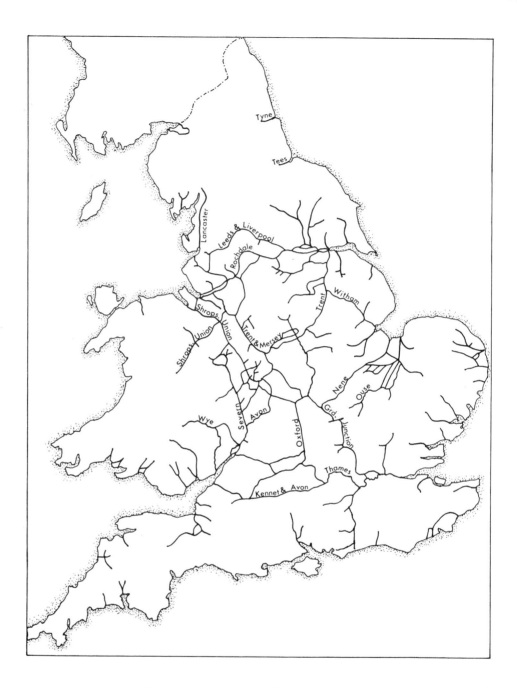

materials like coal and manufactured goods on a scale which was impossible by existing means of land transport. But as soon as rail transport provided a competing network, the canals lost their commercial importance. Outside Britain, the growth of manufacturing industry and the development of the railways proceeded more or less simultaneously, and with the exception of the Netherlands, few other countries had the need to build a canal network. Instead, later canal building was mainly to facilitate ocean transport, with the Suez Canal, opened in 1869, and the Panama Canal in 1914, both designed to save long sea voyages round Africa and South America respectively.

The transition from river to sea trade was made most easily in enclosed seas, where distances were relatively short, and navigation made easier by frequent landfalls. Favourable winds were also important, so that ships with simple sails or rigging could use seasonal wind circulation to complete their voyages. The Indian Ocean was one such area, with Egyptian seamen using the Monsoon winds to sail regularly from the Red Sea to the Yemen by the early second millennium B.C. Later, trade expanded steadily under the Greeks and Romans, and after their power waned, the Arabs maintained an extensive seasonal trade for nearly a thousand years between the Mediterranean lands, India and south-east Asia. The Mediterranean itself was a second major centre of early sea-trade, beginning in the Aegean and then extending over the entire basin under the Phoenicians and the Romans. Under the Phoenicians, the Atlantic coastlands of Europe were brought within the Mediterranean trading hinterland, although movement had already taken place along these seaways from Neolithic times. During the Bronze Age, tin from Cornwall, gold and copper from Ireland, and amber from the Baltic were all included in an extensive trading network which stretched from northern Scandinavia to the Iberian Peninsula and into the Mediterranean. Meantime at the eastern end of Eurasia, trading links developed rather later than in the west. Here the pioneers were Chinese seamen who ventured steadily westward during the first millennium A.D., reaching south-east Asia where they eventually established links with Arab and Indian merchants. Indeed south-east Asia became one of the great *entrepots* of the Ancient World, rather like the western Baltic, Flanders, the Aegean and the Red Sea in the west. From south-east Asia there also seems to have been some limited contact with the islands of Micronesia, but otherwise the whole of the south Pacific, including Australia and New Zealand, and the New World remained totally isolated from the mainstream of ocean trade until the sixteenth century.

These different centres of ocean trade were finally linked in a world-wide system during the sixteenth century. The stimulus came when the Ottoman Turks blocked the traditional caravan route from Europe to the East through Syria, and European merchants encouraged the search for new routes to 'The Indies'. The eastern route round Africa was discovered by the Portuguese seaman, Vasco da Gama in 1498; and the western route across the Atlantic to America was pioneered by Christopher Columbus in 1492. The success of these and later voyages finally shifted the node of commercial and political power from the Mediterranean to Atlantic Europe. Initially Portugal and Spain took the lead, then France and Holland, and finally Britain. Between them they created a new pattern of trade which had a profound influence on world economies. Trade in earlier times was based on the simple exchange of local resources, but in the nineteenth century Britain began to

Figure 6.23
World: major commercial shipping lanes. Notice that the volume of traffic using the route round southern Africa depends on whether the Suez Canal is open to traffic

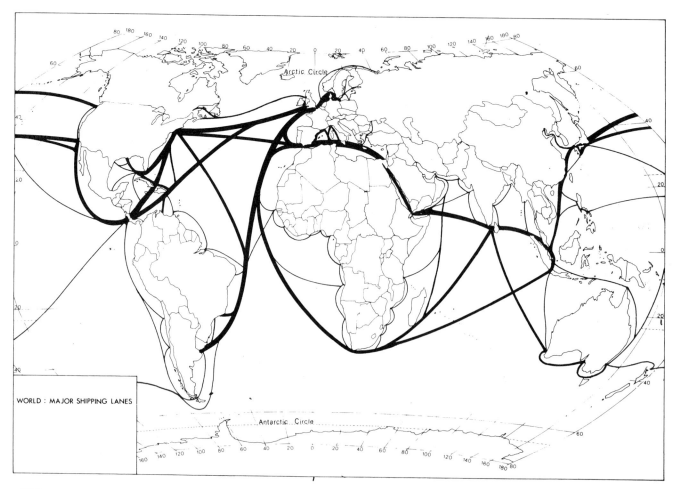

WORLD : MAJOR SHIPPING LANES

import raw materials like cotton, wool and grain, process them, and then export the manufactured goods to the producing countries. Other European countries soon followed, but throughout the nineteenth century Britain controlled the largest fleet of merchant ships in the world, and London was the leading world port. Britain is no longer the world's leading shipping nation, but the greatest volume of world ocean trade is still concentrated on north-western Europe as it was a century ago. Traffic is heaviest on the north Atlantic between Europe and North America, but the sea lanes between Europe and Asia are only of slightly less importance. Most shipping will again use the Suez Canal which was blocked between 1967–75 because of the Arab-Israeli War; during these years vessels took the long route round Africa—long used by oil tankers from the Gulf States, for they were often too large to navigate the Canal.

2.2 Roads and Railways   Unlike ships, which need few fixed points to guide their passage—except for navigational aids like buoys and lighthouses, land vehicles need permanent routes to travel across the earth's surface. Today these routeways form an intricate network linking the settlements of the world's more developed countries. Yet even in these areas, organised land transport is quite a recent development. Before the eighteenth century most road networks were of mainly local significance, focusing on local towns and villages and serving the marketing needs of rural areas. Through traffic to larger towns or to cities such as London simply followed these local routes, many of which were little more than muddy tracks through the fields. Regional and national networks had existed in Europe in Roman times, but these were largely abandoned after the collapse of the Empire. Not until the eighteenth century were similar strategic roads built once again in Europe, as the new nation-states improved the links between their capitals and the major provincial cities. In France, for example, a new network of roads radiated outwards from Paris, and in Britain London was joined to Glasgow and Edinburgh in the north and Holyhead—the packet station for Ireland.

These new trunk roads represented a new approach to land transport, designed and built to the specifications of professional road engineers. But they were intended primarily for the transport of people rather than of goods, and the routes they followed were often of little use to the traffic generated by the new centres of manufacturing industry. Throughout much of the nineteenth century the road network continued to serve mainly local needs, acting as feeders to the canals and railways.

Figure 6.24
Europe: the major
Roman roads

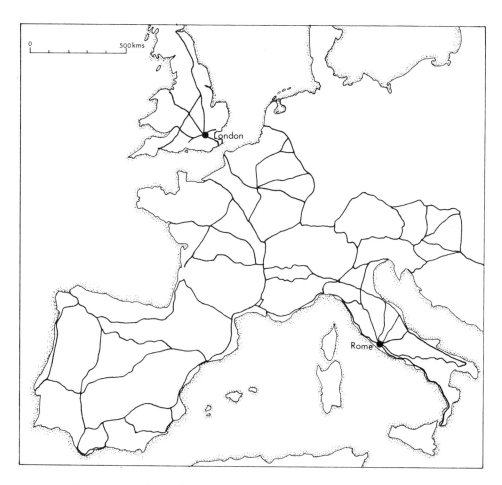

Consequently when commercial freight shifted from the railways to the roads following the development of the motor
vehicle after the First World War, most European road networks became hopelessly congested, at least within the industrial regions. In the 1930s, Germany was the first country to
tackle this problem by building a completely new national road
network, the *autobahn,* designed specifically to provide for high
speed motor transport between major population centres.
Strategic considerations also influenced its design, but the same
principle was later followed in other European countries, including Britain where the building of the national motorway
network began in the 1950s. Meantime the U.S.A., which has
nearly two-thirds of the world's motor vehicles, had largely
completed its own inter-state highway system (Figure 6.21).
Few other parts of the world have national road networks
designed for the motor age, and outside the major towns and

cities, movement by road is still largely geared to local needs, and animal transport.

In such areas railways often provide the main means of moving large volumes of freight and passengers by land as they did in western Europe for much of the nineteenth century. Here they provided fast, cheap and reliable transport that was so vastly superior to that provided by the roads and canals that rail networks spread very quickly indeed. In England, for example, the first line was opened in 1825: by 1840 some 3500 kilometres of track were in regular use, and a decade later this had reached 10 500 kilometres. In its heyday the railway provided a major stimulus for economic growth in the industrial nations, attracting industry to locate near its tracks, opening up mineral resources, developing ports and new towns like Crewe and Swindon and adding enormously to the population of existing towns and cities by making large-scale commuting possible.

The first railways were built for commercial reasons. Like the canals—whose routes they often followed, they linked the ports with the main manufacturing areas. But by the mid nineteenth century the national railway network in Britain was increasingly focused on London; and in France and Ireland a similar pattern emerged, the railways radiating outwards from the capital to the provinces. Regional transport needs were also catered for in the early rail networks of the U.S.A. but here, as in Canada and Russia, trans-continental lines were built mainly for strategic reasons although they also enabled the land to be settled. In colonial territories, railways were built to open up interior areas for commercial development. These 'export lines' typically link a river or coastal port with a specific mineral deposit or group of plantations and rarely link up with each other to form a cohesive network. Many were built in tropical Africa and south-east Asia, and it is in these countries, where the road network is still rudimentary, that the railway network continues to expand. But elsewhere, branch lines and main lines in many countries are being closed down through competition from road transport. For the railway lacks the flexibility of the road vehicle which can carry goods and passengers direct from door to door. Only extreme congestion on the road network, or greatly increased fuel charges are likely to reverse the continued decline of the rail network in advanced countries. (See maps on pages 298 and 299).

Great Britain: a
contemporary
map of the rail
network in 1851.
(*Photo Science
Museum,
London*)

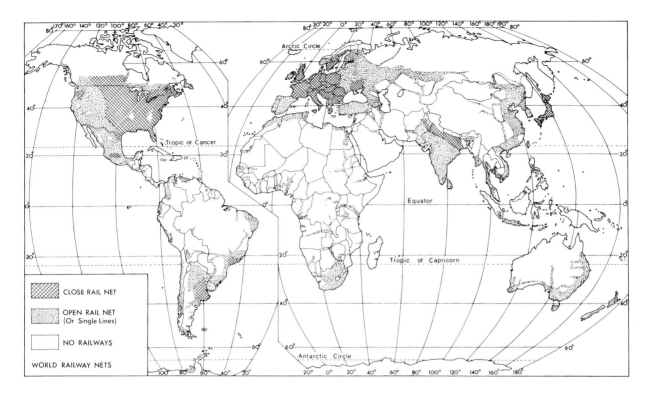

Figure 6.25
World: railway network, 1960s

2.3 Airways The great advantage of air travel is in long distance passenger movement where its speed gives it the edge over rail and sea transport. Indeed air transport has virtually eliminated the ocean passenger-liner for other than tourist cruises, and the transcontinental passenger trains of the U.S.A. But over short distances of several hundred miles, and for most types of freight, surface transport still holds its own. The main drawback of short distance air travel for passengers is that air terminals are usually sited some distance outside cities, and the time taken in ground travel over congested roads more than offsets the time saved in the actual air journey. Air freight rates are also more expensive, except for certain types of goods, such as spare parts for sophisticated machinery or perishable commodities like flowers or vegetables, where the speed of delivery compensates for the cost.

The routes used by major world airlines are largely explained by this traffic, for they are very closely related to the commercial links established by the advanced industrial nations. No less than 75 per cent of the world's air traffic is generated in western Europe and North America, and much of it is concentrated on two major axes: an east-west route linking Europe and North America and extending across the Pacific to eastern Asia; and three north-south routes: North America to South America, Europe to South America, and Europe to Africa. A further transverse route connects Europe with Asia and Australasia across the North Pole. These international routes, most of which were pioneered in the 1930s, are designed to connect major centres of urban population both in the advanced countries and overseas. But their alignment is also intended to avoid certain major environmental hazards, like the mountain chains of the Himalayas or the Sahara desert, which affect weather patterns and create grave difficulties in the event of emergency landings. Hence in the interests of safety, and because most

Figure 6.26
World: major air routes

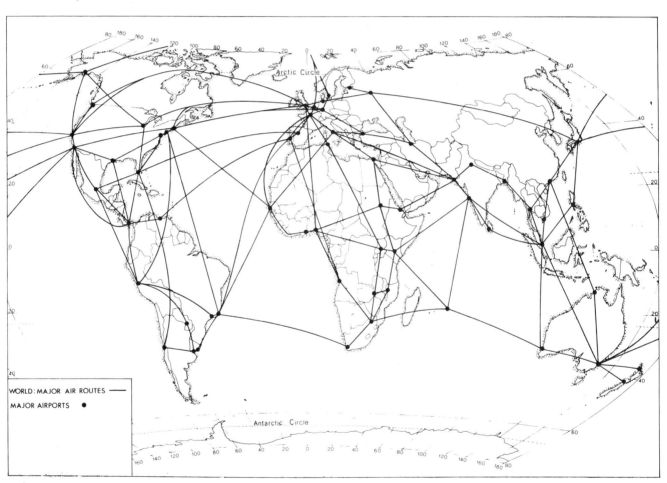

WORLD: MAJOR AIR ROUTES ———
MAJOR AIRPORTS ●

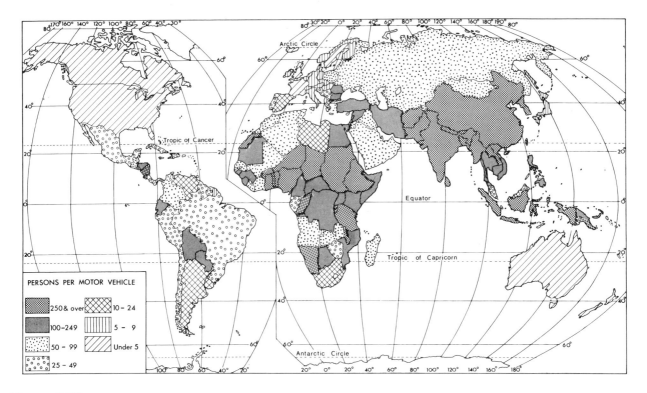

Figure 6.27
World: persons per motor vehicle,
1969 data. Few parts of the
modern world are inaccessible,
but for most people the means of
transport are still primitive

PERSONS PER MOTOR VEHICLE

250 & over
100–249
50 – 99
25 – 49
10 – 24
5 – 9
Under 5

nations are sensitive about foreign aircraft using their air space, most air traffic is concentrated in well-defined corridors.

Apart from their role in intercontinental travel, aircraft have played an important part in the development of certain inland areas where surface travel is difficult, and a landing strip represents only a fraction of the cost of building a new road or railway. This applies in particular to many parts of northern Canada and Alaska, Australia and the Amazon basin. Here local airlines provide an invaluable feeder service, linking these sparsely populated areas to the worldwide network of commercial aviation.

3 Transport Systems

This summary of the development of different means of transport has emphasised the extent of the changes that have occurred during the present century. Not only have new forms of transport and communications been invented, but more and more people have also been connected to existing networks. Today, few parts of the world are inaccessible to modern transport, or too remote to be reached by electronic communications. Of course this does not mean that transport networks are evenly distributed throughout the world: great tracts of the earth's surface are crossed by roads little better than the trails used by prehistoric man; railways are uncommon except in the most densely settled areas of industrial nations; and in most parts of tropical Africa and Asia, scheduled air services operate only from the major cities. But even from the most remote areas—say from inner Mongolia or the heart of Africa, it is possible to reach most of the world's major cities within a matter of days, whereas even a few generations ago the same journey would have taken several months of very uncomfortable travel.

Besides faster travel, many people in the world can now choose between different forms of transport, especially in the advanced nations. For example, it is possible to travel from Cork in Ireland to Cologne in Germany using several different methods: by air, by rail and ship; by car and ship; or by bicycle and ship—besides being able to walk or hitch a lift. Between the same cities messages can also be sent by telephone, telex, radio and television, as well as by letter. Each method offers certain advantages in speed, cost, comfort and security; they compete with and complement each other. This last point is important, for until the end of the nineteenth century there was very little attempt to coordinate transport on a regional, much less on an international basis. Each network operated its own schedule. For example, ships sailed when cargoes were loaded and tides and winds were favourable—and an intending passenger might have to wait on the quayside for weeks before completing his journey. Today we expect to look up a time-table and see exactly how long it will take us to get from Tipperary to Tokyo or Timbuctu—and we can phone ahead to let our hosts know when we will arrive. Needless to say it may not work out quite as we anticipated: fog can disrupt air travel, buses break down or trains fail to run because of labour disputes. But on the whole, modern transport does operate in an efficient and comprehensive way, enabling world-wide circulation on a scale never previously contemplated.

This global system of transport and communications is one of the greatest achievements of twentieth-century technology, for it enables goods and people to circulate freely between the different continents. It completes a process begun nearly five centuries ago, when Columbus' discovery of America and Magellan's voyage round the world finally linked together all the separate regional trade areas. Through trade the world's nations have become increasingly interdependent, a trend which is reflected in the growing number of international agencies and organisations designed to promote economic cooperation and to reduce political tensions.

Indeed the most important feature of the contemporary world is not the conflicts and the dissension which dominate the headlines in newspapers and on television, but rather the cooperation which exists between individuals and nations—even between countries which are deeply divided in political ideologies. All this is a by-product of the twentieth-century revolution in transport and communications. Yet despite these many linkages which draw the world's nations ever closer together, people and places throughout the world remain refreshingly different. Each people has its own pattern of culture, each place its distinctive environment. Explaining why this is so provides the geographer with one of his most rewarding tasks.

FURTHER READING

Balchin, W. G. V., *Geography* (London, 1970)

Broek, J. O. M. and Webb, J. W., *A Geography of Mankind* (New York, 1973)

Chisholm, M., *Human Geography* (London, 1975)

Clarke, J. I., *Population Geography* (Oxford, 1972)

Cooke, R. U., and Johnson, J. H., *Trends in Geography* (Oxford, 1969)

Coon, C. S., *The History of Man* (London, 1967)

Haggett, P., *Geography; A Modern Synthesis* (New York, 1972)

Hudson, F. S., *A Geography of Settlements* (London, 1970)

Johnson, J. H., *Urban Geography* (Oxford, 1972)

Jones, E., *Towns and Cities* (Oxford, 1966)

Mountjoy, A. B., *Developing the Underdeveloped Countries* (London, 1971)

Parker, A. J., *A Geography of Towns and Cities* (Dublin, 1976)

Patterson, J. H., *Land, Work and Resources* (London, 1972)

Perpillou, A. V., *Human Geography* (London, 1968)

Sopher, D. E., *Geography of Religions* (Englewood Cliffs, 1967)

Spencer, J. E. and Thomas, W. L., *Introducing Cultural Geography* (New York, 1973)